SOMOZA
FALLING

SOMOZA
FALLING

A Case Study of Washington at Work

Anthony Lake

THE UNIVERSITY OF
MASSACHUSETTS PRESS
AMHERST

Library of Congress Cataloging-in-Publication Data

Lake, Anthony.
    Somoza falling: a case study of Washington at work / Anthony
Lake. — 1st pbk. ed.
        p.   cm.
    Includes bibliographical references.
    ISBN 0–87023–733–0 (alk. paper)
    1. United States—Foreign relations—Nicaragua. 2. Nicaragua—
Foreign relations—United States. 3. Somoza, Anastasio,
1925–1980. 4. United States—Foreign relations—1977–1981.
5. United States—Foreign relations administration—Case studies.
I. Title.
[E183.8.N5L35   1990]
327.7307285—dc20   90–34788
                                                            CIP

British Library Cataloguing in Publication data are available.

CONTENTS

Preface

IN 1981, AFTER TWENTY YEARS OR SO OF WORK IN WASH-
ington, I began teaching college students about American foreign
policy. I had expected that they would be puzzled about how Washington works, since I knew from experience that the process of
making foreign policy is wonderful in its mysteries. But I have
been surprised to discover that many students are very definite in
their views. Some believe that our foreign policy is made by conspir-
acy, through the secret machinations and slush funds so stunningly
revealed by the Watergate and Iran-contra hearings. Others, who
have read the memoirs of American statesmen, see government
decisions as the products of measured, historic meetings between
the president and his senior advisers. And a few students, those
interested in the study of large organizations, have concluded that
certain laws of bureaucratic behavior control the formulation of
foreign policy. In this view, the machinery of government is operated
by bureaucrats whose only function is to calculate and protect
institutional interests.

There is some accuracy in each of these images. But I remember
a very different picture: of officials operating in the middle reaches
of the State Department and White House, of people (in both
Democratic and Republican administrations) who struggled as best
they could against the limits of time and insufficient information.
The government I worked in was the one described by Woodrow

Wilson when he said that "government is not a body of blind forces [but] a body of men . . . not a machine but a living thing. It falls, not under the theory of the universe, but under the theory of organic life. It is accountable to Darwin, not to Newton."

I decided to write a book about how things work within the world of foreign policy making, a book that would illustrate the working lives of the men and women who shape policy on those many international issues that only occasionally receive the attention of the president and his Cabinet — except when they explode in crisis, as Nicaragua did in late 1978 and again in mid-1979. Who are the middle-level officials in the executive branch, and the reporters and members of Congress with whom they work? What goes on in their meetings? What does a member of the National Security Council staff do every day? How does a press spokesman get ready for a briefing with reporters, and how does the media report what he says? How can a member of Congress influence policy? What is it like to be an assistant secretary or a desk officer in the State Department?

Answering such questions, it seemed, could best be done by telling the story of how our government dealt with one issue. I decided to reconstruct Washington's reaction to the gathering crisis in Nicaragua during 1978 and 1979, the end of the regime of Anastasio Somoza. Somoza's fall was chosen for a number of reasons. It was an intrinsically important event, and understanding it can help us think clearly about the subsequent tragedy of Nicaragua and the role of the United States there. There are, moreover, general lessons to be drawn from this story: about the necessity of relating American goals and American power, about the sources of revolutionary upheavals in the Third World, about the relationship of our domestic politics and our foreign policies, and about the importance of contemplating history if we are to anticipate the future.

In part, I chose this case because it represents a policy failure. President Jimmy Carter and his administration achieved many successes: in the Camp David accords, in the normalization of relations with the People's Republic of China, in negotiating the SALT II treaty, in assisting at the birth of Zimbabwe, and in winning some of their battles for human rights, even if they lost others. But there is more to be learned from failure than from success, even if it is less pleasant to contemplate.

I had a personal reason, as well, for examining our policy toward Nicaragua in 1978–1979. Although I was the director of policy planning in the State Department during this period, I was only occasionally involved directly. Central America was not among my strongest interests, and others on our staff attended most of the State Department discussions described in this book. I remember feeling at the time that I did not know nearly as much about the subject as I would have wished, that there was not enough time to study its history and nuances. This book, then, offered a chance at furthering my education. In addition, because my own role was so limited and undistinguished, I would not be writing a memoir and thus had a better chance of avoiding either an apologia or an attempt at retrospective justification. I hope I have done neither. It is neither modesty nor an effort to distance myself from a failed policy that makes my own appearances in the story nearly as fleeting as those of Alfred Hitchcock in one of his films. I supported the policy and contributed to its fashioning.

This is largely a story about two groups of people within the executive branch and how they sometimes clashed: the career officials who spend their professional lives working under presidents of both parties, and the political appointees who expect to serve only the president who appointed them. Neither group approaches uniformity in its views or actions, but inevitably, there are important differences between them — in their experiences and perspectives, in their styles of work, in what they have to contribute to the formation of our foreign policy.

Too often, accounts of a struggle within the government assume that all virtue lies on one side or the other of a policy divide. The political appointees who were paladins of human rights in some stories become, in other versions, dangerous ideological extremists. The same Foreign Service officers may be seen in one account as wise pragmatists, in another as obstructionist, unprincipled bureaucrats. Yet in this story, neither side had a monopoly on principle. On each side, men and women were acting in ways they thought to be both practical and honorable. Each made arguments in which there was much truth. To anoint either political appointees or career officials as heroes and thus to cast the others as villains would be more than unfair. Such a choice would also imply that the government should be dominated by one group at the expense of the other. Good policy making needs both, for it is seldom that all wisdom lies on one side or the other of a policy argument. Most often, a senior decision maker is confronted by an antinomy, a competition of truths that deserve a full exposition.

I have enjoyed working on this book, largely because of the many people who have been so helpful to me. All of those whom I interviewed were extraordinarily generous with their time and their willingness to try to remember the mistakes as well as the moments of hope. Mary Kennedy and Greg Lagana at the State Department, and the staff of the American embassy in Managua, helped give the story a sense of place. Scott Armstrong and the National Security Archive offered invaluable assistance in providing access to the many cables they have acquired through their Freedom of Information requests. And Alan Rifken helped explore the ways of Congress through his excellent research.

Amy Byrne, Marisa Del Savio, and Sandra Perrin were unfailing in their ability to find the right speeches in old federal records and to track down such obscure scholarly references as the exact words spoken by a character in a Walt Disney movie. (To them and the other young women with whom I have shared classrooms, this note about pronouns: throughout the book I have used *he* when describing generically an official working on American foreign policy, not only because it is simplest, but unhappily because it is more likely to be accurate than *she*. I look forward to the day when some of you have contributed to making this no longer so.) Tammy Sapowsky and Linda Chesky Fernandes were skilled and extraordinarily patient in making sense of tape-recorded interviews and producing manuscripts. I am also grateful to Mount Holyoke College for supporting their work and my own research.

I have been the happy student of William Bowdler, Vincent Ferraro, William McFeely, Daniel Okrent, Robert Pastor, and Viron P. Vaky, whose comments have constantly informed and instructed me. Robert Pastor, in particular, was extremely generous in sharing his recollections and thoughts, as well as a manuscript copy of his excellent book, *Condemned to Repetition*. It is a first-rate history of America and Nicaragua, and it includes a detailed version of a number of the events I describe here.

I am especially grateful to Peter Grose, who knows that direct and detailed criticism is a sign, more than a test, of friendship; to Chris Jerome and her green pencil; to Richard Todd, editorial alchemist and friend; to Eleanor Hard Lake, for her encouragement, her meticulous and skilled suggestions, and so much else; and to Antonia P. Lake, for more than I can record.

Pedro Joaquín Chamorro was driving his Saab slowly along the streets of Managua, crossing the center of the city whose ruined buildings recalled the terrible earthquake five years before. As the publisher and editor of the newspaper La Prensa *drove to work on the morning of January 10, 1978, there was much that might have occupied his mind: his next editorial attacking Anastasio Somoza, the Nicaraguan dictator, or his own political future as the popular leader of opposition to Somoza's rule, or perhaps some less significant matter, even the day's weather, as the cool of the early morning started to give way, at 8:20, to the tropical heat.*

Suddenly a green Toyota pickup pulled in front of his car, forcing it across the curb and into a lamppost. Two men leaped out and appeared at the driver's window of the Saab. Three stunning shotgun blasts were pumped into the front seat. Chamorro collapsed over the steering wheel as his murderers jumped into another car for their escape. The ambulance medics at first thought they were dealing with an automobile accident. By the time they got him to the hospital examining table, Pedro Joaquín Chamorro was dead of multiple buckshot wounds.

The murder rocked Managua. Within hours, riots broke out. When Chamorro's body was released from the hospital, his casket was carried on the shoulders of angry friends first to his home and then to the office of his newspaper. It was followed through the streets by forty thousand mourners.

Years later, Managuans could still recall exactly where they were and what they were doing at the moment they heard the news of Chamorro's death. For it had been not only a sad personal shock to his many admirers. It was the moment from which many would date the slide from power of the Somoza family, a dynasty that had ruled Nicaragua for two generations.

ONE

The Seventh Floor

NEWS OF CHAMORRO'S ASSASSINATION QUICKLY REACHED the Department of State in Washington, through the news reports of the Associated Press and United Press International and by telegram from the American embassy in Managua. The item was important enough to be distributed on the seventh floor of the State Department building — or rather, the Seventh Floor, for this is where the power resides. The secretary, his deputy, the under secretaries, and their staffs have their offices here, along the southern corridor. A command from this area carries particular authority. You hop to it, as much as anyone in the State Department ever hops, when you hear, "The Seventh Floor wants you to . . ."

Even before they were refurbished by Secretary of State George Shultz (at a cost of some $2.2 million, provided by private donors), the suites of offices along the southern corridor were elegantly furnished with antiques, fine American paintings, heavy curtains; the effect is Early American crossed with the Quai d'Orsay. Unlike most offices at the State Department, they largely succeed in overcoming the sterile atmosphere of "New State," the structure completed in 1961 to house a growing if still relatively small agency whose members had been spread among twenty-nine buildings around the city. New State is not insignificant: it covers a two-block area near the Lincoln Memorial and the green expanses of the Washington Mall. But despite the rather formal entrance tacked to the front, New State is more bland than grand, a large rectangular shape redeemed by no distinctive features.

For Foreign Service officers returning from assignments abroad, especially in tropical lands where the colors are vivid and the old colonial buildings notable, the contrast is disheartening. Many of them make a considerable effort to decorate their offices with artifacts and paintings collected during their foreign tours, but the building defeats them. Like a small park in a gray city, the human touch serves mostly to emphasize the sterility of the surroundings. The atmosphere is sterile in a literal as well as a figurative sense. Self-contained heating and air conditioning systems require that no one be allowed to open the windows. Even the Venetian blinds were designed to serve the building rather than its inhabitants. In 1965 *The Foreign Service Journal* complained that the blinds could be opened only downward, toward the street, never up to the inspiring skies, because the architect had wanted a uniform appearance for his creation.

Small triumphs are possible, however. An enterprising occupant may be able to adjust the heating with a bent paper clip. Bribery or pleading may elicit a window key from one of the maintenance people — although a junior officer, having once got one, was deterred from using it by a vision of a terrible depressurization, as in an airplane, sucking thousands of memoranda and cables, as well as himself, through the open window. In the end, the building prevails. As you walk the bravely colored but still somehow dim corridors, the dry air builds up charges of static electricity, to be uncomfortably discharged when you next touch something or somebody. It may be this atmosphere, as well as the demeanor of State Department officials, that once led David K. Willis of *The Christian Science Monitor* to describe the place as "eight floors of good manners, endless corridors of neatness and decorum, platoons of typewriters and innumerable meetings pitched at a sensible, nononsense, low-key hum."

The morning hum at the State Department is first generated by the Operations Center, a few yards down a side corridor from the office of the secretary of state. Here there is no paneling, no elegance. The heart of the Ops Center is a large, windowless room with three desks set on a raised platform manned by the watch officers twenty-four hours a day in eight-hour shifts. Assisted by two operations assistants who sit at smaller desks in the center of the room, they keep track of the most urgent cables flowing in from embassies around the world; of the AP, Reuters, and UPI accounts of assorted problems that spill from the teletype machines near one wall; and of intelligence reports from the Central Intelligence Agency and other agencies that may need immediate handling. (In offices next to the main room, three military representatives are in touch with the National Military Communications Center, the nerve center of the Pentagon, and a watch officer from State's Bureau of Intelligence and Research monitors traffic from the CIA and the National Security Agency.)

Routine messages, the bulk of the thousands of cables sent every day from the embassies, are sorted and distributed by a separate Office of Communications. The telegrams from each post are numbered consecutively, starting anew at the beginning of each fiscal year. By May or June, officials in Washington are referring to "London's 12354" or "Managua's 8768." As a junior staff aide in the mid-1960s, I discovered the post on which my ambitions would wistfully focus. Near the end of the fiscal year, a cable from the American mission in Suva, the capital of Fiji, crossed my desk. It bore the number 2.

Even an event as shocking as the assassination of Chamorro, which was important enough to go to the Ops Center, tends to become simply another item in the torrent of information flowing into Washington. Such an incident is seen primarily as a *problem*, to be analyzed and managed. The blood and dust of a street in Managua is brushed away as officials concentrate on what must matter most to them: the implications of events for American foreign policy. This point was illustrated perfectly by a cable from an American embassy in a small African nation in the mid-1960s. In a sentence or two, it reported that the notoriously violent tyrant of that nation had become incensed when a pedestrian had impeded the passage of his limousine. His chauffeur had kicked the unfortunate to death. A laconic "Comment" at the end of the cable went something like this: "The political implications are not yet clear."

The Ops Center always seems alive: teletypes chatter and telephones constantly ring as the watch officers put senior officials in touch with each other and with American embassies overseas through a complicated system of secure and open telephone lines. (Recently the noise of a television set tuned to the Cable News Network has been added. What is new is CNN, not the television set. Traditionally, on most Sunday afternoons during the fall, an official called to duty in the department has been able to steal a few moments of the beloved Washington Redskins on the Ops Center TV if he has managed to cook up an excuse to drop by.)

The late-night shift is the most important in the Ops Center. Secretary of State Dean Rusk once complained that "every time you go to sleep, two thirds of the world is awake and up to some mischief." As the cables and problems keep flowing in, the watch officers collect and collate the messages for the morning, putting them in folders that hang from "the cart," a metal frame on wheels.

At about 6 A.M., the cart is wheeled out of the Ops Center, bound for the State Department's executive secretary. The Ops Center also provides a summary of the most sensitive cables, together with the Senior Watch Officer's Log of actions taken during the night and a Morning Summary, for wider distribution in the building. The Morning Summary, written with the Bureau of Intelligence and Research, describes in eight or nine lines each the most important pieces of reporting from the embassies, such as the report of Chamorro's death, and offers a comment on their importance or implications.

The executive secretary of the department sits behind a glass wall in an office centrally placed along the quiet corridor between the suites of the secretary and the deputy secretary. There he and his two deputies set the daily agenda for the department and watch over the flow of paper. The executive secretary during the Carter administration, Peter Tarnoff, an elegantly efficient and skilled Foreign Service officer, met at a little after 8 every morning with his deputies after attending a "small-group" meeting with the secretary of state. At these earlier meetings, Secretary Vance reviewed thorny issues with his closest advisers: Deputy Secretary Warren Christopher; the under secretary for political affairs; the under secretary for management; the executive secretary; and the director of policy planning.

At his first morning meeting with his deputies, the executive secretary describes any items the secretary wants from the department's various bureaus: these might include a telegram of instruction to embassy X, a statement for the press spokesman on issue Y, a draft letter to Senator Z. He reviews the most important memoranda from the White House or other agencies calling on State to provide an opinion, a clearance for some action, or a draft of some presidential letter or speech, and these too are farmed out to the relevant bureaus for action. The meeting reviews the status of previous "action items" sent to the bureaus and goes over the responses submitted the previous evening. The group is assisted in this by "the line," seven or eight middle-level officers who sit near the Operations Center. Line officers review the memoranda prepared by the bureaus for their form as well as for content: Is the Prime Minister properly addressed in this letter? Is there a typo anywhere in this memo for the White House? They also hector offices that might be missing a deadline. The acronymic designation of the executive secretariat is S/S; it is easy for an official working against a short deadline to imagine, as the officer from the line calls him for the fifth time, that his tormenter is decked out in a black leather uniform and death's-head insignia.

The executive secretary also assigns distribution of the day's hottest items, deciding which offices should receive the most sensitive messages. Obviously, the daily task of deciding which officials will receive copies of which top-secret messages is no trivial matter. An official who does not know about an emerging issue is not merely uninformed, he will be uninvolved. On matters concerning Central America, the executive secretary made sure that the deputy secretary of state, Warren Christopher, was fully informed. Secretary of State Cyrus Vance was concentrating on other issues that had a higher priority at the time and had delegated to Christopher a primary role on Latin America.

*

The reports of Chamorro's murder went immediately to Steven Oxman, one of Warren Christopher's special assistants. A special assistant serves his superior as an adviser, enforcer, and information source. Typically, he follows a particular set of issues, pushing and probing the bureaucracy for timely analyses, joining the executive secretary in pressing to see that deadlines are met on work needed by his superior, and reviewing draft memoranda and cables before they are submitted to the senior officer. Oxman, a sandy-haired, affable but intense lawyer, was responsible for human rights and Latin American affairs. Just thirty-two years old, he had dreamed of working in Washington since his days as a Rhodes scholar at Oxford, where he had developed an interest in foreign affairs through his academic work on the diplomacy of the World War I years. Subsequent study at Yale Law School and four years at a leading New York law firm had given him a taste for the competitive life of litigation and negotiation. He had wanted to test himself in Washington, to see what that world was like, and he had approached Warren Christopher through a lawyer who knew them both.

Oxman recalls vividly his first, heady days at the State Department: "I was exactly where I wanted to be. I was suddenly working for someone at quite a high level in our government, having access to a tremendous amount of information about what was happening. The day I got there, one of the first documents I saw was the Night Notes [a report sent every evening from the secretary of state to the president on the day's happenings]. President Carter had returned them with his marginal, handwritten comments. I knew that working in a place where I had access to that kind of information was going to be exciting."

He quickly discovered that the culture of the State Department was unlike anything he had ever seen. "I had to make some adjustments," he says ruefully. "There was a large premium on trying to work with people in a nonconfrontational way. I probably was too confrontational. It came from having been a litigator. I had to really work on that." But Oxman soon learned to master himself, to fit in with what he recalls as the "controlled vibrancy" of Christopher's office.

The paneled walls, the carpets, the understated style of the State Department made it seem surprisingly quiet. But the quiet was deceptive; it was the stillness, Oxman says, of "a highly charged atmosphere." Every morning brought a torrent of cables, intelligence summaries, press summaries, and newspapers. The new special assistant was intimidated by Christopher's ability to get through an in box that grew twelve inches every day, snatching moments between meetings to hack away at his paperwork. Oxman found he had to learn to track a large number of issues at once — although fewer, he knew, than Christopher was following. Here, in the daily, desperate battle with the Augean in box and the varied issues packed into it, was the biggest difference between State and a law office. "No lawyer," he notes, "has thirty or so active issues at the same moment."

Because he covered both human rights and Latin American affairs, Nicaragua was one of the thirty or so issues on which Oxman had to concentrate during his first months on the job. But it was not until Chamorro's death that Nicaragua began to emerge from the ranks of small Central American nations with whose dictators the Carter administration had an uncomfortable, ambiguous relationship.

Oxman was saddened by the news of the murder; he had admired Chamorro's courage in standing up to Somoza, and he sensed that this might be a watershed in Nicaraguan politics. The immediate reaction of thousands of Nicaraguans to the assassination made it clear that the regime of Anastasio Somoza was in trouble as it had never been before. Oxman knew that however distasteful he and other American officials found the dictator, years of American association with him meant that trouble for Somoza presaged new problems for Washington.

TWO

Washington and the Somozas

IN EARLY 1978 ANASTASIO SOMOZA DEBAYLE WAS WATCH-
ing his weight as he recovered from a heart attack. But even with
his health in doubt, the aging Nicaraguan ruler remained the very
model of a modern Central American dictator. His father (Anastasio
Somoza García), his brother, Luis, and Somoza himself had accumulated, in some forty years of dynastic rule, a personal fortune of hundreds of millions of dollars — and this in a nation
suffering widespread malnutrition and an obscene rate of infant
mortality. Somoza was reputed to be the richest man in Central
America.

American columnist Jack Anderson had reinforced the dictator's
reputation for venality when he wrote on August 15, 1975,

> The world's greediest ruler is Anastasio Somoza D., the pot-bellied
> potentate who rules Nicaragua as if it were his private state. This
> is no casual selection. We have spent months making the selection.
> After a thorough study of available evidence, we nominate Somoza
> as most grasping of the world's great grabbers. Through his family
> and his flunkies, he controls every profitable industry, institution
> and service in Nicaragua.

Though he may have taken comfort in Anderson's reputation
for hyperbole, such attacks in the American press caught Somoza's

attention, for he and his family had always counted heavily on help from their American friends. He had been educated mostly in the United States, and once told an interviewer that "except for four years all my studies were in the U.S. and [upon returning to Nicaragua from West Point in 1946] I knew the U.S. better than my own country."[1] Somoza loved to banter with Americans in his colloquial if dated English, and had an accomplished hail-fellow-well-met, backslapping manner designed to appeal to American reporters and diplomats. He once greeted a new American ambassador by referring to himself as "a Latin from Manhattan."

Evidence of Somoza's direct complicity in Chamorro's murder has never been found, and it is possible that he had no prior knowledge of so stupid an act. But for many Nicaraguans who already opposed his rule, the reaction was inevitable: Somoza was to blame. Everyone in Managua who knew anything about politics was aware of the bitterness between the two men. They and their families had long conducted a personal as well as a political vendetta. Indeed, as early as age eight, when Chamorro and Somoza had attended school together, they had often fought in the playground.[2]

Chamorro's widespread popularity in Nicaragua was based on personal respect, but it was also a measure of popular opposition to Somoza. At the American embassy in Managua, local employees wept at the news of Chamorro's death and denounced the Nicaraguan dictator. Most of the business community observed a general strike for several weeks. Demonstrations against Somoza, and the organization by the government of counterdemonstrations, led to a decision in Washington to postpone a visit to Managua by Terence Todman, then the assistant secretary of state in charge of relations with Latin America.

But Somoza was in no mood to yield to pressures from within or beyond Nicaragua. When a reporter asked if he would resign, as demanded by members of the opposition, his response was succinct: "Nix." The reporter persisted:

REPORTER: Could you be more elaborate?
SOMOZA: Yes, I would say "No."

REPORTER: The Chamorro incident has obviously affected the nation . . .

SOMOZA: Absolutely.

REPORTER: He was your political enemy for many years. Can you tell us how you personally felt about the assassination, personally?

SOMOZA: Well, I felt like I always thought I would feel. That was the biggest mistake made by anybody, to kill him.

REPORTER: Are you saddened by his death?

SOMOZA: Sure. I'm a politician. I could be killed, too, you know. I'm a human being, too.[3]

Somoza was trying to put up a confident front, but he knew the trouble was serious. For if events in Managua led to a strong reaction against him in the United States, a critical underpinning of his rule would be shaken: the impression, carefully cultivated by his family for two generations, of American favor. At times during the Somozas' four decades in power, Washington's support had been generous. At other times, it had been grudging. There had even been moments when American policy makers had tried to persuade the Somozas to allow democracy to take root in Nicaragua. But always the Somozas had managed to convince the people of Nicaragua and any political opponents that serious opposition to the dynasty was pointless in the face of their friendship with the most powerful nation in the hemisphere.

Indeed, more out of naiveté than calculation, Washington was a midwife to the birth of the Somoza dynasty. In 1932 American policy makers decided it was time to put an end to two decades of interventions by American military forces in Nicaragua. Twin circumstances convinced Washington that the continued presence of American forces was neither necessary nor desirable: the creation of a Nicaraguan National Guard that could keep order, and the election of a Nicaraguan president who appeared to have popular support.

The new president, Dr. Juan Sacasa, consulted American representatives about whom he should choose as the first *jefe* director of the National Guard. The Americans, who had been instrumental in establishing the Guard, envisioned it as an apolitical force that could guarantee the future of Nicaraguan democracy. Who could manage the Guard well, yet be managed in turn by Sacasa? The Nicaraguan president and his American advisers agreed that the best choice would be the husband of Sacasa's niece, a sometime officer in the army of Sacasa's Liberal party named Anastasio Somoza García.

The choice was based on a tragic miscalculation of the man who would become the founder of a dictatorial dynasty, the father of two sons who would also rule the nation. But it is easy to see how Washington and Sacasa could have underestimated Somoza. His hated enemy, the guerrilla leader Augusto César Sandino, belittled him by calling him the Penguin, and one can see why: smooth of feature, rather round in the body and soft in the face, Somoza in the flesh did not evoke the image of a bird of prey. His early career as a toilet inspector and used car salesman did not exactly mark him for greatness. His participation in a military rebellion in 1926 was nearly as unimpressive: after a force he commanded was routed by government troops, Somoza went into hiding for a few days and then emerged to receive a government pardon. The young Somoza's major credential, the one that impressed the Americans in Managua, was his ability to speak English, the result of an American education.

Still, the charming and friendly Somoza was more than a slick American sycophant. He had a shrewd talent for political maneuver, a calculating patience, a determined ambition. A weak character does not establish the longest-lasting and wealthiest dynastic dictatorship in Latin American history. And now, in 1933, Somoza had more than these personal qualities. He had the National Guard. For the next two generations, there might be periods when a Somoza was not president of Nicaragua, but a Somoza would always control the Guardia — and thus, in effect, rule Nicaragua.

The murder of Augusto Sandino soon gave evidence of Somoza's capacities. With the American Marines gone from Nicaragua, Sandino had decided to put an end to his insurgency, agreeing in February 1933 to the partial disarmament of his troops in return for amnesty and economic programs in northern Nicaragua. As the year wore on, however, hostility between the National Guard and Sandino's supporters intensified. Somoza insisted on the total disarmament of Sandino's men, and on February 16, 1934, Sandino went to Managua to clarify matters. After a week of talks he was reaching a compromise with Sacasa — but not with Somoza and his hawkish fellow officers at the Guardia.

On the evening of February 21, a car carrying Sandino, his father, and a number of associates was stopped by a Guardia patrol. Sandino asked to speak to Somoza on the telephone, appealing to their common membership in the Masons. The commander of the patrol passed along the request and Somoza almost agreed, but the chief of the general staff took the telephone away from the *jefe* director and ordered the patrol leader to proceed with the execution. Sandino and two of his companions were taken to a nearby field and shot.

Myth has it that Somoza ordered this murder at the behest, or at least with the blessing, of the Americans. In fact, as historian Richard Millet shows quite convincingly, the American ambassador had not even agreed to an earlier Somoza request that Somoza be allowed to lock Sandino up, and was furious when he learned of the assassination. It also seems clear that Somoza himself, while issuing the fatal order, was pressed to do so by his subordinates.[4] If so, they were merely strengthening his resolve, not his intention. Years earlier, in 1929, he had allowed himself a boast in conversation with an American friend, Graves Erskine: "Erskine, you Americans are a bunch of damn fools. . . . You've got 5,000 Marines down here and you are just not getting ahead, you'll never get Sandino." When asked how he would go about it, Somoza went on: "It would be very simple. I would declare an armistice, I would invite Sandino in, and we'd have some drinks, a good dinner, and when he went out one of my men would shoot him."[5]

With Sandino out of the way, Somoza moved to take complete power, driving Sacasa from the presidency in 1935 through a combination of political and military maneuvers and managing his own uncontested election in 1936. Despite an appeal by three former Nicaraguan presidents that Washington intervene to head off Somoza's power plays, the State Department was determined to avoid muddying even a toe in a new Nicaraguan quagmire. The United States would now be the "good neighbor"; Nicaragua's problems were Nicaragua's affair. American representatives in Managua scrupulously avoided taking sides or even offering advice. The basic American interest in Nicaragua was stability, and order was being maintained by Somoza and the Guard, even if it was at the cost of the American ideal of democracy. While FDR's policy of nonintervention in Latin America was welcomed throughout the hemisphere, for the Nicaraguans who opposed Somoza, the neighbor seemed more indifferent than good.

Somoza soon used the Guardia to solidify his power, firing a warning shot over the heads of any would-be plotters by arresting and briefly imprisoning fifty-six political rivals. He also moved to turn political power into personal wealth. In his first three years in office, Somoza accumulated a fortune of more than three million dollars through forced contributions from Nicaraguan businesses and civil servants, purchases of houses at far below their value from intimidated owners, and improvements on his land by public works projects.[6] A few million dollars was nothing compared to the Somozas' later wealth, but it was not bad as seed money. By the early 1950s, when Somoza had bought up huge quantities of land, the popular Caribbean calypso king Rupert "Kontiki" Allen was not far wrong when he sang "A guy asked de dictator if he 'ad any farms/'E said 'e 'ad on'y one/It was Nicaragua."[7]

American leaders knew Somoza was both despotic and avaricious. While the remark is probably apocryphal, Franklin Roosevelt's famous bit of cynicism in saying that the Nicaraguan was a son of a bitch but "our son of a bitch" caught Washington's disdain perfectly. Americans were wrong, however, if they believed Somoza was ours. He was an American legacy more than an American possession. Roosevelt's remark implied a degree of American support for and influence with Somoza that was not, in fact, real.

Nicaragua was quiet in the late 1930s as events in Europe and Asia took up Washington's attention. To the extent that there was an attitude, the American attitude toward Somoza was one of vague contempt. In Nicaragua, however, Somoza portrayed his relationship with Roosevelt as one of close friendship. He played up a meeting in Washington with Roosevelt in 1939 and declared a two-day holiday in Nicaragua to celebrate FDR's reelection in 1940. And he wrote the American president warm letters — letters that were usually handed to an aide for reply.[8] It is not clear whether Somoza knew that the extraordinary pomp surrounding his visit to Washington was partly the result of circumstance: the Americans were using the arrangements as a dress rehearsal for a visit by British royalty.

As was proper for so close a friend of the American president, when the United States went to war Somoza immediately declared war on Japan, Germany, and Italy. And like other countries in the region, Nicaragua received generous quantities of lend-lease materiel. But the Americans remained determined to avoid involvement in Nicaraguan politics. Messages to and from the embassy in Managua during the early and mid-1940s show a series of efforts by Somoza to identify himself with the United States (for example, asking permission to give a speech from the embassy balcony) and of American stratagems to avoid this. Dr. Frankenstein preferred not to be associated too clearly with his monster.

By 1943 it was clear that Somoza was maneuvering to run again in the elections scheduled for 1947, in violation of the Nicaraguan constitution. Appeals by Somoza's opponents for American help to prevent this were initially disregarded. But in 1945, with the world war won and a new American president in power, American policy shifted subtly. While still professing neutrality among Nicaraguan factions and a policy of noninterference, the Truman administration decided it would take a position on behalf of the Nicaraguan constitution and the principle of democracy. On August 1, 1945, Assistant Secretary of State Nelson Rockefeller warned the Nicaraguan ambassador in Washington that a Somoza run for reelection would seriously affect relations between the two countries. And on December 17, 1945, Rockefeller's successor, Spruille Braden, recorded having told the Nicaraguan ambassador in Washington that

. . . we believe that the best way to practice democracy was to practice it and that sometimes the way was hard. If leftist or anti-American elements should become active, well, that was only a part of the difficult progress toward the democratic goal. [Braden] said that he felt sure President Somoza, being apart from the National Guard, being apart in general from an active political life, would as an elder statesman continue to exercise great influence upon the development of the political situation in Nicaragua along democratic and otherwise favorable lines, and thus write his name large on the pages of history.[9]

Somoza did accept part of the message, backing away from an active candidacy, but he was by no means prepared to be put out to a pasture grazed by elder statesmen, nor was he prepared to lose control of the Guardia. He allowed his Liberal party to nominate Dr. Leonardo Argüello, whom he thought he could control, and then stole the 1947 election for his candidate. Despite pleas by the opposition, the United States had refused to supervise the election unless requested to do so by all parties and joined by other nations.

For once, Somoza had miscalculated. Argüello was of a more independent disposition than Somoza had reckoned. This became clear to the American ambassador in December 1946, when Argüello told him that Somoza was choosing the candidates for the next Nicaraguan congress. Argüello considered them to be of a low caliber and entirely pro-Somoza. "[The congress] is so bad," he said, "and of such a low caliber that I will be able to influence it more readily than I would a group of honest men." The ambassador reported "the distinct impression that he will try to be a real President and to free himself as much as possible from Somoza's influence."[10]

Somoza discovered his miscalculation as soon as Argüello took office. Not only did the new president name a cabinet of his own supporters; he even interfered with Somoza's personal political and economic interests by making a number of appointments in the National Guard and by firing hundreds of bureaucrats who were working on various economic projects for the Somoza family.

Somoza's reaction was swift and predictable: as he had removed Sacasa, now he used the Guardia to remove Argüello and replace him with a more tractable provisional president. The Truman administration reacted by cutting off military aid to the Guardia, removing the American head of the military academy, and — for more than a year — denying diplomatic recognition to what was still, in effect, Somoza's government, despite his offer of anti-Communist provisions in a new constitution and the use of Nicaraguan territory for American military bases in times of emergency.

But Somoza knew his Americans. A few years later, preoccupation with the Cold War had returned political stability to its central place in American policy toward Nicaragua. Democracy was nice, but there were more serious things to worry about. In 1950 the State Department's George Kennan told a meeting of American ambassadors in Latin America, "It is better to have a strong regime in power than a liberal government if it is indulgent and relaxed and penetrated by Communists."[11] The world in which an Assistant Secretary Braden could preach democracy to the Nicaraguans, even if it meant gains for leftists, was gone. And Somoza himself was now again president, elected in May 1950 over an aged rival, Emiliano Chamorro.

In a Cold War setting, the Guardia was no longer seen as an embarrassing barrier to democracy. It was a bulwark against communism. A State Department policy statement of April 17, 1951, referred to "wishful endeavors to emplant democracy where the ground is not yet fertile." As Washington considered reestablishing a military mission in Nicaragua, the ambassador in Managua, Thomas Whelan, cabled his opinion that

> the political opposition to Somoza in Nicaragua harps upon the charge that the United States created the Nicaraguan Army which, according to this opposition, is the force that has kept Somoza in power. . . . Repeatedly oppositionists have called upon this Embassy to help break the chains which they claim we forged to bind them under Somoza's domination. It is possible that restoration of a military mission would intensify this complaint and be interpreted as

our lining up more strongly with the Somoza government. . . . This is the sole political objection I see to restoration of the mission. I do not regard it as particularly important.[12]

An air force mission was soon established.

The indifference of the embassy to the plight of the Nicaraguan opposition was matched in Washington by attitudes among State Department officials. On June 6, 1952, the officer in charge of Central America and Panama affairs wrote: "It is my opinion that, if Somoza keeps his health and remains in control, Nicaragua has real grounds for optimism. . . . Somoza has gone through a necessary period in establishing stability in the country and is giving increasing evidence of a forward-looking determination to do something for the lasting and general good of the country."[13]

The following March, as the Eisenhower administration settled in, the American ambassador in Managua sent a long cable to Washington calling attention to the "strategic importance of the Republic of Nicaragua, not only in relation to Hemispheric Defense but also in relation to the spread of Communism from Guatemala." (The government of Jacobo Arbenz Guzmán in Guatemala had legalized the Guatemalan Communist party and threatened to expropriate the assets of the United Fruit Company there.) The ambassador recommended resuming military aid to the National Guard, noting that the political situation in Nicaragua was stable "for the first time during this century. Despite the widespread impression to the contrary," the ambassador went on, "Somoza is not a dictator in the true sense of the word." One wishes the ambassador had contributed to our etymological education by defining what that true sense of dictatorship might be. Our envoy, however, limited himself to noting that Somoza's political enemies had either joined him or had "grown old and feeble."[14]

A U.S. Army mission was established in Nicaragua, and in April 1954 an agreement for a military assistance program was signed. Somoza offered Nicaragua as a base from which the successful CIA overthrow of the Arbenz regime in Guatemala was launched. There was now no doubt that the relationship had changed: Somoza no longer had to pretend that he enjoyed favor in Washington. For the next twenty years, even if their marriage was not based on love, Washington and the Somozas found their relationship highly convenient. The United States supported the Somozas and the Somozas supported the United States — in votes at the United Nations, in regional councils, and by offering Nicaragua as a base for training and launching the Cuban exile forces that met disaster at the Bay of Pigs in 1961.

In Nicaragua, the face of the Somoza dynasty changed. The old man was gunned down by an assassin in 1955 and was replaced first by his elder son, Luis, and then, after an interregnum in the mid-1960s, by the younger one, General Anastasio Somoza Debayle. Elected president in early 1967, the younger Somoza had already wielded power in Nicaragua for some years through his control of the National Guard.

It was from President Richard Nixon that the Somoza dynasty was to receive the fullest measure of Washington's favor and something close, even, to affection. The relationship was evident not merely in Washington's tangible assistance, but in the occupants of the two great buildings in Managua that spoke of the American presence: the Intercontinental Hotel and the magnificent residence of the American ambassador, set on a hill above the city. In the hotel, the reclusive Howard Hughes rented a whole floor, where he plotted his next forays into the Nicaraguan business world. At the American residence one found Ambassador Turner B. Shelton, whose approach to Somoza would have done an Ottoman courtier proud. A photograph of the two men shaking hands is instructive. Somoza, the dictator, looks like a diplomat. He is standing erect, impeccable in business suit and sensible glasses. He has a pleasant smile on his face and seems to be enjoying the moment in a rather cool way. Shelton, the diplomat representing the greatest power on earth, plays the part of a local pol seeking favor from a party leader. He is leaning in, with head slightly bowed, clutching his friend's limp arm. His eyes are hidden behind sunglasses; his mouth is set in the smile of one practiced in deferential banter.[15] It was a good time for Somoza.

On December 23, 1972, disaster struck Managua when a tremendous earthquake and fire destroyed almost every building in the city. The human toll was appalling: some 10,000 people killed and hundreds of thousands made homeless. Many years later there is still a dark sadness in the voices of those recalling the tragedy, and one can feel the fresh new burst of anger when they describe the contrast between the human misery of the time and Somoza's response. After the disaster, Washington, with other foreign capitals, responded quickly with massive quantities of aid. But Somoza, who had inherited his father's appetite for wealth and his eye for opportunity, hurried to the trough. He and his chief lieutenants in the Guard appropriated building materials for use on personal enterprises, and they went much further: large reconstruction projects, for instance, were steered to land owned by the dictator. Somoza also used the earthquake to expand his political control — with Washington's blessing. He had avoided elections in 1971 by agreeing to give nominal power to a triumvirate of politicians who would "rule" from May 1972 until elections in 1974. But in the emergency following the earthquake, Ambassador Shelton encouraged Somoza to assume total power, and he did so.

Foreign Service officers at the embassy heard the stories of Somoza's looting, and they knew there would be a significant political consequence. It was not only the people of Managua, struggling to rebuild their lives, who were angry. Leaders of the business community were also repelled — by the immorality, yes, but also by the way Somoza was unscrupulously using the disaster and his position to accumulate a new fortune. Embassy officers sought to report all this to Washington, but were quashed by Ambassador Shelton. One particularly courageous staff member, James Cheek, would not be quieted, and exercised his right to forward his views to the State Department through its "dissent channel." (He was later given an award by the American Foreign Service Association for the quality of his reporting as well as his "challenge to conventional wisdom.") Nor could Shelton do anything about reports of Somoza's behavior in the international press.

*

By 1974 it was obvious that Somoza's regime had become unpopular throughout Nicaraguan society. In March a large gathering of business leaders issued a statement accusing Somoza of corruption. Opposition leaders boycotted the September election, which Somoza won against a hand-picked opponent. Leaders of the Catholic church joined opposition politicians in refusing to attend his inauguration. In addition, Somoza and the National Guard faced the limited but burgeoning opposition of the Sandinista National Liberation Front (FSLN). Founded in 1961 with some twenty guerrilla fighters, by 1974 the FSLN had developed a political organization that was especially effective in the rural areas of north-central Nicaragua and among leftist students in the cities. It commanded, also, approximately 150 seasoned guerrillas.

The most dramatic setback to the regime came on December 27, 1974, when thirteen Sandinista guerrillas burst in on a Christmas party held in honor of Turner Shelton, killing the host (a former minister of agriculture) and three security personnel. Shelton had already left, but the Sandinistas were able to take some prominent hostages, including several politicians and two members of Somoza's family. On December 30 an angry Somoza gave in to the guerrillas' demands for the release of fourteen other Sandinistas from jail, a hefty amount of cash, publication of a Sandinista political manifesto, and safe passage for the guerrillas to Cuba. In military terms, the Sandinistas were to fare badly at the hands of the National Guard during the next few years; but politically, they had gained in prestige and in the popular imagination. And the wave of repression launched by Somoza in 1975 was to turn more and more Nicaraguans against him.

Meanwhile, the Watergate scandal had cost Somoza the patronage of Richard Nixon. The Ford administration was to be far less accommodating. A new assistant secretary of state for Latin America, William D. Rogers, replaced Shelton (over Somoza's objections) with James Theberge, a conservative academic expert. On the instructions of the State Department, Rogers and Theberge met with Somoza to tell him that the embassy would henceforth be neutral among competing Nicaraguan political factions, that it was going to make contacts with his opposition, and that it would be keeping a careful eye on U.S. aid accounts.

If Somoza was unhappy with the Ford administration, he feared that worse was to come when Jimmy Carter was elected in November 1976. Still, didn't he have friends in Congress? Hadn't his family always known how to handle the Americans? A friend warned him, "You're going to lose your best friends, the gringos. They are saying that they are going to make life impossible for you. They are going to try and get your ass." Somoza replied, "Aw, you think I have no friends in Washington. I can take care of Carter."[16] He knew, however, that the human rights rhetoric of the new administration spelled trouble. He was upset in July 1977 by the symbolic as well as the financial implications when he was forced to pay for his flight on an American military aircraft when he traveled to a Miami hospital. (He had suffered an attack of angina at his mistress's home.)

But the Carter administration's obvious distaste for Somoza and its concern with human rights were to collide with another of the policies to which it was strongly attached: noninterference in the internal affairs of Latin American nations. Strongly influenced by the recommendations of a report published in 1976 by a commission of Latin American experts chaired by the respected Sol Linowitz, Carter and his advisers were determined to redirect American policy. Latin America would be treated like any other region. The "special relationship" that had produced the paternalistic patterns of the previous seventy years and more would come to an end.

Policy dilemmas are often seen as conflicts between principle and pragmatism. Unhappily, in a complicated world and for any but the most simple of political philosophies, principles themselves — when put into practice — may collide as often as they coincide. So it was with the principles of respect for the sovereignty of other nations and support for human rights.

On the one hand, President Jimmy Carter and most of his lieutenants ranked the international promotion of human rights among the most important of their foreign policy objectives, and there was no doubt that working actively against Somoza would serve that goal. While not the most brutal of Latin American dictators, Somoza during the 1970s had moved up in the standings. American policy makers in 1977 and 1978 thus saw Nicaragua as primarily a human rights problem.

Somoza knew this, and in the hope of deflecting pressures from the Carter administration and Congress he attempted, during the middle of 1977, to curb human rights abuses by his National Guard. On September 19 he also lifted censorship and the state of siege that had given him extraordinary formal authority. This left the Carter administration in a quandary. How could it recognize this relative progress while continuing to put pressure on what remained a corrupt and repressive regime? The answer was a logical but unsatisfactory compromise. The problem was that the existing military assistance agreement with Nicaragua was about to expire, and if it was not replaced, $2.5 million appropriated by Congress but not yet sent to Nicaragua would be lost. The solution was to sign a new military aid agreement — but to refuse actually to provide the $2.5 million or any other aid to Somoza's government. The administration announced that all military aid — and economic assistance — would be blocked until further progress in human rights was demonstrated.

The approach was wonderfully well balanced and subtle. The new military aid agreement created an incentive for further progress on human rights, but blocking the funds made sure that the carrot was only dangled rather than consumed. Unfortunately, the headlines reporting the decision could not convey the nuances of diplomatic strategy or budgetary processes, and what stood out was that the Carter administration had signed a military agreement with Somoza's regime. For many reporters and their readers, the impression was a puzzling one: the Carter administration seemed to be trying to promote human rights by appeasing the Nicaraguan military while penalizing the Nicaraguan people.

As its global interest in human rights led the administration into decisions that were essentially intrusive in Nicaraguan affairs, its regional policy pushed it in the opposite direction and onto the other horn of a policy dilemma. One of the first principles of

Carter's Latin American policy was a new respect for the sovereignty of governments throughout the hemisphere. The predominant view of Carter's senior foreign policy makers (and most scholars of Latin American affairs) was that the days of American arbitration of the internal political disputes to our south had to stop, for those days had seen all too many interventions by American Marines or the CIA, most vivid in memory the Bay of Pigs. Sooner or later, and better sooner, Central American democracy would have to be built by Central Americans. Constant American political and military interventions, even if designed to promote democracy, in the long run worked against it. For a democracy imposed and then manipulated by foreign interests and governments could not be healthy and endure. This did not mean that the United States would or could stay completely out of the internal affairs of Latin American nations, but the presumption would be on the side of Washington's keeping its distance.

Through 1977, the first year of the Carter administration, the tension between a respect for sovereignty and the promotion of human rights could be resolved by an essentially negative approach: a policy of American "distancing" from repressive military regimes. By denying, on human rights grounds, the quantities of military assistance Somoza had previously received from the United States, Washington could distance itself from his regime while putting pressure on him to liberalize his rule. A denial of aid is not a violation of sovereignty, unless one tries to argue that foreign governments have a sovereign right to American largesse.

But as events in Nicaragua deteriorated, as the opposition to Somoza became increasingly violent and the National Guard responded with its own repressive force, such a position became less satisfactory in both conceptual and practical terms. Although a policy of distancing respected the sovereignty of Nicaragua, it neither headed off the human costs of the burgeoning violence there nor prevented the leftward drift of the opposition that might someday replace Somoza.

Thus, the assassination of Pedro Joaquín Chamorro in January 1978 and the popular revulsion against Somoza that followed it brought the concept of distancing into question again. The question was to be raised in Venezuela, where President Carlos Andrés Pérez was determined to push President Jimmy Carter into more assertive action against Somoza. And it was raised also in Washington, where the State Department bureau in charge of Latin American affairs saw an opportunity to reverse the new policy of 1977 and return to more active involvement in Nicaraguan political affairs.

THREE

In Christopher's Back Office

THE KILLING OF PEDRO JOAQUÍN CHAMORRO CAME AS a terrible shock to the president of Venezuela, Carlos Andrés Pérez. It was not only that he was a friend of Chamorro. He also had a strong personal distaste for Anastasio Somoza. And as a committed democrat, the Venezuelan leader was worried that Somoza's autocratic and venal rule could be taking Nicaragua to revolutionary disaster, a disaster that could send ripples of instability throughout the region. The murder of Chamorro made Pérez all the more determined to work for an end to the Somoza regime.

Pérez had developed an unusually close personal as well as diplomatic relationship with Jimmy Carter. Upon hearing of the murder, he wrote a letter to Carter, with whom he often communicated, to urge that the United States and Venezuela do something about the deepening mess in Nicaragua. His call for "joint action" included urging an effort through the Organization of American States to gain a visit to Nicaragua by the Inter-American Commission on Human Rights.

As is customary when letters from a foreign leader are received at the White House, Pérez's message was sent to the State Department for preparation of a draft reply. There, the executive secretariat is responsible for assigning action on such items among the various bureaus and deciding which of the officials on the Seventh Floor should manage any disagreement among them.

It was clear that Deputy Secretary Warren Christopher should have responsibility for deciding the department's position on the reply to Pérez. Christopher chaired the Interagency Committee on Human Rights, the forum in which the Carter administration had made its decisions about Nicaragua. This committee met regularly to thrash out the ways in which American aid policies around the world should be affected by our human rights concerns. The political future of Nicaragua had not yet emerged as an issue deserving high-level attention in its own right; the nation was seen primarily as a human rights problem. So it was natural that Christopher, the senior official most involved in making human rights policies, should resolve any disputes as a response to Pérez was hammered out.

The secretariat decided that three State Department offices should be involved in coming up with the draft reply: the bureaus in charge of Latin American and human rights matters, and the policy planning staff, which often became involved when human rights issues were being considered.

It was almost certain that Pérez's letter would spark a dispute among them, and it did. The letter forced new attention to the old question of how deeply the United States should become involved in the internal political events of its neighbors. The Latin American bureau, formally the Bureau for American Republic Affairs, urged a stronger American role in Nicaraguan politics, including an effort to resolve the dispute between Somoza and his enemies while avoiding the appearance of support for the dictator. The other two offices involved in drafting a reply to Pérez were strongly opposed to this. The human rights bureau (formally the Bureau for Human Rights and Humanitarian Affairs) and the policy planning staff were committed to maintaining the policy of distancing.

An argument over Nicaragua between the human rights and Latin American bureaus surprised no one, because they had been battling on almost every human rights issue affecting Latin America since the beginning of the Carter administration. It was not entirely a struggle over substance. It was also a conflict between the career officers of the Latin American bureau and the political appointees —

the outsiders brought in by the Democrats in 1977 — in the human rights bureau and on the planning staff.

To many of the career officers charged with responsibility for American relations with the nations in the region, the political appointees seemed rigidly ideological and naively idealistic in their emphasis on human rights and their belief in policies of nonintervention. The career people were concerned that an emphasis on the pursuit of human rights would complicate American relations with existing governments, reducing Washington's influence on other issues of importance to the United States. Rhetorical attacks and denials of aid were not, in this view, a human rights policy. On the contrary, human rights were being used to penalize governments that the political appointees did not like. Further, the policy of nonintervention would make the United States irrelevant to the resolution of the very problems caused by its human rights crusading.

For some of the noncareer officials, the resistance among the career officers in the Latin American bureau to the administration's human rights initiatives, as well as to its policy of nonintervention, seemed to be based less on such reasoning than on simple "clientitis": the overriding concern of cautious officials abroad and in the department's regional bureaus that relations with their client governments be smooth. In their view, the career bureaucrats were creatures of habit and hostages to the Foreign Service promotion system. Pursuing human rights involved friction, angry voices, and interference with routine aid programs. This threatened more than an interruption in comfortable daily patterns of work. Whole careers could suffer if trouble with the client erupted during one's watch.

That the career officials were arguing for a relatively more interventionist posture with America's traditional client, Somoza, was seen by the political appointees as a variant on the disease of clientitis. Such an intervention, if it helped Somoza work things out with his opponents, might save his regime. And in any case, it was traditional that the United States step in when instability threatened in Central America. The proposal that the United States become involved in Somoza's disputes with his opponents, some political appointees felt, reflected an interventionist pattern of thought that was deeply ingrained in the Latin American bureau — far more than in the bureaus dealing with, say, Europe or Africa.

Thus, in the eyes of their noncareer rivals, the Foreign Service officers in the Latin American bureau were not so much politically conservative as traditionalist. In this view, the result of traditionalism was opposition to a policy that would correct years of damaging American intervention in the region. And, they thought, internal opponents of the administration's human rights approach failed to understand that the policy would serve not only humanitarian ends but American national security interests as well. For how, the human rights advocates argued, would our continuing to do business as usual with dictators do anything but deepen the repression that was breeding a dangerous radicalism in the region? Frustration with bureaucratic foot dragging led one noncareer official to describe his job as being primarily one of "harassing the Latin American bureau."

All in all, the policy differences between career and noncareer officials were complex and even paradoxical. The political appointees, although more anti-Somoza and more fervent in their views on human rights, were restrained by their commitment to policies of nonintervention. The career officials, generally more cautious in outlook, were the ones pressing for more assertive American policies, in part because of traditional habits of mind about the proper role of the United States in Central America.

The differences between outsiders and career officers took place within as well as among the bureaus. For example, Sally Shelton, a deputy assistant secretary of state for Latin American affairs, sometimes found herself at odds with her superior, Assistant Secretary Terence Todman. Shelton, a political appointee in her early thirties who had worked for Lloyd Bentsen, Democratic senator from Texas, was no human rights ideologue. But at meetings on human rights issues she more than occasionally agreed with the human rights bureau. Once, uninstructed by Todman, she committed her bureau to joining with Human Rights in opposing an economic assistance loan to Nicaragua. On her return to her office she was berated by Todman in front of a number of embarrassed staff members. But she liked Todman, and thought his anger at her position flowed from his concern for the Nicaraguans who would have benefited from the loans as much as from his distaste for the Carter administration's human rights policies.

It was Todman who most frustrated officials working on human rights in Latin America. A career Foreign Service officer, he was vigorous in his opposition to what he saw as the rigidities of the administration's human rights efforts. As a result, by mid-1978 he was reassigned to an ambassadorial post after giving a speech critical of the administration's policies. During his year and a half in the Latin American bureau, many of his actions seemed, indeed, to be obstructionist. But his opponents gave him too little credit. As Sally Shelton observed, he had a genuine concern about the impact of American policy decisions on poor people, and he was not indifferent to the question of human rights. He was later to decline an appointment by the Reagan administration as the first black ambassador to South Africa — again with some undiplomatic public remarks, this time about American policies toward that country.

The early rounds in the struggle went to Todman's opponents, who dominated the human rights decisions of 1977. Members of the human rights bureau and the policy planning staff convinced senior officials that after the Chamorro assassination, Todman's visit to Managua should be postponed. And they were instrumental in gaining the cancellation, on January 30, 1978, of Nicaragua's fiscal year 1979 military assistance loan.

Although differences over policy generally ran along the fault line between career and noncareer officials, and although there was tension between the two groups, it would be wrong to conclude that all Foreign Service officers were subject to clientitis, that all political appointees were aggressive ideologues, or that career and noncareer officials could not work well together and develop close personal relationships. For example, the Latin American bureau and policy planning staff were often represented in meetings on Central America by career Foreign Service officers John Bushnell and Paul

Kreisberg. The characters of both men suggest how wrong a stereo-
typical view of the Foreign Service can be. Bushnell, Todman's
senior deputy, was notable more for his tenacity than for his caution.
He knew what was on his mind, and he spoke it. Paul Kreisberg,
the senior deputy on the policy planning staff, recalls Bushnell as
a skilled advocate: "sharp-edged, cool, and articulate."

For his part, Kreisberg, a career officer, advocated the same policy
of distancing that most of the political appointees supported. Intelligent, honest, and original in his thinking, Kreisberg spoke his mind
in a blunt and friendly way. He sometimes "made waves," a damn-
ing term in an organization devoted to keeping the bureaucratic
waters still. This made him an invaluable member of the planning
staff, whose job included asking difficult questions and warning
of future hazards, but it slowed what should have been a brilliant
career into one that was simply successful.

Kreisberg had been convinced by Richard Feinberg, the Latin
American specialist on the planning staff, that the policy of distancing from Somoza was a correct one. Feinberg argued that Nicaragua
was a test of whether the United States could finally break the
pattern of both American and Central American behavior in which
both sides assumed that Washington was the arbiter of political
events in the region. In too many Central American nations, Feinberg
argued, both the left and the right "had looked to us for problem
solving. We should say to them, 'Why don't you see if you can
solve it for yourself?' Nonintervention does not mean noninvolve-
ment. It means leaving the basic responsibility to them rather than
taking it on ourselves."

This approach made sense to Kreisberg, as did the human rights
policy of the Carter administration. But he did not develop the
kind of emotional commitment to these policies that he sensed in
the political appointees. His sense of professionalism almost pre-
cluded it. "Professionals," he says, "are basically people who do
not live and die over issues. Foreign Service officers have their
own views, and express them. But professionals in the bureaus
deal with one another as colleagues with different views. They
argue for ideas as part of their jobs. Unlike the political appointees,

for most professionals the ideas are not the reason they are in government." So Kreisberg was always direct and vigorous in debate, but never felt or conveyed the kind of personal rancor against his opponents that he felt the "believers" could sometimes show.

The planning staff was included in the action on the letter from Pérez because the answer to it would help set policy, and the staff saw its role as including involvement even on day-to-day business when policy was at stake. This expansive approach to its mandate did not always make policy planning popular with the other bureaus in the department on whose turf it might be treading, but policy flows as much from work on specific items — like the letter from Pérez — as it does from the large, formal interagency "policy reviews" that result in presidential pronunciamentos. Each specific action provides a precedent for future actions, a precedent of which other governments are intensely aware. A formal statement of policy, even a presidential speech setting that policy out in its grandest terms, as such speeches do, is bound to be taken seriously by both American bureaucrats and foreign diplomats. But because policy statements are likely to be broad, their significance may not be deep. Actions are concrete; the elasticity of words, especially as interpreted by diplomats and bureaucrats, can be nearly infinite.

It may seem surprising that while the three offices in State argued over the proper reply to Pérez, a member of the National Security Council staff also became involved in a dispute within the bosom of the department. After reading the many accounts of bureaucratic bloodshed between secretaries of state and national security advisers over the past two decades, one would assume that a member of the NSC staff would be as welcome within the State Department as a retainer of the House of Lancaster at a council of the Duke of York in 1460. But while figurative white and red roses might have been appearing on the pinstriped battle dress of some State Department and NSC officials by early 1978, the happy fact is that bureaucratic relationships turn as much on personality as on institutional rivalry, and common sense sometimes prevails. In the Carter administration, for example, a number of NSC staff members worked far more closely, openly, and cooperatively with their State Department colleagues than their superior, Zbigniew Brzezinski, did with Cyrus Vance or Warren Christopher.

Among these was Robert Pastor, the Latin American specialist on the National Security Council staff. While Pastor was sometimes resented in State's Latin American bureau (especially, it is said, by Todman) for his youth and assertive style, other State officials (especially the political appointees) appreciated him for his friendliness and willingness to work with them. Pastor was only twenty-nine years old when appointed to the NSC staff at the start of the administration, and his smooth features made him look even younger. A compact man with dark hair, he had just served as staff director of the Linowitz Commission, whose influential report in 1976 had recommended that the United States adopt a less interventionist stance in the hemisphere. Colleagues remember that Pastor used the commission report not only as a general guide to policy, but kept score on how many of its numerous specific recommendations for Latin American policy the Carter administration had put into practice.

Pastor brought to his work at the White House a quick intelligence and an ability to write easily and clearly, as well as an extraordinary energy and determination to leave his mark on American policy. Throughout 1977 he had worked with other political appointees — Mark Schneider, the senior deputy assistant secretary at the human rights bureau, Richard Feinberg on the planning staff, and Stephen Oxman on Christopher's staff — to push the Latin American bureau in the new directions set out by the Carter administration and the Linowitz Commission before it. Now, in the letter from Pérez to Carter, Pastor saw an opportunity to engage the interest of Brzezinski and the president in the Nicaraguan issue and to force a clear decision in the State Department in favor of the policy of distancing.

On February 6, 1978, Pastor was to have lunch with John Bushnell, the senior deputy in the Latin American bureau. Pastor was worried about how the draft of the reply to Pérez was shaping up and saw in the lunch an opportunity to push Bushnell toward support for distancing. While noninterventionism was a declared general policy in the region, Pastor believed the American approach toward Nicaragua was not yet clearly enough defined. To be sure, he was pleased when, on the day of his lunch with Bushnell, the department issued a statement reaffirming a policy of nonintervention. Commenting on the turmoil in Managua in the wake of the Chamorro assassination, State Department spokesman Hodding Carter III conveyed U.S. support for "greater freedom and democracy . . . moderation and conciliation." But, Carter added, there would be no American intervention in the affair. When a reporter asked whether "the U.S. may ask Somoza in one way or another to resign," Carter was emphatic: "That would constitute a direct interference in the affairs of that country, and that we are not doing."

The public statement was fine, but Pastor also knew that a day or two earlier, the Latin American bureau had instructed the American ambassador in Managua to make suggestions to Somoza about the organization of his government, an approach Pastor considered incompatible with distancing. John Bushnell was temporarily in charge of the Latin American bureau while Assistant Secretary Todman was on a trip, and Pastor was sure Bushnell favored a reply to Pérez that would go beyond the policy.

The lunch was as contentious as Pastor had thought it might be. The two men argued about the draft reply to Pérez throughout the meal without reaching any sort of compromise. Bushnell argued that the United States was already involved in the Nicaraguan crisis, citing the instruction to the ambassador. Pastor argued that distancing was our public policy and that the instruction had not been cleared by the NSC staff.

Frustrated and a little angry, Pastor returned to his office in the Executive Office Building, next to the White House, and decided to bypass the State Department altogether. He spent most of that evening writing a memorandum to the president that urged a response to Pérez expressing sympathy for his views and cooperation on promoting human rights, while avoiding a commitment to intervening in Nicaraguan political wars. But the next day, Brzezinski refused to forward the memorandum to Carter. It was too complicated, he told Pastor, and besides, there had to be a recommendation first from the State Department. "Do you think the president is an assistant secretary of state?" he asked. Pastor saw that he had been wrong, and turned his attention again to the State Department.

He first went back to Bushnell, but got nowhere. Bushnell suggested that the draft of Carter's letter to Pérez simply not address the question of intervention/nonintervention in Nicaraguan political affairs. Pastor disagreed: the issue could not be avoided in responding to Pérez's points. Nor was Pastor willing to abandon the letter as a vehicle for establishing policy. Since it involved the president and would have to go through the NSC staff, the draft letter offered Pastor a comparative bureaucratic advantage. But Bushnell had the advantage when it came to daily business with the embassy in Managua. That evening Pastor noted in his diary that, as matters stood, Bushnell seemed to have the upper hand. After their conversation that day, he wrote, "Bushnell knew that he had beaten me and he reveled in it."

The next day — Thursday, February 9 — an official in the Latin American bureau called to say that his department would send its draft of the letter directly to the NSC staff for transmission to the president. Pastor responded that the bureau should first clear the draft with Warren Christopher. If he couldn't persuade Bushnell, he would use the clearance process in State to surround and defeat him. So Pastor turned to trying to influence the course of events in the department. He consulted with his customary allies there — Mark Schneider and Richard Feinberg — and Feinberg in turn asked me, as policy planning director, to describe the issue to Christopher if I had an opportunity during the course of the day. This I did.

At the same time, Pastor benefited from a stroke of surprising good luck. When the letter from Pérez had arrived at the White House in late January 1978, Brzezinski had not shown great interest. Now, for reasons having little to do with Nicaragua, Brzezinski decided to get involved in the issue and to push for quick action by the department. Suddenly, Nicaragua had become linked to an issue of deep concern to the national security assistant: the Horn of Africa. The State Department and the NSC staff were engaged in a continuing policy dispute over how best to deal with the growing Cuban and Soviet presence in Ethiopia, and Brzezinski had encouraged the president to write a number of foreign leaders, including Carlos Andrés Pérez, to seek their counsel. In meetings with Pérez some months earlier, Carter had discussed a broad range of global problems (not including Central America!), and Brzezinski knew that Carter respected Pérez's opinion.[1]

Carter's letter to Pérez on Cuban involvement in Ethiopia had crossed Pérez's letter to Carter on Nicaragua. Pastor recalls that on Friday, February 10, "I tried to interest Brzezinski in the various issues raised by Pérez on Nicaragua, but he asked instead about Pérez' response to the letter on the Horn. I called [our ambassador] in Caracas, and learned that Pérez would not receive [him] or the letter until Pérez had received a response on Nicaragua. When I relayed this to Brzezinski, he suddenly took an interest in Nicaragua, and asked for a memo and a draft letter for the President, on an urgent basis."[2] Brzezinski called Christopher and asked that State get the memo and draft letter done by the next day. Christopher could not do so, for he had first to sort out the argument over the draft between the Latin American bureau and its opponents: the human rights bureau, policy planning, and (behind the scenes) Pastor.

The bureaus were therefore told to produce a memo and alternative draft letters by Monday, February 13, and Stephen Oxman, Christopher's special assistant, scheduled a meeting for February 15, in the deputy secretary's office, to thrash out the matter. On Monday, Feinberg met with Pastor and the two worked out a letter satisfactory to both. Feinberg included this version as the policy planning staff recommendation in a memorandum sent to the deputy secretary the next day.

It is rare in the State Department that disputing offices will write separate memos to the Seventh Floor. Senior officials simply don't have time to read long, competing briefs on all the matters that come before them, so the practice is to make the disputants agree on a single memo that fairly states the issue and then presents their alternative views.

The February 14 memorandum on Nicaragua was written by the Latin American bureau and the policy planning staff (with "clearance," or approval, by the human rights bureau). It had "Action Memorandum" written at the top, to indicate that an action would be proposed at the end. (Information Memorandums are just that — and naturally, in offices all around the State Department, they sink to the bottom of the piles of things to do, under the more urgent action items.) The memorandum first made the foreign policy arguments for and against distancing. After stating that Nicaragua faced perhaps the most severe "crisis of regime" in the past forty years and then reviewing the previous year's cuts in U.S. aid to Somoza to penalize him for his human rights abuses, the memorandum suggested two policy options. In outline form it noted the arguments for and against each one. Attached to the document were alternative versions of a letter from President Carter to President Pérez: one reflected a policy of distancing; the other indicated Carter's agreement with Pérez's call for deeper involvement.

The memorandum was very brief, almost cursory, and relied more on logical argument than on analysis of the situation in Nicaragua. In this it followed the pattern of most policy analyses at the State Department and in the White House: state the problem, describe it briefly, identify the options, note the arguments about each. The decision maker then weighs the arguments and decides what to do. No wasted space, to the point, neat. The problem is that the decision may thus be based as much on the force of tidy logic as on the requirements of a messy, illogical situation and a necessarily intuitive sense of its future course.

It is an approach that appeals, however, to senior officials whose schedules allow little time for speculative argument. It is especially attractive to political appointees schooled in the law or the writing of closely reasoned policy articles. Christopher — a man of judicial temperament — was not exempt from this appeal. He had compiled a brilliant record as a lawyer in California and, in the Johnson administration, as deputy attorney general at the Justice Department. When Cyrus Vance was named by Jimmy Carter to be his secretary of state, Vance had only one choice in mind for his deputy: Warren Christopher.

Extremely intelligent, a quick study, humane, self-effacing, Christopher would be a perfect alter ego for Vance. A slender man with dark hair and eyes, he would sit at meetings with a nearly impassive face, listening to the arguments and asking occasional pointed questions. He would then render his judgment. In debate with others — and he was often called on to represent the State Department at interagency meetings — he relied more on the intelligence of his argument and the merits of his case than on the fervor of his appeal, although he was capable of letting himself go when he thought it would be effective. He was aware that his customarily careful approach might seem less than forceful, but he was as often praised for his impeccable attention to the nuances of an issue. His approach was later to prove effective when he played a leading role in helping convince members of Congress to vote for the Panama Canal treaties.

In private, informal conversation, Christopher became far more animated as he led the discourse in search of amusement, his face lighting at a twist of irony or an unexpected observation. And those who watched the pattern of his decisions noted that while his heart was not worn on his sleeve, it consistently led him in the direction of promoting human rights.

Most evenings, Christopher would take home the memoranda he would need for the next day's meetings or the action items he had been unable to deal with at the office. If the papers were less detailed than one might wish, this was a matter of necessity rather than choice. The most seriously underrated factor in explaining Washington decision making is time, or rather the limits thereon. For each meeting there was a briefing memo to be read ahead of time, an instruction to be given afterward. And meanwhile, there were letters and telephone calls that must be managed, speeches to be planned, reporters' queries to be answered or deflected.

When an action assignment produced a memorandum from a bureau, the memo was first reviewed by Christopher's assistants, who usually added a note with their own thoughts about the substance of the issue and how he might wish to handle it. A senior official is seldom allowed by his staff to attend a meeting without a piece of paper describing the event, the issues to be considered, and — often — a "talker" suggesting points the staff thinks might usefully be made. These talking points are often helpful to the senior official. They are always important to the staff members, for they provide one of their best opportunities for influence. When the meeting is with a foreign official, the officers in the department in charge of relations with that nation write the talker; for a meeting of one senior official with others in the department, a talker would come from staff.

This is one of many ways in which a senior official's personal staff helps him deal with the massive workload that flows through his office. The staff assistant is the most junior member, and thus the one who does the scut work: sorting out the deluge of daily messages, making sure the more important ones quickly come to the attention of the senior official and to other staff with an interest in the subject; drafting responses to letters that need not be referred to the bureaus because they lack substantive importance; and overseeing the senior official's daily schedule to make sure he is prepared for every meeting and even for important telephone calls.

Each senior official is also assigned a personal assistant, the most important of the two or three secretaries in his office. The personal assistant manages the schedule and takes care of the most important dictating sessions when the senior official wants to write something himself. A staff assistant can come to grief by thinking that he (usually a he) can tell the personal assistant (usually a she) how to manage the schedule or organize the secretarial staff. He may be led to such folly because he, after all, is an officer, and she is staff (as well as a she). The result of such a confrontation will usually be the departure of the young officer from his position at the left hand of authority for a new job in the lower reaches. Personal assistants have almost invariably been working for or with their bosses for many years, often at the law firms or businesses from which the senior officials were recruited, and they are the best secretaries in the department. It is no contest when one decides that a young Foreign Service officer is invading her turf.

Above the staff assistant in the pecking order come the special assistants like Stephen Oxman, who make sure that their superior is well served by the bureaucracy and sometimes act for him in issuing instructions when they know what he has in mind. Christopher had five of them, one of whom acted as his executive assistant, or chief of staff.

The February 15 meeting on Nicaragua that Oxman had set up was by no means the only item on Christopher's agenda for that day. Indeed, while for Bushnell and Pastor the meeting would be an important test of the strength of their policy and bureaucratic positions, for Christopher it was only one more piece of business during a long and crowded day. So let the reader beware: in any story of how a policy was made over time, it may appear that the decision makers were obsessed with that one issue to the exclusion of others. But that is merely the focus of that particular tale; it may not have been the preoccupation of the people involved. Even in a crisis, other business must be done, other issues managed.

For a senior policy maker, all but the most important issues can seem like sounding whales. They are viewed and pursued, but rarely dealt with definitively before they dive again as events bring another issue into view. The policy maker must deal with those issues when they are in crisis and on the surface; he or she rarely has time to explore the depths. The unwary senior official may easily become the captive of a system and staff that entangle him in so many immediate decisions that they relegate him or her only to the surface of events.

This is why Secretary Vance had turned over primary responsibility for the human rights and Latin American accounts to Christopher, while he concentrated on the issues that most required his personal involvement at the time: negotiation of a SALT II treaty, efforts at peace in the Middle East, normalization of relations with the People's Republic of China, the future of the Panama Canal, and policy toward South Africa and Southern Rhodesia (later Zimbabwe). Vance and Christopher worked with great confidence in each other. Vance always consulted Christopher before making important decisions, and his deputy always made sure that his own decisions moved in the general direction Vance wanted.

The meeting on Nicaragua was scheduled for 4:15 P.M., in Christopher's back room. Tucked away behind the imposing, formal office of the deputy secretary of state is a more intimate space, some twenty by thirty feet, where the deputy secretary, an unpretentious man, liked to hold working meetings with his associates. Like a similar small room that both Henry Kissinger and Cyrus Vance used when they were secretaries of state, Christopher's back office was the place for his everyday work. He and his colleagues could sit around the small conference table in front of his desk and concentrate on their business without having to worry about splashing their coffee or leaning too hard on a Chippendale. His formal chamber was for visitors who needed to be impressed with the majesty of his office. So there was not much room left at the table when Christopher, Pastor, Bushnell, Oxman, Paul Kreisberg representing the planning staff, and Mark Schneider from the human rights bureau had taken seats.

Kreisberg recalls that the debate was calm but intense, with Bushnell pressing his case against a policy of nonintervention in a determined manner. But Bushnell was isolated in the discussion, as his bureau had been in the memorandum to Christopher. The argument followed the lines laid out in the memorandum: Bushnell pushed for an American effort, with Pérez and other Latin leaders, to produce a dialogue between Somoza and his opponents — without seeming to support Somoza. He argued that this could head off a deteriorating situation in Managua without compromising the American position on human rights. As he was later to put it, "The problem with nonintervention is that it is like denying the law of gravity. We are involved and willy-nilly exert great influence. Nonintervention is nonfeasible. The question is *how* to exert influence."

Schneider, Kreisberg, and Pastor pointed to the dangers of trying to affect Somoza's relationships with his opponents: the U.S. might well be blamed if such an effort failed; it would violate the policy of nonintervention in Latin American internal affairs; Somoza would seek to use it for his own purposes; Somoza might well be replaced by military leaders who would be still more repressive. It would be better, they argued, to maintain our distance from both Somoza and internal Nicaraguan political maneuvering.

The argument made by the Latin American bureau did not go as far as some of its members wanted. They believed that so long as Somoza stayed in power, the opposition to him, now led by moderates, would become radicalized and increasingly threatening to American interests. The purpose of a more interventionist American stance should therefore be to find ways to ease him out of power. But the dissidents had no way to demonstrate the accuracy of their predictions and were uncomfortable with calling overtly for Somoza's removal. A more modest recommendation for the establishment of a dialogue between Somoza and his opponents seemed more sensible, more likely to appeal to Christopher.

A punch was pulled on the other side of the argument as well. Nowhere in the memorandum or in the discussion in Christopher's office was there mention of the domestic political implications of the decision (a subject never raised in polite company in the State Department). Yet this was certainly on the minds of at least some of the political appointees in the Carter administration as policy toward Nicaragua was developed. Domestic politics did not determine policy, but it provided a context of which decision makers could not be unaware. After a year in office, Carter was coming under ever harsher attacks for perceived weakness both in his management of the government and in his commitment to the containment of communism. Increasingly he was accused in conservative quarters of waging his human rights campaign more strenuously against authoritarian but traditionally friendly regimes in the Third World than against Communist states. How then could he seek Somoza's removal, as Pérez clearly wanted, without seeming to confirm the charge? What would that do to his political standing, and to his ability to persuade even members of his own party to go along with him on such crucial and difficult issues as passage of Panama Canal treaties?

Although it was very unlikely that he would be persuaded by Bushnell, Christopher, as always, listened attentively. But he was predisposed to the arguments being made by Pastor, Schneider, and Kreisberg. His work on human rights issues during the past year had deepened his distaste for Somoza, and he had no wish to see the United States reduce its distance from him by getting more involved in reconciling Somoza's differences with his opponents. More important, he later recalled, was the meaning for him of "the lesson we learned over and over again about the hostility in Latin American countries to American intervention." He knew too that President Carter and Secretary Vance were strongly committed to the principle of respect for the sovereignty of other nations, and therefore to nonintervention in the internal affairs of Latin American nations. So Christopher came down on the side of a continued distancing from Somoza rather than a more active role for the United States. He therefore also decided that the State Department would recommend that President Carter send the draft letter to President Pérez that had been written by the planning staff — and the discreet hand of Robert Pastor.

As soon as the meeting ended, the State Department draft was sent to the White House. Pastor, who had seen all the maneuvering of the previous week come out exactly where he wanted it, sent the draft letter to the president for signature, under cover of a memorandum from Brzezinski. The president signed it on February 17.

The letter began with the good news for Pérez: Carter promised to work closely with the Venezuelan on human rights issues and to try to gain Somoza's agreement to a visit to Nicaragua by the Inter-American Commission on Human Rights. Then came the bad news, from Pérez's point of view: when it came to Nicaraguan politics, Carter wrote, "We can and will voice our preference for increased democratization. . . . But we will not intervene or impose specific political solutions for individual countries."[3]

On March 28, 1978, Presidents Carter and Pérez met in Caracas.

During the course of their conversations the American reaffirmed his policy on Nicaragua. Pérez warned that if nothing were done about Nicaragua, Somoza could end up playing Batista to a Sandinista Castro. Carter did not disagree with the diagnosis, but he was not prepared to join with Pérez when it came to more forceful action. Carter noted, "As you have requested, we have encouraged Somoza to let in the Inter-American Commission on Human Rights, and we have frozen our aid program. But we have a difficult time proposing direct action to bring about Somoza's downfall." To do so would contradict the American policy of nonintervention. He did not believe the United States should be in the business of changing the governments of small nations.[4]

The result of the conversation was not at all what the Americans wanted. A disappointed Pérez subsequently moved, without Washington's knowledge, to give important support to the Sandinistas. They were fighting Somoza, and the enemy of his enemy deserved his support. Moreover, his assistance might purchase some influence with the Nicaraguan revolutionaries.

Although it was an important moment for the future of events in Nicaragua, the conversation between Carter and Pérez on this subject was quite brief. They had many other topics on their agenda, including the future of economic and political relationships between the industrialized and the Third World nations, global energy problems, and even developments in Africa. Somoza's future was not considered the most important of these issues.

The low priority given Nicaragua in these talks was somehow fitting, for it reflected the process by which the American government had thus far made its Nicaraguan policy. The February decision to reaffirm distancing had been reached largely in the terms of general considerations. The Horn of Africa, human rights, a policy of nonintervention in Latin American internal affairs, domestic American politics — all these were important and legitimate concerns. But none of them involved a careful estimate of what the future held in Nicaragua itself. It is true that to make policy solely with regard to the case at hand would disregard the connections of one case to another and destroy any possibility of coherence in our general foreign policy. But for all policy makers, the temptation is to take refuge in the logic of general policies at the expense of dealing with the complexities of a local reality. It is easier to affirm a respect for sovereignty — or the promotion of human rights — than to predict the evolution of an intricate political danse macabre in a foreign society.

No one at the February 15 meeting in Christopher's office was primarily an expert on Nicaragua. As Harvard's James Thomson has noted, the higher an issue rises in the bureaucracy, the less likely it is that there will be experts in the room.[5] Their presence inhibits the discussion; there might be leaks. Better to exclude them. Even if not excluded, the experts usually sit at the back of the room and seldom speak unless asked for an opinion. This means that at the meetings in which the stakes (like the titles of the participants themselves) are high, the important balance between global policies and local realities is most likely to be skewed toward global considerations. The cost is not only a loss of accuracy about the country concerned; there is also less of a sense of the history of an issue — assuming that the experts themselves have taken the trouble to study it.

Yet even the experts may not have studied history. Paul Kreisberg recalls that in the policy discussions he attended during his twenty-five-year career in the Foreign Service, patterns of the past very seldom came up. An Asian specialist himself, he knew little of the history of Nicaragua. He could have drawn its map, he says, but not described its past in any detail. Why so little attention to history? He argues, with considerable justification, that the answer lies in our whole society; it is hardly specific to the State Department. "We Americans think of ourselves as a people of change," he says. "We look forward, not back. Trying to learn by looking backward is somehow seen as pessimistic. Americans shy away from this, because they don't want to feel bound by history."

In contrast, a visitor to Nicaragua in 1987 found a sense of history everywhere. Before leaving for Managua, the visitor's request at the Nicaraguan embassy in Washington for information about visas stimulated a two-hour discussion about Nicaraguan history. The Sandinistas' consul general in Washington, Leonor Argüello de Hüper, is the niece of a former Nicaraguan president. She remembered meeting, as a young girl, a short, enigmatic man named Sandino. And she does not forget the rivalry of her family with the Somozas. In Managua, the same visitor met a young woman who had worked as an interpreter for the Sandinista government before resigning in disillusionment. She said that she had moved to Nicaragua from Canada after the revolution because she had grown up disliking Somoza and the Sandinistas had captured her imagination. Why? Half Canadian and half Nicaraguan, she was descended from another Nicaraguan president, José Santos Zelaya. Her family had never forgotten that he had been ousted by American Marines in 1909. At the American embassy, a local employee launched into a tirade against the Sandinistas. He had hated them from the start — because, he said, his village still remembers with anger that in the 1920s, Sandino and his followers had murdered a priest there.

For such Nicaraguans, history is alive. History explains almost everything; history shapes their hatreds and loyalties. To policy makers in Washington, Nicaragua is a problem, an exercise in logic and ideological debate. The history of that nation and the record of past American policies toward it find little place in the decision memoranda of the State Department. It is not merely that there is no time for Nicaraguan history, although for senior officials that is certainly true. Sadly, for most in government, there has been little inclination to study it.

FOUR

Questions from the 1920s

IF YOU HAD ASKED MOST OF THE FOREIGN POLICY GENER-
alists in the Carter administration about their policy of noninterference in Latin American domestic affairs, you would have been
told that it represented a break with an American interventionist
impulse that stretched back to the turn of the century and before.
Certainly there were recollections of Franklin Delano Roosevelt
and his "good neighbor policy." But to the degree that they knew
or thought about the history of American policies toward Central
America, the generalists remembered an America all too ready to
send in the Marines.

Yet the issue before Warren Christopher revolved around arguments that were not new. Nor were the officials meeting in Christopher's office by any means the first American decision makers who
had wrestled with a central dilemma: how to let go in Central
America without sacrificing what they believed to be important
American interests there. Even in the bad old days of the 1920s,
when American troops were occupying Nicaragua and chasing Augusto Sandino through its northern hills, most political leaders
and policy planners in Washington wanted to bring our boys home
and put a stop to American military interventionism in the area.
But they did not want to face the immediate cost to American
strategic and economic interests of doing so, or bear the burden
of responsibility for unstable events in Nicaragua that would follow
an American withdrawal.

There were few, if any, references to history or its lessons in the argument before Christopher on February 15, 1978. If there had been, the Latin American bureau might have reminded the others that, fifty years earlier, American officials had realistically come to understand that a withdrawal of American power and influence from the scene in Nicaragua would have consequences both for the American position in the hemisphere and for the Nicaraguans who would suffer from any ensuing outbreak of political violence. Those who favored a distancing from political maneuvers in Managua might have replied, had they recalled history, that the interventionism of the 1920s had produced far more failure than success.

To be sure, the view of earlier American policy makers as reluctant interventionists is not universally shared. Some of the most strenuous critics of American actions in this hemisphere see an imperialistic United States, more than ready for much of this century to send in the Marines or, since World War II, the CIA, whenever American profits have been endangered. The United Fruit Company is the favored nephew, in this story, of a rapacious Uncle Sam.

But a review of the record suggests that the reality is more complex. As Washington floundered through two decades of interventions in Nicaragua, the United States could as easily be seen as an uncertain, sometimes naive giant trapped by vague political fears of instability and radicalism as the Yanqui economic plunderer so dearly hated by the Latin American left. This is neither to excuse nor explain away more than a score of American military interventions in Central America and the Caribbean in this century, the violations of the sovereignty of these nations, the loss of lives, the hostility toward the United States that has been engendered. Nor is it to deny the exploitation of local economies by American companies, especially during the first half of the century. But simple or dogmatic explanations of past American behavior are likely only to suggest simple, dogmatic lessons unsuited to the complexities of both Central America and the making of our foreign policy.

On December 16, 1909, a detachment of 400 Marines landed at Bluefields, on the Mosquito Coast of eastern Nicaragua, to protect American lives and property during an uprising against the govern-

ment of General José Santos Zelaya. Their intervention protected
Bluefields from Zelaya's army and eventually helped the rebels
(whose uprising the United States knew of in advance) to gain
power. The maneuver was produced by a number of impulses that
kept the United States militarily involved in Nicaragua, with one
brief hiatus, for more than two decades. There were indeed economic
motives, especially in the early years, but there were other factors
that also explain the policies of this period: Washington's growing
(and sometimes nearly paranoid) fears of domestic instability or
foreign (other than American) influence in the region; habits of
the American mind, including a belief in a manifest mission, even
responsibility, to bring order and democracy to the lesser nations
of the hemisphere; and the desire of Nicaraguan political leaders
of all stripes to put the power of the United States behind their
own political fortunes.

American hostility to Zelaya was inspired in part by his revocation
of economic concessions to American businesses in the hope of
restoring them at a higher price or selling them to competitors.[1]
Since the 1880s the United States had been vigorously promoting
markets, investment opportunities, and sources of raw materials
in the hemisphere — a process that Secretary of State James G.
Blaine called the "annexation of trade." Hard times in the 1890s
made American businesses all the more interested in foreign markets,
and the expansionist approach of Teddy Roosevelt's presidency
after the turn of the century provided a further boost. American capital flowing into Central America reached unprecedented
levels.[2]

But it was not merely that Zelaya was threatening American
interests. He also was turning to the British and Japanese for new
economic ties, even discussing their helping to build a canal through
Nicaragua that might compete with the American canal through
Panama.[3] Here he struck a nerve. For decades Washington had
been almost obsessive in its suspicion of British political and economic designs in the region, a suspicion largely unfounded, as
James Chace has argued in his book *Endless War*. And Zelaya
was not only raising the British specter; he was threatening the

stability of the region in his attacks on neighboring Honduras. If there is one word that describes the American goal for Central America in 1909, or 1979, or any year in between, it is stability. Stability for the sake of economic interests, yes; but also stability as a barrier to European trouble making, stability as the alternative to political radicalism, stability as a nice, quiet, comfortable end in itself.

A satirical ditty in 1904 caught well the American obsession:

> Urged by motives nowise harmful
>   Beneficial if you will —
> Uncle Samuel's got an armful
>   Of republics infantile.
> Uncle hates their constant riot
>   But he has the knowledge grim
> That he's got to keep 'em quiet,
>   For they all depend on him.
> So he sings in accents gritty
>   This enthusiastic ditty:
> "Don't be scared, you're free from harm.
>   I can't talk your lingo
> But I'll do my best — by jingo,
>   Stop that fightin', San Domingo."[4]

Stability was joined in the minds of American policy makers with the view that Central American peoples lacked the traditions and the power to preserve their own domestic and international peace. Thus the Roosevelt corollary to the Monroe Doctrine, as proclaimed by TR in his 1904 State of the Union address: "Chronic wrongdoing, or an impotence which results in a general loosening of the ties of civilized society, may in America, as elsewhere, ultimately require intervention by some civilized nation, and in the Western Hemisphere the adherence of the United States to the Monroe Doctrine may force the United States, however reluctantly, in flagrant cases of such wrongdoing or impotence, to the exercise of an international police power." Roosevelt himself was not notably reluctant to exercise this power, sending American forces into

Cuba in 1906 and remarking in 1908 with regard to Venezuela that America had to "show these Dagoes that they will have to behave decently."

By the standards established in Washington for the behavior of others in the hemisphere, Zelaya was not behaving decently. His domestic rule had become ever more harshly authoritarian and was leading to insurrection. A threat to American economic interests; a tyrant unable to maintain order; an aggressor against his neighbors — Zelaya was a natural object of American distaste. So limited intervention at Bluefields to protect American economic interests there soon turned to an open break when Zelaya captured and executed two American mercenaries hired by the rebels. This was an affront to the American people. Zelaya tried to mollify Washington by resigning and appointing a reformist successor, but the Americans would have nothing to do with him.

With the help of American naval forces around Bluefields the rebellion succeeded, and the victorious General Juan J. Estrada took power in 1910. Estrada, like Zelaya, was a member of the Liberal party, but his support was drawn from the Conservatives. The distinction between Liberals and Conservatives had little ideological meaning in Nicaragua; the differences between the two parties had everything to do with geographic rivalries (the Liberals based in León, the Conservatives in Granada); with family ties (the hostility between Anastasio Somoza and Pedro Joaquín Chamorro reflected a half century of rivalry between the two families); and with competing claims to political power and the economic benefits it could bring. American favorites in Nicaraguan politics included, at various stages, members of both parties.

In assisting Estrada's revolt, the United States had become the arbiter of Nicaraguan politics.[5] To build the stability Washington so desired, American involvement became still deeper in the years following the rebellion. The pattern for the next twenty years was set.

On taking power, General Estrada made all the right promises. He would hold elections; he would punish the murderers of the American mercenaries; he would end the threat to American economic concessions. But political maneuvering continued, and the

Nicaraguan economy was in a mess. President William Howard Taft decided to apply to Nicaragua his theory of "dollar diplomacy": political stability could be provided through economic stabilization. Washington sent a special representative to Managua, Thomas C. Dawson, and Dawson delivered. He negotiated a truce among the politicians and an agreement paving the way for a customs system that would guarantee loans by American banks to the Nicaraguans.

But Estrada, not a strong character, proved unable to provide stability. In a moment of drunken courage in May 1911, Estrada fired and imprisoned his rebellious minister of war. Then, when the army seemed to be turning against him, he crumbled. On the evening of May 11, he reeled up to the American embassy with his vice-president, Adolfo Díaz, in tow. The next day he fled the country, leaving Díaz, the former employee of an American mining company, in charge.

Díaz, who was better at maneuver than leadership and who was to be known in Washington as "our" Nicaraguan, soon appealed for American help against a gathering rebellion. On August 14, 1912, a detachment of one hundred Marines arrived in Managua, to be followed by hundreds more who fanned out over the country. They were led into combat by the flamboyant Smedley Darlington Butler, who earned his nickname Old Gimlet Eye by battling a 104-degree fever and sleepless nights during the operation. Butler was to achieve fame, but in 1933, bitter at his failure to become commandant of the Marine Corps, he let fly with a remarkable blast:

> I spent thirty-three years . . . being a high-class muscle man for Big Business, for Wall Street and the bankers. In short, I was a racketeer for capitalism. . . . I helped purify Nicaragua for the international banking house of Brown Brothers in 1909–1912. I helped make Mexico and especially Tampico safe for American oil interests in 1916. I brought light to the Dominican Republic for American sugar interests in 1916. I helped make Haiti and Cuba a decent place for the National City [Bank] boys to collect revenue in. I helped in the rape of half a dozen Central American republics for the benefit of Wall Street.[6]

The intervention of the Marines was the first time American troops had fought in Central America to put down a rebellion against a government friendly to American interests. These interests, economic and political, were undoubtedly important in Washington's calculations, but having accepted the position of arbiter of Nicaraguan politics, American policy makers also apparently felt trapped by a sense of responsibility that made it hard not to stay involved. If previous policy had been intervention for the sake of stability, it would be a waste to destabilize the situation by backing out. The habit of responsibility can be seen in a history of the period published in 1918. Writing of elections held in 1916, Dana G. Munro, who was to serve as an American diplomat in Managua and in a variety of posts in Latin America over the next two decades, asserted, "The United States could not well escape the responsibility for deciding which of the three candidates should become President for the ensuing term."[7] What is interesting here is not only the sentiment, but the bland way Munro assumes his audience will accept his assumption.

While Americans easily assumed responsibility for events in Managua, Nicaraguans often succeeded in using Washington in behalf of their own political positions. The game for each politician was to convince the United States that he was the one who held the key to stability and the protection of American economic interests. It didn't matter whether he was in power (Díaz in 1912) or out (Estrada in 1909), whether he was a Liberal or a Conservative. If he wanted to succeed, he turned to the deus ex machina in Washington. The longer the United States played this role, the more it was assumed in Nicaragua — even more than in Washington — that America was responsible for Nicaragua's future. This belief later helped the Somozas hold on to power by maintaining the fiction that they had American support even when they did not. And for critics of the United States, the same assumption about American power offered an easy explanation for Nicaragua's problems: Washington as devil ex machina. One might see in this a picture of innocents in Washington being led by Nicaraguan slickers into the Managuan quagmire. This was not the case. American officials knew the game, as seen, for example, in the contempt in Washington for "our" Díaz. But their own habits of mind, their definition of American interests and ideals, made Washington's policy makers a part of what was a relationship of consenting adults with the Nicaraguan political elite.

President Taft had made America the arbiter of Nicaraguan politics; Woodrow Wilson played the role as strongly as any president in our history — and in other nations in the region as well. While the 2,700 men who had kept Díaz in office were to depart Nicaragua when peace was restored, one hundred members of the Legation Guard stayed on as a warning to any who would rebel against the government. They were to stay until 1925. For Wilson, the American military presence was a civilizing force for democracy, a guarantor of political stability. The central hypocrisy in Wilson's position has often been noted. That he and his "anti-imperialist" secretary of state, William Jennings Bryan, should have allowed their undoubted belief in democracy to propel them into military interventions in the region is often cited as exhibit A in indictments of moralism in American foreign policy.

But there was a more complicated hypocrisy in Wilson's position. Wilson had bitterly denounced Taft's dollar diplomacy, and as president, in a speech in October 1913, he had attacked foreign economic exploitation of Nicaragua. He didn't like United Fruit, and he didn't like the banks. Secretary of State Bryan was still more hostile to Wall Street. Yet in spite of these views, Wilson's actual policies served American business interests as well as Taft's had done. How could the enemy of Wall Street also be the patron of the American banks in Nicaragua? As James Chace argues, Wilson's primary concern was with preventing economic or political inroads into Central America by European or other foreign rivals. American trade would help keep the region free of foreign economic influence. In addition, Wilson made much of the distinction between formal annexation of territories to our south, which the turn-of-the-century American imperialists had favored, and a more restrained position of trade and occasional military intervention for the sake of democracy and stability.[8] Through such distinctions can the willing conscience be salved.

The illusion that the horrors of World War I could produce a world safe for democracy — or a marked change in the nature of international diplomacy — was followed by public disillusionment with Wilson's internationalism. The 1920s were characterized by an American isolationist sentiment that found its expression not only in policies toward Europe and Asia but also toward Central America. It is important to recall, however, that this was not a simple isolationism calling for withdrawal from things foreign. It was also a period of intense nationalism, of America First, of hostility to the communism that had taken root in Russia and seemed even to be spreading to American shores. Within the United States, Attorney General A. Mitchell Palmer played on this fear in his 1920 campaign against radicals, especially foreign radicals. One third of the states in America passed laws to be used against such people. South of our border, the menace of radicalism seemed evident in Mexico. Never mind that the government of Mexico, brought to power by the revolution of 1910, had found it much easier to sound radical in its rhetoric than actually to carry out a revolutionary program. The words were enough to sound the alarm bells to the north.

So while the Harding, Coolidge, and Hoover administrations, reflecting the isolationist currents of the time, took the removal of the Marines as their primary goal in Nicaragua, they also were driven by nationalist currents. American forces could not be withdrawn if this meant political instability and gains in this hemisphere for foreign influence or ideologies. In 1925 an opportunity for withdrawal did seem to be at hand. Elections held in Nicaragua in 1924 were marred by the usual finagling, but the new president, a Conservative, promised honest elections in 1928. Calvin Coolidge ordered the Marines home, and the last of them sailed from Corinto on August 4, 1925.

Within weeks, however, political chaos reigned again in Nicaragua, and in the spring of 1926 the Liberals launched a rebellion on the east coast near Bluefields. As in 1909, a detachment of

Marines was sent there to protect American lives and property. And, as in the intervention of 1909–1912, the force and its role soon expanded. By the end of 1926 more Marines were starting to fan out to various posts around the country in reaction to continued fighting among the Nicaraguans. Despite official U.S. claims that their mission was strictly limited to the protection of Americans and their property, the effect of the Marines' presence again had the effect of supporting the government in power.

It was a mess. Washington wanted stability, but here was a civil war with no end in sight. Washington wanted a legal government, but knew that the regime in place had gained power more through maneuver than through any constitutional expression of the popular will. Washington wanted the Marines out of Nicaragua, but they were back in again, causing "more ill will in Latin America than any other event in our diplomacy with that area during the first sixty years of the century" aside from Teddy Roosevelt's maneuvers in Panama.[9] Once again, Washington and its Marines had become the arbiter of Nicaraguan politics. Unwilling or unable to take a step backward and not daring to let the civil war play itself out lest it bring to power the Liberals (who were seen, because of their support by the Mexicans, as dangerously radical), the Coolidge administration took another step deeper into the affair. In April 1927, Henry L. Stimson was dispatched to Nicaragua with orders to negotiate a satisfactory end to the fighting.

In a month of astute diplomacy, Stimson did so. Through a blend of inducements and threats, he persuaded the chief Liberal general, José María Moncada, to come to terms with the government. In return for an end to the rebellion, the United States agreed to supervise a free election in 1928, to work for a neutral constabulary, and to help disarm the contending armies. These inducements were especially attractive to Moncada (who was to run for president in the 1928 elections and win). Behind them lay a threat that Stimson barely veiled: if the Liberals refused to come to terms, the Marines would assume a more active role and disarm them.

By June 1927, the Liberal military leaders signed the agreement and their troops turned in their arms, with one exception: the enigmatic Augusto César Sandino, whose fight was to bedevil the American Marines during the next five years and whose name and legacy would later bedevil Washington again. A short man with "very white complexion, black hair and brown eyes,"[10] Sandino dressed the part of guerrilla as well as he performed it. He customarily wore a high-crowned, broad-brimmed hat, a red and black bandana, and high boots, with a pistol at each hip. His deep-set eyes appeared rather sad, and he is said to have laughed but very seldom to have smiled. He gave an impression of asceticism and was attracted to mysticism, at times frequenting theosophical and spiritualist groups.[11]

As with any figure at the center of political myth, the picture of Sandino has been simplified and distorted by both his friends and his enemies. Despite the later efforts of Sandinista theorists to place him in a useful ideological niche, Sandino remains a man who was more nationalist and populist than Marxist, more a mystic and romantic than a coherent political thinker. His denunciations of Díaz and the Conservatives focused on their ties to the Americans, not their domestic policies. He was supported by, but then broke with, the Salvadoran Communist Agustín Farabundo Martí. He refused to put his fight in a clear ideological context, writing that

> this movement is national and anti-imperialist. We fly the flag of freedom for Nicaragua and for all Latin America. And on the social level it's a people's movement, we stand for the advancement of social aspirations. People have come here to try to influence us from the International Labor Federation, from the League Against Imperialism, from the Quakers. . . . We've always upheld against them our definite criterion that it's essentially a national thing.[12]

Neither was Sandino the bandit that the American government tried to brand him. His tactics could be brutal with civilians of doubtful loyalty and with his military opponents. But his popularity with his followers and the genuineness of his opposition to the American political and military domination of Nicaragua in the late 1920s seems beyond question. (A sympathetic journalist of the time, Carleton Beals, refused to take seriously accusations of mere banditry. When asked by an American general for his views of Sandino, Beals answered: "He is not a bandit, call him a fool, a fanatic, an idealist, a patriot — according to your point of view; but certainly he is not a bandit." The general's defensive response: "Of course, in the army, we use the word 'bandit' in a technical sense, meaning the member of a band." Beals, by his own account, got the last word: "Then [John Philip] Sousa is also a bandit?"[13]

Born in the mid-1890s, Sandino was the son of a Liberal who had occasionally been jailed for his political activities. Sandino himself left Nicaragua while still a teenager, in the wake of a political scrape in his hometown. After travels through Honduras and Guatemala, he worked in the oil industry around Tampico, Mexico. It was here, he later said, that he became committed to fighting American imperialism.[14] Still a Liberal partisan, he returned to Nicaragua in 1926 to join Sacasa's rebellion.

When Moncada agreed to American terms the following year, Sandino took a small band of followers to the hills of northern Nicaragua. This did not, at the moment, seem a significant event. The American government was committed to maintaining a military force in the country in order to preserve order through the 1928 elections, but Washington still wanted the American presence drawn down, and the first seventy Marines were removed in mid-June 1927. The prospect then was somewhat encouraging: although Nicaraguan politicians were still wrangling and seemed more committed to their own fortunes than to the future of a true democracy, if an apolitical National Guard could be trained and stability restored through the elections, a complete withdrawal of the Marines could be foreseen.

As it was to do fifty years later with the Sandinistas, Washington underestimated the strength and determination of Sandino and his few armed men. On July 16, 1927, Sandino led some five hundred troops in an attack on a U.S. Marine and Nicaraguan National Guard detachment at Ocotal, a town near the northern border with Honduras. The attack began successfully, but Sandino's force was then driven back by what was probably the first dive-bombing operation in history. Five De Havilland biplanes peeled off from 1,500 feet to carry out strafing and bombing runs at 300 feet. The guerrillas suffered heavy losses and headed back into the hills.

Sandino had lost at Ocotal, but he had won the serious attention of the Nicaraguans and new support in the northern region. He certainly was not daunted. Messages to the American commanders and troops who were fruitlessly to pursue him during the next few years included advice that they make out their wills before entering his mountains; the image of a guerrilla about to decapitate a fallen Marine with the message "What do you think of this?"; and a written sally signed "Your obedient servant who wishes to put you in the tomb with handsome flowers."[15]

The 1928 election was relatively fair, and Moncada was solidly ensconced as the Nicaraguan president. In 1929 the newly elected Herbert Hoover, a critic of intervention, and Henry Stimson, his secretary of state, oversaw the development of a plan for total withdrawal of the Marines. And indeed the number of American soldiers was constantly reduced, from 5,000 in January 1929, to 1,800 by the end of the year, to 1,412 by January 1931.[16] But it was to be January 1933 before the withdrawal was complete. Hoover and Stimson did not move more quickly for a variety of reasons. There was the recollection of the events following the withdrawal of 1925. There was Sandino's insurgency. And there was slow progress in building up a Nicaraguan constabulary that could keep order after the Americans had left. As later with "Vietnamization," Nicaraguization was a slow and iffy proposition.

Hoover's hesitations reflected these immediate concerns, but they were also part of a general pattern throughout the 1920s and earlier. Like his predecessors, he saw in Nicaragua more trap than opening, more trouble than opportunity. To understand the impulses and constraints that defined the American dilemma in Nicaragua is to understand an important central truth about this or almost any foreign policy: with very rare exceptions, foreign policy decisions represent *compromises*. Reading the memoirs of former officials or the analyses of historians, one might suppose that all successful foreign policies were planned from the start in accordance with some grand strategic design. Such designs are indeed useful as a definition of desirable goals, but it is rare that any nation has the power and will to impose its vision on history. For the most part, foreign policy makers in all nations seek to find means to wend their way successfully through competing national interests and ideals, contradictory international dangers and opportunities, and the claims of contending domestic political, economic, and bureaucratic interests.

Success in foreign policy is seldom absolute triumph. It is usually the achievement of modest progress, or the avoidance of disaster, through the effective pursuit of some compromise course. Failure usually proceeds either from the single-minded pursuit of one goal at the absolute expense of other interests, or the adoption of a compromise policy that provides a refuge from reality rather than a vehicle for effective action.

American policy toward Nicaragua in the first decades of this century (except for the Stimson mission) was an example of the latter kind of failure. Throughout the Taft, Wilson, Harding, Coolidge, and Hoover years, Washington's policy can best be seen as a quest for that most perfect of all instruments, a device by which one may eat one's cake and have it too. Faced with pressures for intervention and constraints against the use of force, American policy makers convinced themselves that their policies would protect American interests without requiring active intervention. The result was an unsatisfactory compromise: sincere protestations of non-interventionist intent contradicted by the presence of the Marines.

The interplay of impulses and constraints was complex:

Economic Interests: American bankers protested the State Department's plans for the withdrawal of the Marines in the early 1920s. The return of the Marines in 1926 and the deployment of the occasional warship off Nicaraguan shores followed requests for protection by American fruit, lumber, and other business concerns operating in Nicaragua. The protection of American property as well as lives was an important political consideration. Even Democratic politicians critical of American policy nonetheless insisted on this principle.[17]

But economic considerations were less important in the 1920s than in the previous decade. It has been estimated that by 1928 there was less American investment in Nicaragua than in any Latin American nation save, perhaps, Paraguay.[18] Indeed, economic concerns were used to justify actions taken primarily for other reasons. Under Secretary of State Robert E. Olds, in a candid memorandum concerning the reintroduction of the Marines in 1926, wrote, "Usually it has been sufficient for us to intervene on the sole pretext of furnishing protection of American lives and property . . . but it is beginning to appear conclusively that . . . in view of the substantial support which the insurrectionists are receiving from Mexico . . . unless we are willing to go beyond measures appropriate for the mere protection of American lives and property . . . the government which we have recognized will be driven from power."[19]

Ideological and Strategic Fears: Under Secretary of State Olds was clearly more worried about Mexican radicalism than about American corporate profits. His first concern was that neither the people of Central America nor outside powers come to believe that the United States would countenance instability and changes in the status quo. If Nicaragua went to the radicals, others, encouraged by American weakness, might be tempted to follow suit. One suspects that he would have used the image of dominoes falling, one by one, had he thought of it. Olds also may serve as a prime exhibit of the American habits of mind, cited earlier, that uncritically accepted the responsibility of the United States for events in Central America. In arguing for strong action against the Mexican-supported Liberal insurgency in 1926–1927, he wrote that:

> The Central American area down to and including the Isthmus of Panama constitutes a legitimate sphere of influence for the United States, if we are to have a due regard for our own safety and protection. . . . Our ministers accredited to the five little republics stretching from the Mexican border to Panama . . . have been advisers

whose advice has been accepted virtually as law. . . . We do control the destinies of Central America and we do so for the simple reason that the national interest absolutely dictates such a course.

There is no room for any outside influence other than ours in the region. We could not tolerate such a thing without incurring grave risks. At this moment [January 1927] a deliberate attempt to undermine our position and set aside our special relationship with Central America is being made. The action of Mexico in the Nicaraguan crisis is a direct challenge to the United States.

. . . If this Mexican maneuver succeeds it will take many years to recover the ground we shall have lost. . . . Until now Central America has always understood that governments which we recognize and support stay in power, while those we do not recognize and support fall. Nicaragua has become a test case. It is difficult to see how we can afford to be defeated.[20]

Olds and like-minded strategists were concerned about the Monroe Doctrine, about the Panama Canal, and about rights to a future canal across Nicaragua. But they were also in the grip of an obsession about the spread of radicalism in the hemisphere. In fact, in supporting the insurgents in Nicaragua and in its radical rhetoric, the Mexican government was largely posturing for the benefit of its own people, to disguise its unwillingness to pursue the revolutionary domestic program to which it was committed. The Mexicans' favorite in Nicaragua, Dr. Juan Sacasa, was no Marxist. But for many in the United States, bolshevism was on the way. Appearing before the Senate Foreign Relations Committee on January 12, 1927, Secretary of State Frank Kellogg cited various pieces of evidence indicating Communist designs in the hemisphere. While some editorialists were skeptical of such State Department claims, others were of the same mind as American officials. *The New York Herald Tribune,* for example, warned that the "bolshevization of Nicaragua" would endanger the Panama Canal and Nicaraguan canal rights.[21]

Manipulation by Nicaraguans: The state of mind in Washington made it easier for Nicaraguan politicians to appeal for American intervention to save Nicaragua (including the political fortunes of the criers for help). In 1924 and 1925 a Conservative president pleaded that the Marines not be withdrawn. In early 1926, before they turned to armed rebellion, the Liberals, whose support by Mexico was to worry American policy makers, in turn appealed for Washington's help. Then, in the summer of 1926, the Nicaraguan government speeded the return of the Marines by announcing that it could not protect American lives on its own. And in December 1926 the government rang the most evocative changes in Washington by asking the Americans whether they really wanted to see it surrender to the Liberals and their (gasp!) Mexican backers.

Even Augusto César Sandino was prepared at one point to see an exercise of American power if it would mean the defeat of his Nicaraguan enemies. In 1927, before he took up arms, he reportedly suggested the establishment of an American military government in Managua until fair elections could be held in 1928. This was preferable, in his eyes, to the continued hold on power by a political rival who could cook the elections in the traditional fashion.[22]

American Representatives in Managua: On the ground in Nicaragua, seeing rather than reading about "instability" and subject to appeals for action by Nicaraguan politicians, American representatives in Managua were almost always ahead of the State Department when it came to recommending action, either diplomatic or military. This was true in 1909, when the American consul in Bluefields issued statements attacking Zelaya before Washington had moved toward the same position. It was still true in 1927, when Henry Stimson had to battle the State Department before he could commit the United States to supervising the 1928 elections. In a message to Washington arguing that he had to use the threat of action by the Marines in order to get a settlement, Stimson pointedly reported that Nicaraguans thought "we are held back from decisive action by vacillating and timid policy."[23]

Less strenuous argument had sometimes sufficed. On September 6, 1925, the American minister in Managua cabled Washington: "It is believed that the appearance at Corinto at this time of an American war vessel would have a stabilizing effect." The next day he dashed off a brief: "[The] President has just requested me to ask the Department to be good enough to despatch an American war vessel to Bluefields and another to Corinto immediately."[24] The tone of the message seems, to the modern eye, about as dramatic as the murmured plea for a glass of sherry by a parched British club member. But Washington agreed.

More eccentric was the extraordinary behavior of the American chargé d'affaires, Lawrence Dennis. Acting on his own, he launched during the fall of 1926 a series of confrontations with the Nicaraguan president that helped produce the latter's replacement. Dennis retained his independent spirit after leaving Nicaragua. By 1932 he was producing books ardently advocating American fascism.

All of this — calculations of economic and strategic interests, fears of radicalism and foreign influence, habits of mind, events in and appeals from Nicaragua — was enough to keep the United States deeply involved for more than two decades. But as Stimson put it, American policy makers were more vacillating and timid than bold — more like Hamlet than Henry V. From the start, there were important reasons why Washington policy makers wished they could see a safe way out of Nicaragua.

It may seem inexplicable that our policy makers could have been anti-interventionist in their desires yet interventionist in their actions. An explanation (which should not be taken as a justification) lies in the simple fact that policy makers are human beings. All of us do things we believe are necessary, even if we know those things are shortsighted or wrong.

Thus the fact of intervention does not deny the reality of anti-interventionist constraints. Inhibitions about intervention flowed from four sources: principle, American politics, the price of interventions, and protest in the region.

Principle: The moral ambivalence felt by many in Washington was notably expressed by President Wilson in his repeated expressions of anti-imperialist intent, and also by Elihu Root. As secretary of war under William McKinley and Theodore Roosevelt, Root had helped guarantee future American political influence in Cuba through the Platt Amendment. Yet as a senator during the Wilson administration he was a leading critic of the American policy of propping up ineffectual Nicaraguan leaders. They lacked legitimacy, he argued, precisely because they relied on the Marines to stay in power. Similarly, Warren Harding in 1920 attacked the Wilson administration for its hypocrisy in using bayonets to promote democracy.

Politics: Both Root and Harding were, of course, carrying out their attacks in a political context. The political appeal of opposition to American intervention was clear. It had an idealistic element, especially during the first decade of intervention in Nicaragua, for there remained a strong anti-imperialist constituency within the American public. Later, in the 1920s, the political appeal was to isolationist sentiment as well. Yes, most Americans agreed, we should protect American lives and property. But did this require twenty years of occupation and the active fighting involved in combating Sandino?

Will Rogers put it succinctly: "Why are we in Nicaragua and what the Hell are we doing there?"[25] As the Republicans had attacked Wilson on the issue, so now the Democrats (joined by isolationist Republicans such as William Borah) sought ways in Congress to block involvement in Nicaragua.

Price: The politics of the issue involved not only idealism and isolationism, but the costs of the adventure as well. The pursuit of Sandino through the hills of Nicaragua was difficult and dangerous. All told, 136 American soldiers died during the second American intervention — 47 by enemy action, 24 of disease, 41 by accident (including one fall in a shower and another from a horse), 11 through homicide, and 12 by suicide. The deaths of eight Marines in a guerrilla attack on New Year's Eve 1932 produced a wave of editorials and resolutions in Congress. Stimson soon concluded that the withdrawal of the Marines must quickly be completed.

Indeed, Stimson had to worry about more than the political impact of the casualties. The Marine Corps was spread thin in the mid-1920s, with 4,000 men in China and a contingent in Haiti.

By 1930 the gathering Depression made the financial costs of Nicaragua less supportable. And there was also a special diplomatic cost: Stimson's appeal to world opinion to oppose the Japanese invasion of Manchuria in 1931 was vitiated by the occupation of Nicaragua.

Protest in the Region: American policy makers also knew that military intervention was unpopular throughout the hemisphere. While the Nicaraguan elite tried to elbow their way into American favor, the public there was far from enthusiastic about the American presence. Despite the Nicaraguan government's efforts to prevent their departure, the withdrawal of the Marines in 1925 was greeted with popular approval in Managua. Moreover, Sandino's fight seems to have enjoyed significant popular support in the area of his operations. One of his American pursuers reported "all people encountered . . . unquestionably strong for Sandino."[26]

Criticism of American policy was also widespread in other parts of Latin America. Sandino was famous all over the continent and even in China, where Chiang Kai-shek named a military division after him.[27] Throughout the 1920s Latin American governments embarrassed American representatives at regional meetings by introducing resolutions condemning interventionism. The Americans cannot have enjoyed the casuistry of the responses they lamely offered in the name of international law.

Caught between their fears of instability in Nicaragua and the costs of intervention there, American officials sought an easy way out, a device by which to preserve a comfortable quiet without serious costs. As each policy proved illusory, they moved on to another. The sequence of policies provides a history of American efforts to shape events without exercising power, to be dominant without seeking domination, to rule without violating anti-imperialist ideals.

First there was the notion of an international agreement that could produce stability within each of its signatories as well as peace among them — a kind of Central American version of the Congress of Vienna. Treaties signed in Washington in 1907 by the five Central American republics had required noninterference in one another's affairs and nonrecognition of any government that came to power through unconstitutional means. But within a year the leaders of the republics, including Nicaragua's Zelaya, were back to bickering, interfering, and fighting among themselves.

Then came the dollar diplomacy that could provide stability the easy way. President Taft and Secretary of State Philander C. Knox argued that economic solvency could produce peace and stability in Central America; they would substitute dollars for bullets. Woodrow Wilson added his own twist, suggesting that American trade, together with free elections, could produce stability. But economic progress does not necessarily promote tranquility. Indeed, it can increase the political competition for the economic spoils power can bestow. And elections in Nicaragua had proved not to be the answer, since in Nicaraguan hands they were hardly fair and free.

So in 1923, American hopes were again pinned on international diplomacy. Another Central American treaty was negotiated, committing the signatories once more to refuse recognition of any unconstitutional government. This proved no more effective in deterring coups and conflict than had the original effort in 1907.

In 1925 Washington hit upon an instrument that finally let it remove the Marines without leaving instability in their wake — but with consequences it did not foresee. Largely at American insistence, the Nicaraguan government began to develop a constabulary that could replace the army in keeping internal order. It was called the Guardia Nacional: the National Guard. Gradually trained and brought up to strength, officered by Americans, the Guard played an important part in the fight against Sandino. By the spring of 1931, as Stimson publicly explained the plan for complete withdrawal of the American Marines at the end of the year, he could cite the presence of the Guard as one of the reasons for his decision.

This time the United States meant it. Once out, it could and would stay out. Before the 1932 Nicaraguan election, the American assistant secretary of state wrote to the American minister in Managua about Washington's refusal to guarantee arrangements among the Nicaraguan political parties concerning their postelection behavior. "What I want to avoid," he wrote, "is the continuance of the feeling in Nicaragua that they can turn to us to settle all their problems. I think they ought to be made to feel that the country is now being turned back to them and that it will be their responsibility, and solely their responsibility, to get together in some way which will insure stability and peace."

In the American conception, the National Guard would be an agent of this stability. It would provide an apolitical force that would serve all constitutional Nicaraguan governments impartially. It would be the guardian of democracy. This was to prove a naive miscalculation, and one of monstrous proportions: a triumph of optimism and good intentions over good sense and knowledge of either Nicaraguan history or politics. Arthur Bliss Lane, the American minister in Managua during the mid-1930s, later wrote of this miscalculation, "In my opinion, it is one of the sorriest examples on our part of our inability to understand that we should not meddle in other people's affairs." For the Guard was quickly to emerge as the guardian not of democracy but, in Richard Millet's words, of the Somoza dynasty.[28]

Perhaps if they had had time to ponder the history of American involvement in Nicaragua, American officials in 1978 might have learned some practical lessons from the defeats and occasional successes of their predecessors. Of course, they might have been misled, for one can as easily learn too much from history as too little. Particularities of time and place are tremendously important: it would have made little sense to base policy in 1978 on the circumstances of Nicaragua in 1928. American policy makers were far too reliant on analogies when they looked on Vietnam as an Asian Berlin, or as a latter-day Czechoslovakia coveted by a Hitler masquerading as Mao Tse-tung. Nor did the American debates over El Salvador in the early 1980s gain greatly in their sophistication when opponents of Reagan administration policies drew an absolute parallel between that Central American nation and Vietnam.

But if there is danger in learning simple lessons from history, there is wisdom in learning at least the questions it poses. The debates of 1978 and 1979 would have been enriched by more attention to certain fundamental questions. If, for example, the United States were to distance itself not only from Somoza but from its role as arbiter of Nicaraguan politics, was it prepared also to live with instability and the possible triumph of radicals in Managua? Would there be a rerun of the dismal events of 1925, when a withdrawal of influence was quickly followed by a new, costly intervention?

On the other hand, if the United States were actively to seek Somoza's removal in favor of his moderate opponents, would it bring sufficient power to bear to achieve its purpose (as Stimson had done in 1927)? Short of the threat of military intervention, were there levers of American influence that could move Somoza? And if the Carter administration sought such an end, would it run afoul of the conservative constituency that the Somozas had built up in the United States over the previous decades?

Or suppose Washington finally decided on a compromise policy somewhere between distancing and intervention against Somoza? For example, if it were to promote a negotiated solution among the Nicaraguan parties, would Washington use its power to ensure a satisfactory, democratic solution? Or, as in the late 1940s, would its promoting democracy be more a posture than an effective policy? Were there tighter limits to American power in the 1970s than in the 1920s, when a small number of Marines could keep a government in power?

Beyond such questions of policy, the history of the matter posed an issue of moral obligation. Having created the Nicaraguan National Guard and then having allowed the Somozas to use it to rule and to accumulate their riches, was the United States obligated to undo the damage it had done by replacing both Somoza and the Guard with something better? Did the bitter result of the intervention of the 1920s provide an obligation to tidy up? Or was the lesson of the 1920s very different: that any intervention in Nicaraguan politics was likely to produce new dilemmas — and new American responsibilities?

FIVE

State: The Bureaus

SENIOR GOVERNMENT OFFICIALS CANNOT POSSIBLY FIND the time to write all the speeches, memos, and letters that bear their names, although most insist that the words be drafted and redrafted until they suit the individual. Foreign Service officers are thus quite wrong to judge their professional progress merely by their rank. If a hot young officer keeps careful track, he can celebrate his bureaucratic baccalaureate when he finds that he is repeating more words written for him than he is writing for others.

He can also tell how he is doing through geography, which in the State Department imitates power. The higher the floor on which he works, the greater his clout. This is not only true on the Seventh Floor, where the secretary, his deputy, and the four under secretaries wield their authority. Just below them, from the sixth floor, the assistant secretaries of state and their deputies manage the fifteen substantive bureaus that are the heart of the department. Ten of the bureaus deal with functional matters — economic and business affairs, international organizations, public affairs, congressional relations, human rights, and the like. The five regional bureaus — for East Asia and the Pacific, Africa, Europe and Canada, the Near East and South Asia, and Latin America — are the oldest and most prestigious. It is here that the policy-minded most want to work, for the regional assistant secretaries and their subordinates are the ones to whom both the Seventh Floor and the embassies first look for support.

Geography is also a guide to power within each bureau. On the floors directly below each assistant secretary sit the members of that bureau. Usually, the officers working on policy are located on the fifth and fourth floors; administrative officers may work on floors below them. A visitor may therefore surmise with some accuracy the contents of the piece of paper clutched by that official scurrying by. If the sighting is in an ascending elevator, the text of a draft is probably being delivered to some superior. If in a corridor, the hurried official is probably off to persuade a counterpart in some other bureau to clear such a draft before it can go upstairs.

Each bureau is divided into offices. In the regional bureaus, the substantive offices are divided along geographic lines, each headed by a country director. In a region with numerous smaller nations, an office may work on relations with more than one country.

Wade Matthews, director of the Latin American bureau's Office of Central American Affairs in 1977–1978, was charged with six: Nicaragua, El Salvador, Guatemala, Belize, Honduras, and Costa Rica. A tall, graying, professorial Foreign Service officer whose pleasant baritone is smoothed by a southern accent, Matthews was strongly opposed to the Carter administration's policy toward Nicaragua. The policy of disassociation, he believed, was a "feelgood" policy. Refusing to deal with Somoza might make clear the administration's distaste for the dictator, but it did nothing, in Matthews's view, to promote American interests or a solution to the gathering crisis in Nicaragua. He felt that only by gaining Somoza's confidence could the United States persuade him to reach an accommodation with his enemies and agree to an orderly transfer of power to an acceptable alternative.

Matthews was the official primarily responsible for the department's day-to-day business on Central America. As he recalls his work on Nicaragua in 1977–1978, his voice becomes edged with frustration. Every letter to a member of Congress, every decision concerning economic or military assistance projects in Nicaragua, indeed almost everything he did had to be cleared with a number of other offices in the department. For example, State Department approval of any sale of arms to Nicaragua had to receive the clearance of at least three internal offices — and almost invariably involved a fight with the human rights bureau.

The battle Matthews remembers most vividly was notable for the small ground on which it was fought: the provision of sling swivels to the Nicaraguan National Guard. A small item costing only a few cents, the swivel attaches a rifle to its carrying sling. A few years before the Carter administration took office, an American company had sold a few thousand rifles to the Nicaraguan government. Defective swivels had rusted, and in mid-1977 the company agreed to replace them free of charge, but Human Rights refused authorization. It opposed the provision of any arms to Somoza, including the parts of any weapons.

The struggles on such matters between the human rights bureau and Matthews's Latin American bureau were laborious affairs. Human Rights would often refuse to clear a sale, sometimes simply sitting on the paperwork. If it thought the item important enough, the Latin American bureau would seek to dislodge the matter by referring it to the Seventh Floor. Matthews, together with a Human Rights officer and a member of the Bureau of Politico-Military Affairs, would hammer out fair descriptions of one another's arguments as they drafted a joint memorandum. And when the decision was returned to them, usually from Deputy Secretary Christopher, the Latin American bureau had almost invariably lost.

In the case of the swivels, Matthews recalls that in October 1977, after some months of direct wrangling, he turned to a flanking maneuver. He knew that Mark Schneider, the senior human rights deputy, was adamantly opposed to letting the swivels go to Nicaragua, so on a Saturday, when Schneider was out of town, Matthews got Patricia Derian, Schneider's superior, to sign a memorandum that included the positions of both bureaus. He then gained support for his view from the under secretary for political affairs, Phillip Habib, the third-ranking official in the department and its most senior Foreign Service officer. When Schneider, on his return, and Derian learned that Habib had sided with Matthews, they launched a counterattack, insisting that the matter go immediately to Christopher, who had to approve Habib's decision. Christopher was in any case sympathetic to the human rights position — although innocuous in themselves, the swivels were after all parts of guns — and he denied the Latin American bureau's appeal.

The swivels were probably of greater use to the critics of the administration than they would have been to the National Guard. Matthews remembers that when he met Somoza in 1977, the Nicaraguan went into a tirade against President Carter and used the swivels as prime evidence that no matter what he did to gain Washington's approval, Carter would deny him even the smallest assistance in his fight against the Sandinistas. Referring to the American president as a "son of a bitch," Somoza swore that he would outlast him in office. Texas congressman Charles Wilson, a leading Democratic opponent of the administration's approach to Somoza, first lent his support to the Latin American bureau in calls to the State Department and then publicly denounced the final denial. Matthews smiled enigmatically when asked later if he had let Wilson know about the bureaucratic battle.

The swivels war, one of many disagreements between the two bureaus, was not a sign of systemic breakdown but an indication that the system was working, even if the nature of the struggle was sometimes unpleasant. The divisions between the human rights and Latin American bureaus reflected bureaucratic perspectives. It was the function of the human rights bureau to fight for these issues as a central goal of American foreign policy. That is why Congress had mandated the bureau. It was the Latin American bureau's job to manage the full range of American relationships with the nations of this hemisphere. It was natural that the two would collide over a crucial foreign policy issue of the time: the priority to be given to human rights as concrete, practical decisions were made in the day-to-day business of American diplomacy. The Seventh Floor benefited from hearing both sides of those arguments.

The disputes also reflected the differing backgrounds, policy views, and principles of the people in the two bureaus. Although neither was homogeneous and each had allies in the other's camp, the contrast between them was clear. Human Rights was led by political appointees who passionately believed in their mission and who had brought to the State Department a highly assertive style of argument. The Latin American bureau was led and staffed primarily by Foreign Service officers who were trained in the gentler ways of diplomacy. For the former, veterans of domestic political and congressional battles, controversy and confrontation were simply a part of life. For the latter, vigorous discord was beyond the pale, a barrier rather than an aid to illuminating and settling differ- ences. It was a clash not only of principles and policies but of cultures.

In the human rights bureau, Derian and Schneider knew that they faced a tactical choice in how best to do their job. They could try to do business in the State Department fashion, or they could argue with voices raised, when necessary, and push their issues to the hilt. They chose the latter course, out of both inclination and calculation. Derian, who had been a political and civil rights activist in the South, was noted, as Raymond Bonner has put it, for the way she "treated dictators and strongmen, even if they were heads of state, with all the respect she would have shown a redneck southern sheriff."[1]

Mark Schneider was no less firm in arguing the Human Rights position. He recalls that he once went to a senior official on the Seventh Floor to make an unabashedly emotional appeal against some decision his bureau had opposed, only to sense almost immedi- ately that he had lost his audience. The official politely heard him out but throughout the meeting took refuge in arranging and re- arranging the papers on his desk. Schneider knew that when he crossed swords with officials such as John Bushnell, the senior deputy in the Latin American bureau and a respected Foreign Service officer, it cost him points with career officials. But he was expressing what he thought and felt. And lacking a network of natural support in the other bureaus, he was certain that a more muted approach would simply blur the Human Rights position.

Despite the disarming smile that often appeared on his expressive, bearded face, Schneider was intensely serious about his business. He was always prepared to state, with direct argument and emotional appeal, his conviction that human rights concerns should be at the core of American foreign policy decisions. When asked how he came to such a view, he begins with a legal and historical answer. Until World War II, he argues, international relations were seen by governments, scholars, and legal experts as relationships among states. Human beings were seen only as the occupants of those nations, as the beneficiaries or victims of the game of diplomacy. After the Holocaust, however, the United Nations recognized for the first time — in the Universal Declaration of Human Rights — that people could legitimately appeal to the international community to rectify the abuses of their governments. Schneider believed that the Carter administration was the first to try to make this a central principle of its foreign policy, and he was happy to be given a chance to take part.

Schneider saw in this issue more than an international legal proposition. He was raised in an ethical Jewish tradition that was reinforced by his experiences as a Peace Corps volunteer in El Salvador in the 1960s. He remembers his outrage when he and a group of Salvadorian friends were rousted by a group of National Guardsmen, put up against a wall, and then sent home, when they simply had been standing on a corner eating refried beans one evening. He and other volunteers heard and retold stories of people taken away, people beaten. When he returned to the United States, he became chairman of a human relations board in Pittsburg, California, where he could draw on his ability to speak Spanish.

Schneider went to Washington in 1970 and joined the office of Senator Edward M. Kennedy, where he became one of a small number of congressional staff members with expertise on both Latin America and human rights. He was thus a participant in the efforts of the early and mid-1970s to force the Nixon and Ford administrations to integrate human rights into the mainstream of American foreign policies. When offered a job as Derian's deputy, he leaped at the chance to fight from within. And fight he did, earning particular criticism from opponents of the Carter administration's human rights policies as a leftist radical. Somoza went so far as to tell an American official that Schneider was "connected

with the FSLN . . . the Communist FSLN."[2] What really offended
his opponents was the vigor with which he acted, not the nature
of his political views (actually rather traditional in their liberalism).
Hanging a leftist label on him was the easiest way to strike at
him. To accuse him of a radical attachment to human rights would
hardly have had the effect they sought.

For Wade Matthews, the career officer, the pursuit of human
rights was a legitimate national concern, but he believed that the
Carter administration was promoting human rights at the expense
of more important national interests. In early 1977, Matthews,
then working in the office concerned with the Organization of
American States, wrote a memorandum attacking what he saw as
the view of the incoming Carter administration: that Central America would be an excellent testing ground for its human rights policies
because the United States lacked vital interests there. In April, Assistant Secretary of State Todman read the memorandum, agreed
with Matthews's views, and elevated him from the OAS office to
be the country director for Central America.

Wade Matthews's concern reflected a point often made by critics
who claimed that the Carter administration was applying double
(or multiple) standards in implementing its human rights policies.
Since Central America was seen as less important than, say, the
Persian Gulf or South Korea, the administration had unfairly chosen
Somoza and neighboring despots as the primary targets of its human
rights crusade. (One observer sharing Matthews's view suggested
in 1977 that if bananas were oil, Somoza would have been treated
with the same consideration as a despotic sheik.)

A policy of disassociation from Somoza, Matthews thought, represented an abdication of American responsibility in a double sense.
First, the United States was walking away from its traditional involvement in Central America and thus from its share of responsibility for events. In addition, it was failing to pursue its own interests
there. As Matthews was to write in 1980 in a paper for the State
Department's Executive Seminar, "the advancement of the national interest (hopefully but not necessarily enlightened and bene-
ficent to all) is the proper goal of foreign policy. . . . The sub-

stitution of some other goal, no matter how ethically laudable, is not politically sustainable in the current world."[3]

Matthews saw the pursuit of those interests — the deterrence or defeat of potential adversaries, the avoidance of catastrophic damage in doing so, the protection of foreign raw materials sources and markets — as a duty, indeed as the purpose of his work as a Foreign Service officer. He believed that human rights activists were "supra-nationalists" who believed that "the accomplishment of moral or ethical purpose above and beyond the welfare of the nation is the supreme national goal." The consequence of the administration's approach, he wrote, was the antagonism of other nations engendered by our "moral imperialism," the destabilization of friendly governments, their replacement by hostile regimes, little actual improvement in human rights, a concentration on issues peripheral to our "endangered national security," an inconsistent application of human rights policies, and — by deciding policy on the basis of others' internal policies — interference with Washington's ability to gain international support by consistently rewarding friendly acts and penalizing those who oppose us.[4]

On the other hand, most policy makers in the Carter administration believed that integrating human rights into foreign policies would promote American national interests as well as broader moral concerns — that repressive dictators were sowing revolutionary whirlwinds that would someday benefit the Cubans and Soviets, that democracies make the steadiest allies, that when other peoples see America defending their rights, a long-term political benefit in goodwill and trust is gained. Moreover, polls showed that the American people overwhelmingly supported a foreign policy that emphasized human rights.

Although it is true that the concern for human rights was applied with inconsistency, for many policy makers this was a sign of a serious, pragmatic effort to go beyond doctrinal simplicities. Different approaches were necessary to suit different local circumstances. In one case, sanctions might help; in another, positive encouragement might be most effective. They also argued that the promotion of human rights was only one of a number of American interests, and that realistically, a different balance among those interests should be struck depending on the strategic and economic importance of each nation with which the United States was dealing. Matthews understood this, but it was his job to promote American interests in Nicaragua, and he thought the policy of disassociation from the Somoza regime would only damage them.

Just as Schneider was attacked for his radicalism when in fact he saw the promotion of human rights as serving both national and broader interests, so Matthews was seen by some of his bureaucratic opponents as an apologist for Somoza. In fact, he believed (and wrote in a number of memoranda within the bureau) that it would benefit Nicaragua if Somoza stepped down. He even recalls telling Somoza, when he met him in 1977, that his regime suffered from an incurable fatigue. It was not, Matthews thought, that Somoza was worse than the other despots in the region; the Nicaraguan people simply wanted a change after decades of rule by the Somoza family. Distancing would not persuade Somoza to leave, nor would American sanctions, which only made him dig in his heels. Somoza, he later noted, "was as much American as Nicaraguan. He had a contempt for his own people, but listened to Americans and understood the give and take of American politics." If Washington had gained his confidence in 1977 rather than hectoring him, an appeal might have been made to his anticommunism as well as to his venality. It could have been suggested that his departure from office before 1981, leaving a strong National Guard in place behind a broadened Nicaraguan government, would head off political instability that would benefit the Communists. And while it did not need to be made explicit, it would be clear that Somoza could retire outside Nicaragua with much of his wealth.

Thus Matthews persisted in opposing measures that would penalize the Nicaraguan regime. It would be inaccurate, however, to see that work as a series of exciting or frustrating meetings and exchanges of memoranda explicitly on policy. Every young Foreign Service officer wants to make policy, or should want to. Involvement on issues of national importance — even peripheral involvement —

makes work in the State Department especially exciting. But while a successful Foreign Service officer does get to participate in meetings at which policy is to be decided, most of his work is more routine than romantic.

It is the country directors like Matthews who get the everyday work done. Each weekday at 8 A.M. or so, Matthews left his house in suburban Virginia for the traffic jams at the bridges across the Potomac. A country director is just high enough in rank to be allowed that most coveted State perk: a parking space in the basement of New State rather than on Washington's crowded streets. An elevator took Matthews from the basement to his fourth-floor office at the center of a suite shared with Agency for International Development officials working on Central America. Next to Matthews, in smaller offices behind glass-windowed partitions, were his "desk officers," each responsible for following the affairs of one of the Central American countries.

Matthews had been unable to find a desk officer with political experience in Nicaragua, and so had brought on a competent former consular officer. Matthews himself had never been to Nicaragua before taking his job. His previous academic training and experience had focused more on South America than Central America. Why were there no officers with substantive experience in Nicaragua available for service on the desk? Some, Matthews recalls, were on foreign assignment; others simply didn't think, in 1977, that work on Nicaragua would be very interesting.

Matthews would get to his desk at around 8:45, in time to go through the thirty or so cables from the embassies that had arrived during the night. Four or five usually required close reading. He would also look through reports from the CIA and scan *The Washington Post,* if he hadn't had a chance to read it at home. Then, after checking quickly with the desk officers about any hot items, he would head up to the sixth floor for the Latin American bureau staff meeting. Here, the assistant secretary or his senior deputy would go around the room discussing with the office directors the major items on their agendas for the day, passing along instructions from the Seventh Floor, prodding for quicker action on work

that was lagging. Matthews would then meet with his desk officers
to report on the meeting and give them any guidance necessary.
At midmorning he could settle in at his desk to attack his own
day's work.

Always there was paper. There were draft responses to letters
from members of Congress, for signature by one of the department's
senior officers. (As the situation in Nicaragua deteriorated, the
volume of such congressional mail increased from one or two letters
a day in 1977 to ten or more by late 1978.) There were telegrams
to the embassies in Central America asking for information, instruct-
ing ambassadors to raise issues with the local governments, inform-
ing them of decisions reached in Washington, or simply taking
care of administrative matters. There were memoranda on arms
sales, policy papers, statements for more senior officers to use in
appearances before congressional committees. And there were
"guidances" — questions and suggested answers — for the department's spokesman to use at his daily press briefing.

Almost every draft produced by Matthews's office had to be
cleared by officials in other bureaus. The clearance process is perhaps
the most laborious, frustrating, and time-consuming of all bureaucratic tasks. After the thrill of creation — the drafting of a telegram,
a policy paper, a speech — comes the agony of gaining approval
by all of the offices, bureaus, and agencies with some interest in
the item's content. Each official providing the clearance initials
the document at the bottom, where all the agencies and names
are shown under "Clearances." In some cases the clearance may
be designated as "in substance," which means that the document
was not read in detail but approval was given for its general content.
(Some have argued that the department's work could be conducted
much more efficiently if more clearances were given in substance,
but it requires a fair dose of trust to let someone else characterize
your views in a memorandum you'll never see in its final draft.)

Except in unusual circumstances, the system demands that all
those with an interest in a topic be allowed to check any document
for accuracy and to express their own opinions. This is not irra-
tional: senior officials need to know all sides to an issue before

deciding it. But in practice, the product of this process is more likely to be blandly conventional than boldly creative. There will, of course, be differences of opinion, yet the overwhelming impulse is to soften rather than to sharpen such differences, to disguise convictions in the passive voice — the safe, impersonal voice of bureaucracy ("It is believed that . . ."). Why? Because the drafting officer needs clearances from officials at his own level, and where differences are irreconcilable, the argument moves to higher levels for resolution. This does more than make work for one's superior; it suggests a failure of bureaucratic skill: the offending officer could not take care of business at his own level. Thus the halls of the State Department and the larger embassies are trudged by officials in search of clearances and, on all but the most contentious of issues, of consensus through the lowest common denominator.

Because Matthews held strong views on Nicaragua (as did most of the officials he dealt with in other bureaus), his clearance process was more interesting than usual. But it was also more time-consuming for him than it would have been for an office director working on a less controversial region. And time was short. Beyond the numerous papers to be written or read, there were meetings: meetings to hammer out joint drafts, meetings of senior officers at which Matthews might be asked to take notes and offer occasional opinions, meetings with a stream of visitors — other officials seeking clearances, officials from the CIA or Defense Department (perhaps once a week), lobbyists from human rights organizations (and only rarely from businesses or conservative organizations), ambassadors from the embassies of Central American nations (each dropped in perhaps once a month), officials or opposition figures from Central America who were visiting Washington, reporters (four or five a week), and, occasionally, congressional staff members or even a member of Congress if he happened to be in the building visiting a senior official. Occasionally his work was set aside for trips to Central America or travels in the United States for speeches on administration policies. (Matthews was always careful to begin his public statements with the phrase "the administration believes." He did not want to describe the administration's views as his own, since he disagreed with them, but he believed he should not publicly voice his disagreement with the government he served.)

Most days, Matthews ate lunch at his desk or in the cafeteria on the ground floor, where the quality of the food lies somewhere between edible and enjoyable. He was rarely taken out to lunch by a reporter on an expense account; more often they would go dutch at the cafeteria. His afternoons sped by, and it was usually seven P.M. — and often eight or nine — before he could think of home. About once a week there might be a party, a diplomatic reception at an embassy, or an evening with friends. Matthews recalls once going a week without seeing his children, who were in bed before he got home and off to school before he arose. Sundays were his own, except during crises, but most Saturdays he worked into the middle of the afternoon. It was frustrating to be working when most of Washington was out enjoying the weekend, but at least one could create a little of the feel of a holiday by leaving suit and necktie at home. On weekends, sports shirts and even tennis shorts are often sighted; blue jeans have yet to become part of the uniform for the weekend diplomat.

One casualty of the weight of Matthews's work was the opportunity — even the inclination — to read. At the end of the day he might look through *The Economist,* but it is an almost universal complaint of officials like Matthews that their days of memos, cables, and letters drain them of the will to read more at night — especially on the same subjects with which they have just been wrestling. Ask any former official and he will almost certainly tell you that it was only after leaving government that he started to read *Foreign Affairs* or even *The New York Times* with anything approaching care. The result is that while officials are immersed in classified reports, they lose touch with how those outside the government perceive the world. Another result of his workload was lack of time to sit back and contemplate policy. While Christopher was besieged by competing policy problems, Matthews, at the "working level," was frustrated by the way the trivial competed with policy matters. After all, it was the chance to work on policy that made the grind worthwhile.

Since policy toward Nicaragua was being made largely in the context of the administration's human rights initiatives, the most interesting battles in 1977 came within the framework of Christopher's Inter-Agency Group on Human Rights. A working group chaired by Mark Schneider for the human rights bureau and a deputy assistant secretary from the economics bureau screened all foreign assistance projects and military sales to determine whether any should be brought before the Christopher committee for debate at a more senior level. Matthews either attended or prepared the staff work for others to attend its meetings.

It was in this process of reviewing foreign military sales that, in May 1978, the Latin American bureau scored one of its few triumphs against Human Rights. The previous fall, the administration had suspended all new economic assistance projects in Nicaragua pending improvement in that government's human rights record. This included two loans from the Agency for International Development worth $10.5 million, for rural education and nutrition improvement. Under congressional pressure, the administration reconsidered the matter in the early spring. The Latin American bureau favored the loans, arguing that Somoza had not returned to the repressive ways of early 1977, even after the turmoil following Chamorro's assassination in January. The policy planning staff favored all such loans on the ground that the administration was committed to promoting economic as well as political rights, and that to deny basic economic assistance would penalize poor people for the sins of their government. The human rights bureau opposed the loans, arguing that such assistance should not be offered in cases like that of Nicaragua, whose government it considered to be particularly loathsome.

In May, Christopher approved the AID loans. The reason had more to do with congressional power than with the force of the bureaus' competing arguments. Congressman Charles Wilson convinced Henry Owen, a senior White House aide who was becoming the central administration figure in setting international economic policy and shaping aid legislation, that Wilson would use his considerable influence against the whole aid bill if the two loans for Nicaragua were not forthcoming. Owen then persuaded Christopher. In a letter to Ambassador Solaun in Managua (Solaun had opposed the loans), Matthews noted with some satisfaction,

> Wilson decided that since persuasion had been unsuccessful in changing U.S. policy toward Nicaragua, coercion should be tried. Using the Freedom House ranking of political liberties as the only available ranking that had some sort of objective criteria, Wilson told various U.S. government officials that he intended to introduce and lobby for an amendment to foreign assistance legislation prohibiting the various sorts of aid which we were withholding from Nicaragua on allegedly human rights grounds to any country which Freedom House rated equal or lower than Nicaragua. . . . This included such nations as Peru, Bolivia, Panama, Thailand, the Philippines, and most of the African countries. . . . The general consensus of [senior] officials was that the issue of sending . . . political signals to Somoza had to take a clear second place to preventing serious damage to our world wide aid programs.

Matthews's letter to Solaun went on to suggest that there be a further push for more such loans, and even expressed optimism that the hold on military items might be loosened. He was wrong. In the end, while the two economic loans were signed in August, they were never implemented while Somoza remained in power.

Announcement of the two loans in mid-May was accompanied by a statement that the action represented no shift in the administration's approach to Somoza and his regime. Reporters did not accept this. A May 16 headline in *The Washington Post* read: "U.S. Frees Aid to Nicaragua in a Policy Reversal." Once an administration develops a reputation for some particular frailty, reporters are delighted to find new evidence confirming the impression. By 1978 the press was leaping at every sign of the inconsistency for which the Carter administration was being criticized.

The decision on aid to Nicaragua was bad enough in this regard, and worse was to come when the president decided to send a friendly letter to Somoza that might encourage him to new progress on human rights.

On Wednesday, June 21, Robert Pastor, the NSC staff member charged with Latin American affairs, received a memorandum from Zbigniew Brzezinski:

THE WHITE HOUSE

WASHINGTON

June 21, 1978

MEMORANDUM FOR: Bob Pastor

FROM: Zbigniew Brzezinski

SUBJECT: Human Rights in Nicaragua

As you know, President Somoza indicated on Monday that Nicaragua would cooperate with the Inter-American Human Rights Commission. Somoza further indicated:

Nicaragua is studying the possibility of ratifying the Inter-American Convention of Human Rights.

Amnesty for political opponents is negotiable with the opposition; and

"The Twelve" [members of an exile opposition group] are free to return anytime they choose.

In response to the above, the President stated that a message should be prepared for him to send Somoza encouraging these moves. Please respond by close of business Thursday. Also clear the message with State and Fallows.[5]

Carter had read a report of Somoza's statements in an intelligence summary prepared by the Situation Room on June 20. Pastor did not find the president's decision to send a letter to Somoza surprising. Carter had sent similar letters of encouragement to Generals Pinochet in Chile and Videla in Argentina, both major league abusers of human rights. (Similarly, the president had surprised everyone in his New Year's Eve toast in Teheran by praising the shah.) This was perfectly consistent with Carter's general policy directive on human rights, issued on February 17, 1978, which stated that the United States should use the full range of diplomatic tools in pressing for progress, but "should emphasize positive inducements."[6] But Pastor was uneasy, and expressed his doubts about the letter to Brzezinski. Somoza, he suggested, might use it as evidence that he enjoyed American favor after all. The national security assistant ordered Pastor to include his objections in a memorandum to the president covering the draft letter.[7]

Pastor drafted a letter noting Somoza's statement and encouraging him to implement his promises. The draft arrived at the State Department on June 22, with a request for comments by 3 P.M. that same day. Copies were sent to the Latin American and human rights bureaus, to policy planning, and to the under secretary for political affairs. Mark Schneider of Human Rights had already heard about the draft in a telephone call from Pastor, and remembers that he went through the roof. It was, he thought, a stupid idea, since Somoza was sure to publicize the letter. He went to the Latin American bureau to argue strongly against it. Matthews was on vacation, but others there agreed that the letter was dangerous. (On his return a few days later, however, Matthews was to welcome the idea, since he believed in encouraging rather than bullying Somoza.) The two bureaus quickly passed their objections to the Seventh Floor, where the issue went to Warren Christopher. When Christopher called Pastor to ask him about the source of the letter, he learned that Pastor had not told his colleagues in the department that the idea was the president's. (To do so would have suggested disloyalty, that he was trying to distance himself from President Carter.) Christopher was clearly trying to ascertain whether Pastor was acting for the president or on his own, and he told the deputy secretary that it was Carter who wanted the letter. The conversation was very brief: Pastor did not offer his own views of the letter, and Christopher simply thanked him for the information before hanging up.

Objection to sending the letter seemed useless, so State made marginal changes in the draft and returned it to the White House with a recommendation that the letter be delayed a week while the Inter-American Commission negotiated with the Nicaraguan government about a visit by its representatives to Managua. Pastor then wrote a covering memorandum recommending against sending the letter lest Somoza use it for his own purposes. Brzezinski deleted Pastor's warning, since he did not want to oppose the State Department on what he saw as a relatively minor matter when he was fighting it on such contentious issues as policy in the Horn of Africa.

Thus President Carter was unaware that the two bureaus in the State Department with most knowledge of the subject, as well as his own NSC expert, opposed the idea. An inveterate editor, he made a number of changes in the draft. Where Pastor had written that the president noted Somoza's statements with great interest, Carter added "and appreciation." At the end, he also added, in his neat script, "and appreciate very much your announcement of these constructive actions." The president then ordered that his letter be sent a week later, as the department had recommended.

These additions led Pastor to write another memorandum on Nicaragua to Brzezinski on June 28. It began:

> Now that the President has added a touch of warmth to his letter, I really regret that I had not requested a second time that you send in the longer memo to him explaining the political situation there. Somoza is not just another leader whose professed interest in human rights can be translated into real actions by Presidential nudges. Furthermore, our historical relationship with Somoza makes it very difficult for us to take any step which could be interpreted as supportive of Somoza without it antagonizing the democratic opposition in Nicaragua and our human rights supporters in Nicaragua.

His memorandum was ignored.

Why did State and Pastor not push harder to get their objections before the president? Why did Brzezinski not forward Pastor's memos? For all officials, there is a proper concern about overloading their superiors with too much information, too many issues, and — especially — too many complaints. To fight and be prepared to die over every issue is to guarantee being effective on none, for soon the superior will dismiss the pleadings as tedious and the pleader as unsound, a person incapable of making distinctions between the important and the trivial. Thus the power of the "effectiveness trap," which suggests to every bureaucrat that caution on the unpleasant issue at hand will increase his effectiveness on other issues. The essential calculation is correct: an official should not squander his bureaucratic capital on unimportant issues. This implies, however, a willingness to fight when the importance of an issue merits it. James Thomson suggested the effectiveness trap as a powerful device for explaining bureaucratic behavior on the Vietnam War. Many officials, he argued, decided that a fight on Vietnam would mean ineffectiveness on other issues. In that case, of course, the other issues were of far less importance, and the calculation became simply a rationalization for self-serving caution.[8]

The president's letter to Somoza should have gone out on June 30, but State procrastinated. According to a chronology of events later written in the Latin American bureau, the bureau waited until July 3, when it received the actual signed copy. It then spent five days "consulting with the NSC and the Deputy Secretary's office on an appropriate course of procedure" — i.e., how to send the letter. (In the standard operating procedure for delivering such letters, the text would be cabled to the embassy for delivery, with the actual letter to follow by diplomatic pouch.) On July 8 the cable finally went out, with an instruction that Ambassador Solaun deliver the text of the letter to Somoza as soon as possible, but suggesting that "if [Solaun] had objections as to substance or timing he should so indicate."

On July 10, Pastor called Solaun to instruct him to inform Somoza, when he gave him the letter, that it was confidential presidential correspondence and to ask that Somoza treat it in that fashion. On July 11, Matthews called Solaun to ask if he had an appointment to see Somoza. Solaun said that he did and was about to leave for the meeting. The ambassador said he thought it would be best simply to make an oral presentation of the points in the letter rather than to leave a copy with Somoza. There being no time to seek White House guidance, Matthews told him to use his own judgment but to cable the department with the rationale for his decision. Thus Solaun gave Somoza only an oral message.

The requested cable from Solaun arrived at State on the fourteenth. He argued that violence had been increasing since the president had signed the letter, Somoza's opponents were planning a general strike for July 19, and he was sure Somoza would not respect the confidentiality of the letter. It would be better not to deliver a text. But on July 17, the signed letter arrived by diplomatic pouch in Managua. On the twentieth, after consulting with the White House, the Latin American bureau instructed Solaun to proceed with delivery of the letter, emphasizing its confidentiality and expressing the president's concern about the increase in violence. Finally, on July 21, a full month after Brzezinski's instruction to Pastor (giving him one day to provide a draft for the president), the letter was delivered to Somoza.

Somoza immediately saw the value of the letter. As he wrote later in his memoirs, "I was not interested in a collector's item, and without being able to use the letter, that's what it was."[9] He arranged a secret meeting with his enemy, President Pérez, and laid the letter before the astonished Venezuelan. Pérez was not moved, and told Somoza, "I don't care what Carter says. Our position is firm. You have to go."

Private embarrassment for President Carter with his friend Pérez became a public setback on August 1 when *The Washington Post* published a front-page story under the headline "Carter Letter to Somoza Stirs Human Rights Row." The article said that the letter had been forced on the State Department by the White House, and indicated that the idea had come from the NSC staff. "State Department officials," it said, "are concerned that revelation of the letter . . . will raise questions about the sensitivity of the Administration's human rights policy." Officials in the White House were furious about the leak, which seemed clearly to have come from State and to be aimed at the NSC staff. Pastor was especially upset, since the leak seemed directed personally at him. After reflection, he found solace in the thought that in suffering the blame himself, his standing with Brzezinski and the president might have been strengthened. But the incident still rankled.

Pastor checked with Schneider and then assured his superiors that their first suspicions were incorrect: Schneider was not the source of the leak. He was, after all, a friend of Pastor, and would

not use such a leak to harm him. Years later there was still considerable speculation about the source. Some former officials believe it
was a congressional friend of Somoza; others point indirectly at
each other. The day the article appeared, Somoza told an American
diplomat that he had shown the letter to no one. He was lying;
he had shown it to Pérez. But the leak does seem to have come
from State. Pastor says he was later told by the reporter that it
was a "senior pro–human rights official" in the Latin American
bureau who let the matter slip at a social event. He also notes
the self-destructiveness involved in such an official's accomplishing
through the leak precisely what he or she professed to be worried
about: public harm to the president's human rights policies.

In subsequent days the White House tried to explain the context
and purpose of the Somoza letter to reporters, without much success.
The effect of the incident was to deepen the divide between the
NSC and State. As always happens after leaks, the circle of decision
making was narrowed. The human rights bureau was less likely
thereafter to be included in any interagency deliberations on Nicaragua controlled by the NSC. And despite the fact that the letter
had indeed proved ill-advised, the procrastination of the Latin American bureau and the embassy in delivering it rankled. The staff
secretary of the NSC shot a memorandum at State. The target
seemed to include Pastor as well as the procrastinators at the department:

NATIONAL SECURITY COUNCIL
WASHINGTON, D.C. 20506

July 10, 1978

MEMORANDUM FOR: Peter Tarnoff
                         Executive Secretary
                         Department of State

SUBJECT: Forwarding of Presidential Letters

It is our assumption that the Department forwards Presidential letters
to Heads of State or Government immediately upon receipt by the
Department from the White House. To prevent a situation similar
to what happened with President Somoza's letter from recurring,

if the Department or an Embassy wants to recommend a delay in delivery, please be sure to inform me immediately. It is not enough to have the bureaus speak to the NSC staff members.

Christine Dodson
Staff Secretary

The reprimand may have had some cathartic effect in the White House but it did nothing, of course, to repair the damaging public impression of further inconsistency in the administration's Central American policies.

SIX

State: The Embassy

THE AMERICAN EMBASSY IN MANAGUA IS A SMALL AFFAIR, and there are few who have loved it — or at least who have wanted to serve there. Until very recently the most ambitious young Foreign Service officers have not often been drawn to Latin American affairs. Service in one of the big capitals in South America or in Mexico City might offer a chance to write an important dispatch or cable, and perhaps to work with senior diplomats who might use their weight to push along one's career. But the region is dotted with smaller posts, many in Central America and the Caribbean, where the older officers seem to have been put out to pasture and their younger colleagues feel unnoticed. Even in 1928, when Managua was hot in a figurative as well as a literal sense, a Foreign Service officer wrote to Washington, "It would help if men who specialized in Latin America knew they would not ordinarily be sent to posts like Buenaventura and Puerto Cortez where they would get no valuable experience. A man with the right spirit ought not to mind going to Managua or Tegucigalpa, if he knew that it was not necessarily a disgrace to be sent there."[1]

One would think that the smaller posts would be popular with junior officers, for they offer a chance at a wider range of responsibilities than do the larger, more bureaucratic American missions. But the small posts are small because they are located in the backwaters. Only when these waters become roiled can a junior officer take advantage of the opportunity.

That is what happened to Patricia Haigh. When she arrived in Managua in March 1977, she held few expectations of adventure. She was a junior officer assigned to the economic section of the embassy. It was her second assignment in the Foreign Service. Little in her training or experience prepared her for the important work she was to carry out over the next two years: it fell to her and a few of her colleagues in the embassy to report to Washington on a gathering revolution.

Her previous assignments and training had been more random than rigorous. A graduate of Wheaton College and the Wharton School of the University of Pennsylvania, Haigh joined the Foreign Service in 1974 largely because of a desire to live abroad. Applicants to the Foreign Service choose one of four specialties — political or economic affairs, consular work (including such matters as the granting of visas to foreign visitors or immigrants and assistance to American citizens abroad), or administration (involving everything from personnel management to making the embassy motor pools run on time). Haigh chose administration. It interested her, and the service was always seeking administrative officers.

She was first given five weeks' training at the Foreign Service Institute in Rosslyn, Virginia, just across the Potomac from Washington. The course covered matters more procedural than substantive, including information on the ways of the State Department, security concerns, how an embassy works, and the like. Thus armed for her career in administration, she went with the rest of her class to a ceremony in an ornate diplomatic reception room on the eighth floor of the State Department. After being welcomed to the Foreign Service by a senior officer and swearing to uphold the Constitution, she and her fellow junior officers were joined for coffee and cookies by friends and a number of personnel officers from the various bureaus in the department. She chatted with an officer from the Bureau of African Affairs, and the next day was more surprised than she should have been to receive a call inviting her to come and discuss a job in that region. Most junior officers are simply assigned to a post, but she was offered a choice because the job was rather unusual: she could replace a roving administrative officer in West Africa who had been taken ill. Haigh wasn't so sure: she lacked the experience to be an administrative trouble-shooter, she knew little of Africa, and the indisposition of her predecessor was hardly encouraging.

Haigh accepted the job because she had said she was available for duty anywhere in the world. She was relieved, however, when the department's personnel office called to say they were terribly sorry, but the job in Africa was no longer available. "Thank God," she thought, trying to sound disappointed. Would she mind going to Italy instead? "Anything for my country," she told herself, and accepted an assignment to Genoa. Her two years there seemed to go quickly, in part because of a lively social calendar. A gregarious young American was invited everywhere. Haigh led a life "that a middle-class kid from Rhode Island had never seen before." Even the diplomatic receptions, at which foreign representatives and local dignitaries were packed into tight, uncomfortable masses of small talk and large drinks, were enjoyable. It was surprising how much one could learn at them — "not political secrets," she recalls, "but information about doings at the port, and economic deals and problems."

Drawn to economic affairs, Haigh pursued a specialty in commer-cial work, including reporting on economic events and the promo-tion of American business interests abroad.[2] She was offered a choice of Managua or Quito, Ecuador, for her next post, and chose Quito. She was duly assigned to Managua. Some twenty-four weeks of intensive instruction in Spanish were followed by two weeks of "area studies" for officers going to Latin America. The latter included a morning on Central America during which a visiting professor reviewed its countries, noting the differences among them. There was a section on the history of Latin America as a whole, but little specifically on the story of American relations with Nicaragua and its neighbors. This did not seem surprising to her. "Who had heard of Nicaragua in 1977?" she says. On learning of her assignment there, she had had to look up the country in an atlas: "Ah yes; it's two nations up from the Panama Canal."

In late March 1977, Haigh left a heavy snow storm in Rhode

Island for the heat of Nicaragua. As she was driven from the airport to the Intercontinental Hotel in the heart of Managua, she was struck by the paucity of tall buildings in the city. The 1972 earthquake had left in its wake an extended village rather than a city. The hotel was an exceptional survivor: it dominated much of the area by virtue of its position on a hill and its odd, pyramidal shape.

A mile or so away, from another hill, the American embassy dominated another part of Managua. (The United States was given the building and its site by Anastasio Somoza García in 1946 in return for rights to the Corinto naval base, which was to be liquidated after World War II. According to *The New York Times,* Somoza had wrested the residence away from its Nicaraguan owner for a price far below the value he set on it when trading it to the Americans.)[3] Set on a few acres of well-tended lawns and gardens, the building is considered the most beautiful in Managua. On one side, its large, high-ceilinged rooms offer views of the city and far beyond; on the other, they look out over the lawns and a fine swimming pool. Out of sight are a softball field and various outbuildings. In this residence the American ambassador lived, in a style only the most plutocratic of his fellow citizens could hope to afford.*

For many American ambassadors around the world, the contrast between these residences and their homes in the middle-rent districts around Washington is stunning. Obviously, the architectural dominance of such residences conveys an unfortunate political symbolism. Would it not be better for our representatives to live more modestly abroad, as the wily Benjamin Franklin tried to pretend while wandering around Paris in his coonskin cap? Wouldn't more modest quarters be better suited to a republic founded on the rejection not only of Old World repression, but of its frippery and pretension as well? There are strong arguments to be made for

* Under diplomatic tradition and international law, the ambassador's residence, not the building containing his and his subordinates' offices, is technically the embassy. The local government has no legal claims on or within an embassy, which is considered part of the territory of the government it represents.

such a view, and cost-conscious congressmen have made them. But much of diplomacy is representation, and large nations are expected to be represented by grand embassies.

The embassy on the hill had survived the earthquake unscathed. At the bottom of the slope, a half mile or so away, the embassy's office building had been destroyed. Thus Haigh found her working quarters in a structure built as a temporary replacement but on its way to achieving an ill-deserved permanence. Centered in a walled compound covering a few acres, the work space consisted of prefabricated Bailey building units joined together in unhappy union. The compound, which also contained separate quarters for the motor pool and an enclave for consular officers, was itself quite pleasant: modest gardens and flowering trees made hot days seem a little cooler. But the mood was lost as one entered the main building, with its artificial light, linoleum floors, and wall-board. Mice (or rats, depending on one's imagination) occasionally left droppings on the desks of the fifty or so people working there. A few years after Haigh's tour in Managua, a cat fell through one of the flimsy ceilings as it pursued the miscreants.

The embassy was staffed in the normal pattern. At the center, where two modules joined, were the offices of the ambassador and his deputy chief of mission. Elsewhere, in much more modest offices, were the political, economic, consular, and administrative sections; a modest number of rooms for representatives of the United States Information Agency, the Voice of America, and the defense attachés; a small section for the Central Intelligence Agency station chief and his staff; and space for fifteen or so representatives of the Agency for International Development. Access to the building was controlled by a Marine guard.*

Haigh quickly found life at her new post very pleasant. At some of the 280 or so Foreign Service posts around the world, American officials are housed in compounds. In Managua they lived "on

---

* Each guard stands an eight-hour shift. Embassy work is popular duty in the Marine Corps, which provides six weeks of training in such varied topics as the State Department and its embassies, counterterrorism techniques, and etiquette, including table manners and seating arrangements.

the economy." Haigh found a pretty little house with a rose garden on the southern outskirts of the city. With four other houses, it shared a common fence that offered dubious protection against robbers. And like most Americans living in Managua, Haigh hired a live-in maid and cook. (For many Americans in the Third World — reporters, officials, business people, even volunteers working on development projects — hiring servants is at first uncomfortable, an affront to our egalitarian sensibilities. But those who do not soon find that their work suffers as they spend time tracking down the necessities of life.)

Work at the embassy began at 7:30 A.M., in the glorious, fresh coolness of tropical mornings. Haigh's day was spent meeting with Nicaraguan businessmen, reading reports on the economy, writing reports to Washington, answering inquiries from American businesses. At 4:30, official hours were over, and most people would leave the air-conditioned haven of their offices to enter the heat of the late afternoon. More than jewels or a Mercedes, the air conditioner has become the most important mark of elite life in the tropics. At the embassies, modern business buildings, the more important government offices, the tourist hotels, and the best houses, cooling machines make midday efficiency possible. Typewriters click rapidly above the hum of the air conditioners. Outside this world, where there is no artificial invigoration, people live in sticky heat. Understandably, they work at a slower pace, sometimes to the irritation or amusement of air-conditioned observers. An irony of modern life: once the tropical rich moved more slowly than the poor, because they could afford languor. Now, when they wish, they move more quickly, because they can afford air conditioning.

In the late afternoons, if their work was done, Haigh and her colleagues might play tennis or swim. And in the evenings, when the air was warm and soft, the city's elite would drink and dine on verandas and in dining rooms far removed from the life of most of Managua. The parties were often formal. A Foreign Service officer who might trot out a dinner jacket or evening dress once or twice a year for parties in Washington found them in regular use in the Nicaraguan capital.

Haigh was low on the embassy totem pole. She never, for instance, attended a meeting of the "country team." (At all American embassies, the ambassador and his deputy regularly meet with the chiefs of all U.S. agencies and the heads of their own political and economic sections in an effort to coordinate their actions.) But according to a number of visitors to Managua at the time, Haigh was soon one of the embassy officers who understood best what was going on in the country. Visitors also remarked that this was not a strong embassy. Under Turner Shelton, American ambassador in the early 1970s, the main function of the embassy had been to hold the hands of Somoza's followers while the ambassador held Somoza's. Shelton had actively discouraged meetings with Somoza's opponents and tried to block reports by embassy officers that appeared critical of the regime.

Shelton's successor in 1975, James Theberge, began to broaden the embassy's contacts in Managua, and Mauricio Solaun, who was sent to Managua by President Carter in 1977, encouraged embassy officers to go still further in talking to Somoza's growing number of critics. Unfortunately, Solaun, a quiet former professor, was not noted for forcefulness in his dealings either with Somoza or with Washington.[4] And a number of visitors and reporters remarked on the caution the ambassador and most embassy officers displayed about venturing outside the capital city.

Haigh, though, was happy to make numerous contacts in Managua. She was gregarious and enjoyed social life. The business community in Nicaragua was not large. Everyone knew — even seemed to be related to — everyone else, and the conversation was heavy with political as well as personal gossip. It didn't hurt at all, in a society where the men prized their machismo, that Haigh had reddish hair and *ojos azules*. This is by no means to suggest that being a woman with blue eyes offers an advantage in the Foreign Service. Even women who experience little overt discrimination often report a sense that the men seem resentful of their presence, that they think the women might be there only because they were admitted through some special hiring program at the expense of male applicants, and that a woman's place is in something like cultural affairs or administration rather than political or economic work. Such prejudice is seldom made explicit: the State Department is a very polite place. It was a long time ago, in 1909, that sentiments were put as baldly as they were by the assistant secretary of state who wrote that "the greatest obstacle to the employment of women as diplomatic agents is their well known inability to keep a secret."[5]

The department has made particular efforts over the past decade to increase the number of women in the service, in part because of the emphasis put on the issue by President Carter and Secretary of State Vance, in part because of a class action suit brought in 1976 by a number of female Foreign Service officers. Yet by the mid-1980s only twenty-one percent of Foreign Service officers were women, a figure comparable to the percentage of women holding positions on the professional staff at the United Nations or receiving Ph.D.s in international relations and political science. And despite similar efforts with regard to minority groups, only 252 of 4,000 Foreign Service officers in 1987 were black.[6]

As a commercial officer, Haigh was well placed to observe the growing opposition to Somoza among the middle and upper classes. The crucial event in this ground swell was the assassination of Pedro Joaquín Chamorro in January 1978. Even before the murder, many young businessmen had expressed distaste for the dictator, but now distaste turned to anger. A few members of the middle class had already opposed Somoza openly: indeed, in October 1977, twelve of them, including businessmen, priests, and intellectuals, had signed a statement praising the Sandinistas. Dubbed Los Doce, they became during the following months the chief lobbyists for the Sandinistas, traveling to foreign capitals where support or sympathy might be drummed up. For most members of the Nicaraguan establishment, however, the issue in late 1977 had been reform, not revolution. They supported calls for an end to economic and human rights abuses by the regime, not an end to the regime. But after the shock of Chamorro's murder, the issue became Somoza's rule itself.

Before the assassination, life in Managua had generally been quiet for Haigh and her colleagues at the embassy. In October and November 1977, the Frente Sandinista de Liberación Nacional (FSLN) had launched a series of guerrilla raids against National Guard outposts, but it was clear that the Sandinista bands were small and limited to activities far from the city. After the assassination, sleepy Managua awakened. The Unión Democratica de Liberación (UDEL), an organization of anti-Somoza businessmen formed in 1974, called for the strike of January 24. The next day, eighty percent of the country's economy was idle.

It was clear to Haigh that her Nicaraguan friends had been irrevocably politicized, that in the most fundamental terms, Somoza had lost his legitimacy. One had only to speak to the Nicaraguans working at the embassy to see the strength of the reaction against him. Conrado Godoy, a thin, elegant Honduran, was working in the radio section as, among other things, a Voice of America correspondent. Godoy was one of many foreigners employed by our government abroad. The State Department relies on almost twice as many "locals" (approximately 10,000) as Americans at its foreign posts. The work of the locals ranges from chaffeuring and general maintenance to clerical duties and interpreting. Although they are generally paid less than Americans, their salaries are quite generous compared to those of most people in Third World nations, and besides, work at an embassy conveys a certain prestige. Godoy, who had been a successful television announcer in Managua before joining the embassy, recalls with an ironic smile that as much as his friends envied his "earning green," they envied his title, which was as long as that of the president of a republic: he was the *jefe de la seccion de radio de la embajada Americana*. The ability of embassies to attract good people like Godoy means that the locals are often far more competent than the level of their duties would suggest. A junior Foreign Service officer may learn more from the clerks with whom he works than from his American superiors.

Godoy recalls, "The reaction in the embassy to the Chamorro assassination was stunning. All the employees just stopped working. There was a lot of crying. It was definitely the beginning of the end with Somoza. . . . There was no sympathy for him. Even the

American officers hated him. He was incredible. After the assassination, there was nothing he could do but go out." Although the local embassy employees did not join the strike, they sympathized with the strikers.

In July and August 1978, sporadic clashes between the protesters and the National Guard, and frustration at the failure of the Americans to remove Somoza, led many opponents of the regime to come together in a new organization: the FAO, or (in English translation) the Broad Opposition Front, which included the opposition political parties, the major labor unions, and Los Doce. On August 21 the FAO issued a program for the future, which included Somoza's departure from power. The FAO did not include the Nicaraguan Chamber of Commerce, but after some hesitation the chamber joined the FAO in calling for a general strike at the end of the month.

Meantime, although they remained limited in number and torn by internal disagreements, the Sandinistas had taken advantage of the anti-Somoza current in the country to build up their strength. The two more ideological of the Sandinista factions — the Guerra Popular Prolongada and the Proletarios — were, ironically, relatively cautious, arguing for a gradual buildup of their numbers and mass support. Members of the third faction, the Terceristas, were more pluralistic in their ideology and more inclusive in their efforts to attract bourgeois recruits and allies. Led by Daniel and Humberto Ortega and the charismatic Edén Pastora, they urged a spectacular action to dramatize the cause and give it new momentum.*

On August 23 the Terceristas struck in an action named Operation Pigsty. Disguised as members of the National Guard, Pastora and a group of twenty-five followers bluffed their way into the National Palace and then stormed into the Chamber of Deputies, killing

---

* Robert Pastor suggests that the Sandinistas were also aware of plotting against Somoza by disaffected National Guard members. Fearing that this might produce a more moderate, popular regime, the Sandinistas hoped a dramatic act of their own might forestall the plotters.[7] In late August eighty-five members of the Guard were arrested by Somoza for conspiring against the regime.

one guard in the process. The frightened deputies, most of whom had retired under their desks as Pastora and his three squads burst into the room, were taken hostage, together with a large number of other officials and journalists.

After repelling a counterattack by a passing National Guard patrol, the small group of Sandinistas settled in for two days of tense negotiations with Somoza. Concerned for the safety of a family member as well as for so many of his followers, and turning a deaf ear to the hawkish advice of Michael Echanis, an American mercenary in the National Guard, Somoza finally gave in to the raiders' demands: Sandinista manifestos were printed in the government newspaper, some fifty political prisoners were released, $500,000 ransom was paid for the hostages, and perhaps most important in political terms, Pastora and his followers were allowed to make their triumphant way on buses to the airport and thence abroad. Their route was lined with thousands of Managuans cheering and chanting anti-Somoza slogans. Few were probably Sandinistas, but Pastora and, to some degree, the revolution had captured their imaginations. Even at the embassy, the local employees enjoyed this twist to Somoza's tail.[8]

Apparently inspired by Pastora's bravado, young Nicaraguans in Matagalpa, north of Managua, spontaneously fought with the National Guard for five days. The FSLN, meanwhile, was planning a major, coordinated series of uprisings. The Sandinistas had to act quickly if they were to capture leadership of a genuine popular revolution in the making. On September 9 small bands of Sandinistas struck at National Guard outposts in Managua, Estelí, Masaya, León, and Chinandega. Except in Managua, the attacks produced days of fighting between the Guard and local citizens even after the FSLN cadres had slipped away. The fighting was most serious around and in Estelí.

At the embassy, reports to Washington on the fighting relied largely on information from the Nicaraguan government or secondhand information (a nice word for rumors) from Nicaraguan contacts in Managua. It was only by accident that one embassy officer gained a firsthand view of events in Estelí. "It was a holiday,"

Patricia Haigh recalls, "and after waking up, I had a sudden passion
for pancakes, I had to have pancakes. I went to the Hotel Intercontinental, which was the only place I knew that served them. There
were a lot of reporters there, to cover the fighting outside Managua.
I was enjoying my pancakes when an attractive wire service reporter,
Tom Fenton — not the Tom Fenton on TV — came up and said,
'Look, we're going out to look at the situation in Estelí, why don't
you come along? It might do the embassy some good to see what's
actually happening.' It sounded interesting, so I called the DCM
[the deputy chief of mission], since I would be going two hours
upcountry. He said to go ahead, but to be careful."

Fenton, Haigh, and a photographer had driven an hour or so
from Managua when they hit the first of what were alternating
zones of FSLN and National Guard control. They knew they were
in Sandinista country when "we started seeing strange things. First
there were enormous rocks in the road to be driven around, and
then a trench across it, maybe four feet deep and three feet wide,
to be skirted. We saw this young boy, no more than fourteen,
with something long wrapped in a mat. I'm so dumb, I asked,
'What is that?' Of course it was a rifle.

"Finally, maybe three miles from Estelí, we came to a checkpoint,
a tractor-trailer across the road as a blockade. There was a young
man there, a Sandinista, standing with his red and black bandana
over half his face. He asked who we were. I was masquerading
as a journalist with a camera around my neck. I didn't know how
to use it, but the photographer had showed me what button to
push in case I had to pretend. I had my diplomatic passport with
me, but I'm embarrassed to say it was hidden in my pants because
I did not have a purse. Tom Fenton had told me to take my watch
off, that if we got stopped they would ask for watches. We told
the kid that we were journalists and were going to look at Estelí.
He said fine and pulled the truck off the road, and away we went.

"Another mile or so down the road we saw three other American
journalists waving to us to stop. They had been strafed by a National
Guard plane and had pulled their car under a tree. We did, too.
They wanted us to go with them to look for a fourth member of

their party who had gotten separated from them during the strafing. They thought I should stay with the car, but I was terrified. I didn't want to stay by the car alone. You have to understand that I'm a middle-class kid who'd never seen anything like this before, my first tour had been near the Riviera. So I went with them, and we walked down the road carrying white flags and trying to make our cameras conspicuous.

"We were getting near another National Guard zone when an orange jeep went by with white flags flying. There was a family in it, obviously going in to get their relatives out. It was a couple in their early forties and a kid, I would guess eighteen or so, unarmed. Just after it passed us, we reached the crest of a hill. Suddenly there was an enormous *chaboom!* in front of us and the road exploded. We all jumped — the five men went one way into a ditch and I went the other, into a gulley on the far side of the road. It had one little bush in it — it seemed like a very little bush — and I put my head under it. The National Guard was strafing us from the air, with a machine gun in the door of an old DC-3, I think. Thank God it's very hard to hit someone from the air. I had orange on, which wasn't very helpful — and high heels. I was really dressed for this safari.

"The strafing stopped and Fenton, being chivalrous, stood up and called 'Patricia!' They didn't know where I was. I was so terrified being over there by myself that I stood up and started running across the street to jump in their ditch. Suddenly it was like the Keystone Kops. As I ran across, bullets followed me. It was a Somoza tank, parked down the road. Thank God those people were terrible shots. They were also shooting with rifles. I don't know how they could have missed me, but in the circumstances, I was pretty fast . . . There were bullets everywhere, and the six of us crawled through the bush and hid under a large oxcart under a tree and waited for the firing to stop."

The group finally returned to their car and found the missing member of their party. Haigh and the reporters had been caught between Sandinista and National Guard units which had been shooting at objects on the road without much discrimination. The Na-

tional Guard tank crew had killed the family in the jeep — the
first explosion Haigh had heard. The missing reporter had been
near the tank and had heard the commander yell that the people
in the jeep were Communists.

Haigh recalls the relief when the group got back to their cars:
"We decided to speed on back to Managua. We weren't going to
be able to get into Estelí and see the fighting, although we could
see the strafing from where we were, and we wanted to get out
of there before we got killed. We had thought the fighting had
almost stopped, or we wouldn't have gone. It probably had, and
then started up again. It was hard, in Managua, to know what
was going on because as soon as the fighting started anywhere
the telephones would go bad . . .

"When we started back to Managua, we soon ran up against
the truck and the young Sandinista with the bandana. This time
he wouldn't let us through. He sent us up to a house off the road,
the local FSLN command post. Six other journalists who had also
been trying to get out were there. The FSLN soldiers stood us in
two circles of six. Some of the journalists said that they must let
us go back to tell the world how the Guard were killing innocent
people. The Sandinista leader seemed to agree, but first had the
radio journalists turn on their tape recorders for a speech on the
need for freedom in Nicaragua. I thought it was over, but then
he said: 'Do any of you have contact with any of your embassies?'
Fenton kind of looked at me but no one said anything. 'You tell
your embassies that they are killing innocent people,' the Sandinista
said. Now I thought we could go.

"But we heard only more bad news. He asked to see our press
passes. I was the only one who didn't have one. The only thing I
had was a diplomatic passport and I certainly wasn't going to
show them that. But there were other women in the group and I
figured maybe they would skip us. No such luck. They started
with another woman.

"I was about fifth in the circle and Fenton was glancing at me.
I was thinking, 'Dear Lord, what am I going to do?' It was like
an agonizing movie. . . . After the first reporter they went on to

the second one and then to the third. They got to Fenton, who was standing next to me. And then it was me. What could I say? Well, why say anything? I turned and grabbed Fenton and kissed him passionately on the neck. And they skipped over me . . . I guess they thought I was the local squeeze.

"So they let us go. We drove by the kid with the gun and back to Managua. I went into the embassy with dirt on my face and said there was a war out there."

It had already become apparent to Haigh and others in the embassy that the rupture between Somoza and the great majority of his countrymen was complete. During the late summer Haigh had spent considerable time preparing a long cable on the reasons for the deep opposition to the dictator within the Nicaraguan business community. The root of the problem, she wrote, was the corruption of the regime, its use of political power for economic gain at the expense of businesses not connected to the Somoza family. Not a new insight, perhaps, but Haigh documented her point at some length. She also suggested that especially for a number of the younger members of the community, there was an idealistic dimension as well. They had received some of their education in the United States, and were frustrated and humiliated by the denial in their own country of the political values they had studied.

When she had finished drafting her report on the causes of opposition to Somoza, Haigh presented it to other sections of the embassy for comments and clearance, and then to her superiors for authorization to send it. (The cable, like all such messages, would not bear her name, but the name of the ambassador.) Then the message was typed on a distinctive green telegram form (since changed) and taken to the communications unit. As at all American embassies, the communications clerk worked behind a small window with security bars on it. If he was in one of the back rooms working with his coding and transmitting devices, he could be summoned by pressing a buzzer next to the window. In Managua, the clerks worked in a dingy room adorned chiefly by water and air-conditioning pipes running across the ceiling.

Haigh was extremely pleased when she learned that the assistant secretary for Latin American affairs in Washington had read her analysis of the situation. This was no small thing. Her cable was long — more than ten pages — and busy bureaucrats do not reach first for the items that take the longest to read. Moreover, her report was but one of a huge number of cables pouring into Washington every day. In 1978 the department received as many words from its embassies each day as it had received in the entire year of 1930.[9] The era when an ambassador in Managua had requested a warship in a cable of a few sentences belonged to antiquity. Now, personal ambition as well as professional pride lead Foreign Service officers abroad to churn out reports on everything of any possible relevance to policy concerns in Washington — and much that is of little relevance to anything. An officer who does little reporting may be judged lazy or incompetent, and an embassy that has not reported an event covered in the Washington newspapers is an embassy embarrassed. (Might the firing of the local minister of urban affairs appear in an AP report? Better to report it just in case.)

It was also a tribute to Haigh's cable that it was read in Washington even though it was not highly classified. Paradoxically, the more closely restricted a cable is in its distribution, the more likely it is that lots of people will actually read it. The reason is obvious: if a document has a low classification, it probably contains little that is important and can be put at the bottom of the reading pile. On the other hand, a cable labeled NODIS, especially if it also contains the magic words EYES ONLY, is hot and worth reading.

It is surprising that so many officials receive copies of NODIS and EYES ONLY messages. There was a time, back in the mid-1960s, when NODIS meant "no distribution except as personally authorized by the secretary of state." It was a time when such words had meaning, when the only eyes meant to gaze on an EYES ONLY cable were the secretary's. Cables marked EXDIS were to go to a carefully selected few, while LIMDIS messages were for a limited but somewhat wider audience in the lower but still responsible reaches of the department. Another set of designators was established to indicate how urgently a message should be handled. A cable marked PRIORITY was meant to move quickly over the wires and to be placed near the top of each recipient's daily take. An IMMEDIATE message would take still higher precedence with the code clerks and cable sorters. A FLASH was intended to be so rare that it would go like lightning through the system, signaling that troops or missiles somewhere were about to cross a border.

While putting NODIS or EXDIS on a cable gave the sender a means of influencing its distribution in Washington (or at the embassies if sent from the department), and using FLASH or IMMEDIATE could influence the speed with which it was sent, the classifications — TOP SECRET, SECRET, CONFIDENTIAL, and LIMITED OFFICIAL USE — would determine how carefully it was handled and how many years it would be before it was released to the public.

For a brief while, all this was taken rather seriously. But soon the system fell victim to a kind of grade creep. Who could resist the temptation to proclaim his or her best work worthy of the attention of the secretary by making it NODIS? If Ambassador Jones in the country next door or a fellow officer in the political section of your own embassy keeps getting his cables there faster by marking them PRIORITY, why not mark your own IMMEDIATE? It might even help you get "immediate" action from Washington. If you believe your work is important, as you should, don't the events surrounding you seem all the more dramatic? So that (and this is an actual case), if you heard a rumor of the death of Chiang Kai-shek (years before it took place), wouldn't you send the news in a FLASH message? And who would take seriously a secret you learned at a diplomatic reception if you merely call it CONFIDENTIAL? No, better to make it SECRET.

Soon after the system was in place, there was a rising stream of NODIS messages, many of them unworthy of attention by the secretary but of concern to his chief subordinates. Any message from the field with serious content was designated at least SECRET.

In reaction to the flood, Secretary Dean Rusk asked that messages that were really — yes, really — meant for him be slugged NODIS CHEROKEE, for the county of his birth in Georgia.

The most inventive use of a FLASH message was one by Richard M. Moose, the irrepressible and effective assistant secretary of state for African affairs in the Carter administration. During a 1980 trip to Ghana, at a luncheon given by the American ambassador, Moose fell into conversation with the local ministers of agriculture and finance. They were lamenting the Ghanaian taste for white bread made with imported wheat because Ghana produced quantities of corn. Sensing a chance to demonstrate simultaneously American efficiency and the culinary glories of his native Arkansas, Moose went to the ambassador's telephone and called the Ops Center in Washington. A watch officer called Moose's home and got his grandmother's recipe for corn bread, sending it — at Moose's instruction — by FLASH message to the embassy in Ghana. It was delivered to Moose before the conclusion of the lunch. The ministers were delighted, and the next day the government of Ghana issued a press release featuring the recipe and a ringing call for consumption of more corn bread. Management types in the State Department were neither delighted nor amused, however, and reprimanded Moose when he returned to Washington. Moose tried to appear abashed but was not completely successful.

Despite the debasement of the classification system, reporting from the embassies is on the whole quite good, even if they produce too much of a good thing. The standard of writing is high, certainly for government officials. There is even occasional humor from a post with a puckish ambassador. But there are problems with quality as well as quantity. Beyond the failure of many posts to distinguish between the important and the trivial, some fall into the trap of clientitis. It is natural to develop an affection for the society in which one lives, especially if, like most Foreign Service officers, one is drawn to life abroad. Our diplomats also tend to be diplomatic in describing foreign personalities and events. Their reporting can thus easily become protective rather than objective.

But charges of clientitis have been overstated and are sometimes damaging. Superpatriotic congressmen and commentators regularly charge that the State Department is better at recognizing the interests of other nations than it is at promoting our own, and Foreign Service officers are just as regularly outraged at such attacks on their patriotism. Understanding of foreign societies and the interests of foreign governments is central to the task of any diplomat. An objective report on how the world looks to a Fidel Castro or some other left-wing tyrant unpopular in Washington can easily be seized upon as evidence that the author of the report has gone beyond understanding to active sympathy. Such charges discourage the Foreign Service from performing its most important function: helping decision makers recognize the nature of foreign realities.

These critics of the Foreign Service fail to see the ironic fact that clientitis is an infection that becomes most virulent when Washington is limited in its thinking by an ideological fixation on the survival and success of some foreign client. In such a case an American ambassador is judged in large part by his ability to influence our client while maintaining friendly relations with him. A contretemps with, or even an unfavorable report about, such a leader suggests worse than undiplomatic behavior: it can be seen by Washington as a sign of disenchantment with the policy itself. The temptation is thus to leave some of the warts out of the picture of America's friend, and to report conversations with him in ways that make both the friend and the ambassador seem wise and sensible.

Under Mauricio Solaun, however, the embassy in Managua showed no sign of treating Somoza with the sympathy shown by Turner Shelton. Haigh's report on the disaffection of the business community in Nicaragua pointed to one of the reasons for the deep trouble in which the dictator now found himself, but opposition to Somoza went far beyond the angry commercial community. The fighting around the country was as much a product of spontaneous revolt as of Sandinista organization, suggesting that his regime was in trouble with almost every level of Nicaraguan society.

The dramatic events of August and September 1978 had overtaken the policy of disassociation. Policy could no longer be made only in the context of human rights concerns, for Nicaragua itself had become an issue. In Washington, Viron ("Pete") Vaky, now well ensconced as assistant secretary of state for Latin American affairs, knew that Somoza had irrevocably lost any mandate to govern. The *fuerzas vivas* — the "live forces" — in Nicaraguan politics were nearly united against him. Vaky was determined that American policy turn in the direction of Somoza's early removal, before repression and revolution so fed on each other as to drive out all moderate possibilities in Nicaraguan political life.

SEVEN

The Sixth Floor and the EOB

WHEN PETE VAKY SPEAKS OF THE MEN HE HAS ADMIRED in the Foreign Service, one learns a great deal about Vaky himself. "My first boss was Francis Styles," he says. "A professional. He took a great interest in young Foreign Service officers, in training me to be a part of a *profession,* even in the smallest things. The first time I wrote a memo to him, I referred to a 'dispatch' to Washington. He came into my office and said, 'In the *Foreign Service,* we spell it *despatch.*' And he was a man of great dignity, always aware that he was representing the United States. He was always calm. More than calm, he was careful and steady. Things never became a great crisis with him.

"Willard Beaulac, who held about ten ambassadorships in Latin America, was also a professional of the old school, I think the first graduate of Georgetown's School of Foreign Service. He knew human nature in its original sense yet had an old-fashioned sense of morality. I remember that near the end of his career, in the mid-nineteen fifties, he told me how much he objected to our close relationship at the time with Rafael Trujillo [the Dominican dictator] because Trujillo was 'an *evil* man. I don't see how we can look him in the face.' And Beaulac *ran* his mission, even reading all the official mail sent to and from his subordinates. He was confidently in charge. He took responsibility.

"And there was Tony Freeman, my ambassador in Bogotá, Colombia, when I was chief of the political section in the late nineteen fifties. He, too, ran his mission with a strong and sure hand, and he was a master at operating in a foreign society. He knew how to stay in touch with everyone, and he wanted to know everything. He persuaded the foreign minister to have an informal lunch with him every week, just to stay in touch. And he was an excellent negotiator, because he knew that to get the other person to compromise with you, to take as much of your position as you can get him to, you first have to understand *his* interests, to get into his skin. That way, you understand both how each side sees its interests and what each thinks the power relationships are, too."

A lively, friendly man with wiry gray hair, at fifty-three years of age Vaky was already one of the most senior American diplomats, respected by the Foreign Service for the very qualities he respected in others: a calm and intelligent competence, an ability to understand other societies with sympathy rather than with sentimentality, an "old-fashioned sense of morality," and a willingness to take responsibility — a virtue much admired, if too seldom imitated, by less successful Foreign Service officers. An energetic and tough bureaucratic operator, the new assistant secretary of state in the Latin American bureau had an obvious taste for Washington warfare, but by all accounts he succeeded in limiting these struggles to affairs of policy rather than to personal prerogatives. Vaky knew what many forget: that allowing policy disputes to become personal vendettas is damaging to oneself as well as to the misguided colleague one opposes. In short, he thought of himself, and was seen by others, as a professional. Ever since high school in Texas, when an English teacher had led him to the memoirs of an American diplomat in Latin America, Vaky had loved the Foreign Service and its ways.

Vaky was now returning to a job he knew well. He had served as acting assistant secretary for Latin America in the late 1960s. From his paneled sixth-floor office, he was to make sure that the bureau successfully managed day-to-day relationships with more than forty-seven American posts (sixteen consulates and thirty-one embassies), while simultaneously serving the Seventh Floor; managing an Interdepartmental Group (a coordinating body of assistant secretary–level officials from other agencies); representing the State Department at numerous other interagency meetings; and testifying before congressional committees on issues that did not require a higher-ranking representative. In addition he would resolve any disputes with other bureaus and agencies that did not have to be sent to higher levels; coordinate the most important daily business with the White House staff; keep in touch with members of Congress who had particular influence on Latin American issues; and serve as the official to whom Latin American ambassadors in Washington usually turned when they had business to do with the U.S. government.

There was plenty on his daily agenda as Vaky took charge in August 1978. But Nicaragua was the issue that came to dominate his schedule, his thoughts, and his emotions. By September he was spending more than two thirds of his time on the problem. Delegating most of the work on other problems to his deputies, he began drafting the important cables and memoranda on Nicaragua himself: he knew exactly what he wanted them to say, and besides, the office director for Central America, Wade Matthews, disagreed with him on the best policy to pursue. Matthews tried to serve his superior as Vaky wanted him to, reserving his disagreements for separate memoranda, but the two men were simply on different wavelengths, and the daily work suffered. By the end of the year Vaky moved Matthews out of the bureau. Matthews held no grudge, and later noted that had he been in Vaky's shoes, as a professional matter he would have done the same thing.

Vaky came to Washington from service as the American ambassador in Venezuela, and he was obviously influenced by the thinking of Somoza's enemy, President Carlos Andrés Pérez. Indeed, after returning to Washington, Vaky still received phone calls from Pérez, who was as consistent about the Nicaraguan ruler as Cato the Elder had been about Carthage: *Somoza delendus est*. Like Pérez, Vaky was convinced that if the United States did not force Somoza's early resignation in favor of the moderate opposition, the Sandinistas would become stronger and eventually replace him. Time and again during the next few months, Vaky was to remind other American officials of a precedent: the fall of Batista in Cuba.

Others in the State Department and on the NSC staff were also worried about the course of events in Nicaragua. In early August, Robert Pastor at the NSC recommended to Zbigniew Brzezinski that there be a formal interagency review of policy toward Nicaragua, but Brzezinski did not agree to order one. At State, the policy planning staff was making the same proposal to officials in the Latin American bureau, but Vaky was resistant. "I had just gotten there," he recalls, "and I didn't think that was the way to make policy. You have to bring in everyone with any interest at all in the issue — the Pentagon, the economics agencies and bureaus — and the discussions are unwieldy. I remember that soon after I arrived, Secretary Vance asked that we put together a general strategy session on Mexico. Everybody was there at the first meeting — maybe ninety people — to be sure their bureaucratic interests weren't affected. Policy is made on the fly; it emerges from the pattern of specific decisions. Its wisdom is decided by whether you have some vision of what you want, a conceptual thread as you go along."

Of course, it was also to Vaky's bureaucratic advantage to keep policy making out of formal interagency channels. As assistant secretary he was at the controls when it came to the daily decisions that can be the stuff of policy. It was in his Latin American bureau that the cables to the embassy in Managua were written, the letters to members of Congress drafted, the daily guidance for the department's press spokesman shaped. Important items had to be cleared, but his bureau dominated the daily process. On the other hand, a formal interagency review, especially one leading to a broad policy decision by the president, would give the NSC staff a comparative advantage, since it had the last word in submitting recommendations to the president. Within the State Department, the policy planning staff was charged with co-authorship of all formal interagency policy papers, but on operational matters it did not even need to be consulted.

This did not mean that Vaky could or wanted to avoid all interagency discussion of Nicaragua. On August 29, 1978, in the wake of Edén Pastora's sensational raid on the National Palace, Vaky convened an informal discussion of the course of events in Nicaragua and what might be done about it. The participants, including Robert Pastor and State Department officials from the Latin American bureau, the planning staff (including me), and the human rights bureau, sat around a long table that almost filled the sparsely decorated, narrow room. They listened first to Vaky as he outlined his view of the problem: if Somoza did not go soon, the Sandinistas would be the ones to replace him. Richard Feinberg of policy planning, who had just been to Nicaragua and had met with Somoza, described his trip and agreed that the dictator had lost his legitimacy.

Vaky then proposed his solution to the problem: the United States should seek the early removal of Somoza. This could be accomplished by our passing the word in Managua, and especially among the leaders of Somoza's own National Guard, that the old man would no longer enjoy any kind of American support. This would result, Vaky said, in a split within the ruling Liberal Nationalist party and action against Somoza by the National Guard.

Pastor and I agreed with Vaky's point that Somoza was the problem. The spreading violence in Nicaragua had made it clear that an American policy of distancing ourselves from him would no longer do. Somoza's attacks on his moderate opponents in the wake of Pastora's raid and his evident unpopularity required a more active American approach. The situation would obviously be improved by Somoza's departure, but Pastor and I argued that the United States should not assume the responsibility for removing him. Our main argument was one of both principle and policy: the Carter administration had committed itself to respecting the sovereign right of other societies to govern themselves, and in the past, when the United States had acted to overthrow another government, for reasons noble or base, the result had rarely served our or the other nation's interests. Pastor had in mind here the sad history of American interventions in Central America and, most recently, the consequences of American complicity in the overthrow of the Allende government in Chile. The United States had aroused the anger of Latin Americans when it intervened in their affairs, and many successor governments were as bad as or worse than those overthrown. Pastor knew that there were two principles to which President Carter was strongly attached in his Latin American policies: nonintervention and multilateralism. A unilateral American action to depose Somoza would violate both principles. Pastor knew too that the president had repeatedly said that he would not order an intervention in another country unless direct American security interests were threatened, and no one had convinced him that this was the case in Nicaragua.

In my own mind was the experience of the American-approved coups in Saigon in late 1963 and early 1964, which had ushered in a period of severe instability while convincing many Vietnamese (inaccurately) that the American embassy was calling all the shots in Vietnamese politics. The United States was blamed for the ensuing political chaos, and confirmed the view of many highly nationalistic Vietnamese that successor governments were creatures of the Americans — a fatal disability in a war for "hearts and minds."

For Vaky, arguments about *principles* were useful because they clarified goals and values, and in general he shared the values of the Carter administration. But, as he was later to say, "The important thing to look at was *consequences.* Do you use your power to shape the outcome even if it violates the spirit of nonintervention? Or do you hold to the principle at the cost of putting self-imposed limits on your power to resolve a worsening situation? It was a question of what is good versus what is right."

The Carter administration, Vaky believed, was making two mistakes regarding Nicaragua. It was failing to exercise its available power because of an excessive attachment to general principle, and it was concentrating too much on the protection of individual rights. Vaky believed in promoting human rights but, he later remarked, "the issue was not only civil rights; most fundamentally, it was the political future of Nicaragua."

However, his opponents at this August 29 meeting, and those who were to disagree with him at many meetings during the coming weeks, did not believe they were asserting principle at the expense of pragmatism. For them, the principle they were defending was rooted in practicality: in the lessons of the past about the dangers of interventionism and in questions about the future. They wanted to know whether Somoza could be removed as easily as Vaky suggested, since the dictator was at the time particularly vehement about retaining his hold on power until the 1981 elections. If we told Somoza to depart and he did not, would we not look impotent as well as interventionist? Might we then be forced into actively plotting a coup against him? Besides, who would replace him? Would it necessarily turn out to be the moderates, or could it be a still more repressive regime led by the National Guard? Conversely, was there not the risk of a rapid collapse, including that of the National Guard, that would create a vacuum for the Sandinistas before a substitute military structure could be formed?

Vaky suggested that Somoza would depart or be removed by the Guard once the United States slipped him the black spot, simply because of the overwhelming influence we had traditionally wielded in the area. The American word had far greater impact, he said, in Central America than it had in Asia or Africa, the areas I knew best. His point reflected his frustration at the meeting. He *did* know more about Nicaragua and its history than most of the others there, and he was sure of his analysis of the future if Somoza were not removed. But he neither produced a scenario of events showing how Somoza could be safely removed nor showed how democratic moderates rather than a new dictator of the left or right could come to power in Nicaragua.

This was the sticking point for Warren Christopher as the argument escalated to his level in subsequent meetings. "The Latin American bureau wanted us to oust Somoza," he recalls, "but they never really showed us *how,* or what would follow." In retrospect, Vaky agrees: "If I could do it over again, I would work out the scenario. I never did that, and wish I had." But he remains convinced that a firm word in Managua would have sufficed, and that the moderates would have come to power if the United States had acted to remove Somoza in 1978, before the Sandinistas became stronger and the moderates more divided.

While it did not come up at the August 29 meeting, or in all but the most guarded terms at later interagency discussions, most of the political appointees involved in discussions on Nicaragua had in mind another factor: the impact in Washington of action by the Carter administration to remove Somoza. The president was already coming under assault for being soft on foreign leftists and hard on foreign conservatives for their human rights abuses. If he were to remove Somoza, his domestic political opponents would have a field day in political attacks on Carter himself and in undercutting him in Congress on such issues as agreements concerning the future of the Panama Canal and ratification of a SALT II treaty (then under negotiation). "See," they could say, "the man is even prepared to overthrow a friend fighting Marxists in Nicaragua. How can we rely on him to drive a hard bargain with Moscow on arms control? A president like that is not securing future rights to the Panama Canal — he's giving it away."

Nicaragua was now becoming an issue in its own right, rather than one of a set of human rights problems to be settled in the Inter-Agency Human Rights Committee. The Nicaraguan whale was rising again into the sight of senior policy makers. But it was by no means the largest on the surface of a very rough sea. Would it be worth taking a gamble on Nicaragua at the possible cost of success on what were perceived to be larger issues? During the autumn of 1978 the White House, Secretary Vance, and most of the Seventh Floor were focused elsewhere. The negotiations for a SALT II treaty were reaching a critical stage. Talks on the establishment of formal diplomatic relations with the People's Republic of China were about to bear fruit. The president pulled off his extraordinary feat at Camp David with Anwar Sadat and Menachem Begin. And there were other delicate diplomatic ventures under way, including the search for settlements of conflicts in Southern Rhodesia and Namibia, negotiations for an extension of our base rights in the Philippines, and human rights *démarches* with a number of governments. Newspaper headlines trumpeting the American removal of Anastasio Somoza Debayle would only be an impediment in persuading Congress to go along with the administration's approach elsewhere. Robert Pastor was sure that there would be such headlines if we told Somoza to step down. He suspected (rightly) that Somoza was taping his conversations with American diplomats, and Somoza would undoubtedly leak any conversation that might offer ammunition to his friends in Congress and embarrass the administration.

Soon a crisis would arise that would make the administration all the more hesitant about attacking Somoza lest it lend ammunition to its conservative critics: the revolution in Iran. If the coming weeks were to be, for Vaky, an autumn and winter of discontent, for most of Washington the coming season was to be the fall of the shah.

Thus, in the August 29 meeting the lines were drawn over the central point of an argument that was to continue through the events of the next five months. On the one hand, Vaky, a career officer, was trying to get the American government to take the bold action that his experience and judgment told him was necessary to avoid disaster in Nicaragua. On the other side was a political appointee, Pastor, whose perspective from the White House told him that taking the action Vaky proposed might not succeed in Nicaragua and could lead to disaster on other fronts. Add to this the fact that the State Department and the NSC staff were traditional rivals, and it might seem that this was a classic recipe for intense bureaucratic conflict.

Both Vaky and Pastor understood very well the natural tension between State and the NSC staff. Since its creation in 1947 to serve the newly created National Security Council, a Cabinet-level coordinating body, the NSC staff had been steadily expanding its influence at the expense of the State Department and, to a lesser extent, of Defense and other foreign policy agencies.[1] The NSC had originally been designed strictly as a planning and broad policy setting body. But as presidents discovered the need for a staff that could protect presidential interests and promote the perspective of the White House in a rapidly expanding foreign affairs bureaucracy, the role of the NSC staff shifted to a far more aggressive involvement in the daily business of the government. This transformation took place largely under President John F. Kennedy and his national security assistant, McGeorge Bundy. With this shift in its role came a great increase in the size of the NSC staff — from fewer than a dozen substantive staffers under Kennedy to twenty-eight in 1969, the first year of Henry Kissinger's reign as national security assistant, and to fifty-two by early 1971. The staff was reduced under Brent Scowcroft in the mid-1970s and cut still further under Zbigniew Brzezinski; but with almost forty active professionals in 1978, it still went far beyond the scope of the staff under Eisenhower or even Kennedy. The staff was to grow rapidly again in the Reagan administration, with grand titles strewn among its members. Under Admiral John Poindexter there were four deputy assistants to the president for national security affairs (Brzezinski had had one); a special counsel; ten special assistants to the president; forty directors, and nine deputy directors.

Perhaps even more important than the growth in numbers at the NSC staff were two other developments, one in the types of people on the staff, the other technological. The creator of the NSC, Harry S. Truman, made the staff part of the president's executive office, but he wanted it to be part of the permanent government, "to serve as a continuing organization regardless of what Administration was in power."[2] In this conception it would be manned on the British model, by apolitical civil servants. But thirty years later, the opposite was true. Now each administration tended to load the staff with its own loyalists. People who had worked on the presidential campaign would most zealously protect the president's interests and promote his policies, and it was they who deserved the jobs in the White House. Such men and women were likely to be more aggressive operators than career officials. A second development — changes in communications technology — helped them stay on top of the bureaucracy. Built in the 1960s and constantly improved since, new communications networks flowing into and from the White House Situation Room allowed the NSC staff to monitor the cable traffic of the foreign affairs agencies with much greater efficiency and, through "back channels" — usually provided by the CIA — to communicate with American embassies and foreign governments without the knowledge, much less the approval, of the State Department.

Foreign governments were by no means unaware of the growth in power and size of the NSC staff, and it was natural that they should increasingly turn to the staff when they wanted something from the American government, especially if secrecy was important. (The State Department's terrible reputation for leaks has been only marginally worse than its actual performance.) Henry Kissinger, with the blessing of President Nixon, was himself drawn to secret negotiations with foreign governments. He was an effective negotiator, the talks remained secret because State was not informed, and Kissinger's power grew at the expense of the department. Thus, by 1977 the NSC staff was not only much more powerful within the government than had been envisioned; it was also deeply engaged in dealings with foreign governments. President Carter, who had criticized Kissinger's "Lone Ranger" diplomacy during the 1976 campaign, had pledged to bring about an orderly foreign policy process in which the national security assistant would coordinate policy but stay out of diplomatic operations. The intention was genuine, but by the following year, Brzezinski was pressing already for an operational role.

For decades, then, there had been competitive tension between NSC staff members and the assistant secretaries with whom they primarily dealt. Even Vaky, for all his devotion to the State Department, had quickly realized during a tour of duty on the NSC staff that a president needs an assertive staff. However much State thought that as the primary foreign affairs agency it deserved the deference of the NSC staff, this simply was not possible, any more than the Defense Department could be left to shape military policy and budgets by itself. "I had always thought the State Department was the most objective agency in Washington," Vaky says. "But when I got to the NSC staff I saw that State, too, had its own point of view and its own style. I could look at a piece of paper and tell immediately what department it was from. If it was indirect and long, with an 'on the one hand, on the other' approach, it was from State. If it was a frontal assault, filled with facts and statistics but not particularly clean or clear in its argument, it was from Defense. The CIA produced the best analysis. An NSC staff member has to keep after all of them to get a full and fair analysis of the options for the president."

But an assertive NSC staff means trouble with the State Department. As Robert Pastor notes, "Any good assistant secretary of state wants to make policy. To work with an NSC staff member runs the risk that someone else might make it." Indeed, the more competent and the more interested in policy both are, the greater the likelihood of conflict. This is especially the case when the national security assistant and the secretary of state are themselves locked in struggle, and by the fall of 1978 the competition over policy between Brzezinski at the NSC and Cyrus Vance at State was becoming more intense. The president was unable to reconcile their differences over how best to deal with the Soviet Union, and Brzezinski was also starting to take an operational diplomatic role in negotiating normalization of relations with the People's Republic of China.

Vance, who was playing the lead role on the Middle East, SALT II, and southern Africa, had at first refused to react to Brzezinski's diplomatic maneuvering and his increasing contacts with the press, even though they tended to undercut Vance's own standing. But in mid-1978, despite his considerable distaste for battles over turf, Vance had gone to the president to insist on a clarification of their roles. The president had reaffirmed Vance's position as principal foreign affairs spokesman, yet in practice little had changed.

By the fall of 1978, therefore, there was every reason for Pastor and Vaky to collide over Nicaragua: the history of NSC-State competition; the differences of the two men in viewpoint, background, and style; the depth of the concern that both felt about the issue; the drive of each to make policy; the friction between their superiors. How could it not add up to war? The two fought for their positions through whatever bureaucratic strategies they could devise, Pastor trying to move policy decisions into the formal interagency process and rounding up allies at State to attend key meetings; Vaky keeping himself at the center of action and guarding as much of the department's information as he could. If Vaky thought that a decision he found unwise might possibly be reversed, he might delay its implementation for a day or two. In addition, his good relationship with Warren Christopher, who admired Vaky's competence, usually prevented Pastor from wielding the same influence on the Seventh Floor that he had used in the February 15 meeting on the letter from President Pérez.

Yet Vaky and Pastor worked very well together. They argued and competed, but fairly and without personal malice. Neither attacked the other in background leaks to the press. They were open in their differences, and neither tried to freeze the other out of the action, although they did not necessarily share all of their information with each other. They got together before key meetings to shape any possible areas of agreement while trying to define their differences with precision and spoke on the telephone five or six times a day about operational matters. There *was* a bit of a problem about the telephone calls. Vaky was a morning person: he liked to do the toughest business of the day early, when he felt most effective. Pastor, a slow starter, tried to save his most important conversations for the afternoons and evenings.

Each understood that he needed the other. During Vaky's time on the NSC staff under Henry Kissinger, in 1969 and 1970, Kissinger and William P. Rogers had fought the first — and probably the worst — of the battles between national security assistants and secretaries of state. As a Foreign Service officer assigned to the White House, Vaky had been caught in the middle. Kissinger was keeping Rogers in the dark on a number of important matters, and the State Department knew that its leader was in a weak position. Rogers did not want his authority weakened further by direct dealings between the NSC staff and individual bureaus in State that would circumvent the Seventh Floor. Happily, Vaky and the senior deputy assistant secretary for Latin American affairs at the time, John Crimmins (like Vaky a career Foreign Service officer), understood that especially at a time when their bosses were at loggerheads, the key link in getting foreign policy business done is that between the sixth floor at State and the Executive Office Building, home of the NSC staff. It was better for Crimmins to hear from Vaky about the likely White House reactions to Latin American bureau proposals early on, in informal meetings at State, than to be surprised later when affairs had escalated to higher levels. So Vaky and Crimmins went on working together without heeding the higher-echelon spite between State and the White House.

(Vaky did pay a price, however. At the end of his two-year tour at the NSC his name routinely went to the Foreign Service personnel office for onward assignment, and he was given a very attractive one. The personnel office was then overruled by Secretary of State Rogers, apparently in revenge for Vaky's having served at the White House. It took a year's cooling-off period, while Vaky enjoyed himself as a diplomat in residence at Georgetown University, before the personnel office could get Vaky a senior assignment as ambassador to Costa Rica.)

Vaky welcomed the fact that Pastor could bring to meetings at State a broader White House perspective, as Vaky himself had once done. In any case, an effort to freeze Pastor out of State's business could lead to a retaliation that would serve neither of them well. Principle, personality, and self-interest combined to make Vaky want the system to work. Just as the assistant secretary understood through experience the value of cooperation with the NSC staff, Pastor was no less interested in working closely with Vaky even as they competed to influence policy. In part, Pastor's reasons were personal. After a year and a half of struggle with the Latin American bureau, Pastor was delighted to work with an assistant secretary who understood and accepted the role of the NSC staff. In early August, soon after Vaky's arrival, Pastor wrote in his journal, "Procedurally and substantively my relations with State have changed 98%, all attributable to Vaky. He is very impressive and open, insists all important policy matters get cleared by me. This is the first time that ideas and initiatives are not just coming from me but from [the Latin American bureau]."

Pastor also welcomed having an older, more experienced colleague to consult, without fear that what he said might be used against him to an unfriendly associate or reporter. Articulate and open in his opinions, Pastor exuded a level of confidence unusual even for an NSC staff member. If there is a single characteristic shared by successful foreign policy professionals, it is this ability to convey confidence in their opinions. (Of course, the confidence may be unwarranted: estimates of the consequences of most foreign policy decisions are guesses based on incomplete information. As Dean Rusk once said, "At press conferences, 80 percent of the time the right answer to a question could be 'Damned if I know.' ")[3]

But a foreign policy expert will seldom admit to uncertainty or ignorance. In public it would expose him to ridicule, and in meetings with his superiors it would diminish his standing. Because the stakes are so high and the future so unpredictable, presidents, senators and even the public want reassurance that the experts to whom they are listening are more than merely good at guessing about the future on the basis of some — but never enough — facts. Most patients do not want their doctors to confess to worry or doubt. And, rather like doctors, foreign policy experts often come to feel the necessary confidence; it offers a kind of psychological self-protection. Constant agonizing over decisions that involve life and death would lead to personal and professional disaster. The problem, obviously, is that this necessary decisiveness can produce an arrogance and absence of feeling that may be just as dangerous as filling each day with a hundred indecisions.

Pastor had the necessary confidence, but he was also young — he had just turned thirty — and he recalls "moments when I was uncertain that I had enough experience or wisdom to offer the kind of advice to Brzezinski and the president that I was being asked to offer. And at the NSC, I was the only one working on Latin America. During the first eighteen months, I sometimes felt very alone, especially when dealing with the State Department. There were times, when I was on the offensive, moving from bureau to bureau, that I felt very confident. But there were also times, when I was exhausted or under attack, when I felt that the whole government was closing in on me. And there was seldom enough time to be sure that the recommendations I was making were the right ones. So I would try, if I could, to call people whose judgments I respected — like Richard Feinberg at policy planning — and bounce ideas off them."

With the arrival of Vaky in Washington, Pastor had a colleague at the Latin American bureau with whom he could think things through "and feel a little more secure that the recommendations would be more solid." If there were still many moments of doubt, it was nevertheless "exhilarating to be at the center of things." This was just what he wanted to do. Pastor was an "inner/outer," one of those people whose careers include jobs both outside and — when the political times are right — inside the government. A generation earlier, noncareer officials appointed to foreign affairs positions tended to be lawyers, bankers, and sometimes professors, whose careers were centered on their law firms, banks, or universities. By the 1970s a new class of foreign policy professionals had emerged that saw government service not as an occasional tour of duty but as a prize always before their eyes. Some were primarily idealists; others had a lean and hungry look. Most were impelled by a mixture of belief in their policy views and personal ambition. They wanted to be in government, but only to work for a president with whom they agreed. For some, private careers were shaped to enhance the chances of future public service — occasionally in ways that twisted their true interests and beliefs. As one cynic put it, "Power corrupts. And the absence of power corrupts absolutely."

When not in government, foreign policy professionals often find bases — in think tanks, at universities, or in businesses and law firms that offer a degree of personal freedom — where they can write policy articles and books about the issues that most interest them, attend foreign policy conferences, and every four years offer assistance to presidential candidates who might help them return to a government position. Because they spend so much of their time on foreign policy issues, they bring more knowledge of foreign affairs to their government work than the earlier generation of political appointees were likely to have. But this expertise causes friction in their relationships with career officials, for the new foreign policy professionals are less likely to consult the Foreign Service. Are they not, also, foreign policy experts? And because they are more overtly partisan and politically active than the inners and outers of the 1950s, they are more likely to be assertive in trying to impose on the bureaucracy the new directions of a newly elected president.

The route Pastor had followed to the NSC staff was typical, in most respects, of these policy professionals. While at Lafayette College he had become fascinated by Latin America and traveled through the region on his own, doing research for a thesis on Guatemala. He had started by getting a job on a banana boat making the run between Bluefields, Nicaragua, and Tampa, Florida, unloading bananas and then cleaning the empty hold on the way back to Nicaragua. Pastor recalls this as the worst job he ever had because of the snakes that had come on board with the bananas and resisted leaving the darkness of the hold. After graduation he worked on Latin American issues for the Congressional Research Service of the Library of Congress, and then served in the Peace Corps in Malaysia. Next it was on to Harvard to get his Ph.D. in government, and then to the staff of the Murphy Commission, a group of scholars and practitioners studying government organization for the conduct of foreign affairs. While there, he was asked to write a few papers for the Linowitz Commission on American policy toward Latin America. A clear and prolific writer, Pastor was happy to do so. This led to his being named staff director of the commission. Columbia University professor Richard Gardner had been hired as a commission consultant, and in 1975, when Gardner and Brzezinski were recruiting volunteers to help Jimmy Carter on foreign policy issues in his presidential campaign, they included Pastor. Brzezinski liked Pastor's work and took him along to the NSC staff.

Pastor had been assigned an office on the third floor of the Executive Office Building, next door to the offices later made famous by Colonel Oliver North. Separated from the White House only by a narrow roadway, the EOB provides office space for a large number of the president's staff. Because the most senior of the president's advisers have their offices in the West Wing of the White House, near the Oval Office, being in the EOB confers a somewhat junior status. But this is offset by the charm of the building itself, a splendid baroque wedding cake in the midst of the boring boxes that house most Washington bureaucrats. Extended porches, dormers, and small columns — nine hundred of these last — appear all over the facade. Inside, marble halls, granite stairways, and bronze balusters recall the time when architects (in this case A. D. Mullet) and builders could let themselves go. Not everyone loved the building when it was completed in 1888 (Henry Adams called it "Mr. Mullet's architectural infant asylum"),[4] but most people today find it wonderful.

Pastor's office, like most in the EOB, was far more elegant than anything to be found in the ordinary reachhs of New State. It had a high ceiling, ornate nineteenth-century woodwork, and two large windows overlooking an interior courtyard. The EOB was once the State Department's building, and one imagines there a nineteenth-century pace: messengers bringing dispatches on trays and waiting respectfully while policy makers pen judicious replies, desk officers dozing in hushed offices in the years before the fall of every sparrow around the world seemed to affect some American interest. Now, it is not the dignified building that seems an anachronism but the jangling telephones, high-speed typewriters, and shredding devices.

For Pastor, there was little quiet. His job used all his energy and filled his life. He found that his Latin American duties on the NSC staff fell into three general categories: seeing to the daily needs of the president, the national security assistant, and other senior White House personnel; coordinating the most important work of the various foreign affairs agencies; and planning policies and new initiatives.

The first task — serving the president and Brzezinski — was much the most time-consuming and often the most frustrating. A colleague at the time, Madeleine Albright, points out that the NSC staff is essentially parasitic: it has to rely on the agencies to provide information and drafts of documents. No NSC staff member covering a region like Latin America could possibly find the time to write most of the speeches and toasts needed for diplomatic occasions, the responses to letters to the president from members of Congress and others, the likely questions and suggested answers for press conferences, the briefing books, including "talkers," for meetings with foreign leaders and others. So the White House asks the relevant agency — usually State — to provide the speech, letter, or briefing book required. And because the clearance process at State allows each office to add its own points while taking the interesting edge off any passage it finds objectionable, the State draft is usually barely on time, long, unobjectionable, and uninteresting. So an NSC staff member eventually redrafts the document — before the White House speechwriters and then the president redraft it once again.

A presidential trip abroad, such as Carter's to Venezuela in March 1978, requires a full briefing book for each stop. Inside a large blue loose-leaf binder are an overview paper describing the purposes of the trip and the scheduled meetings and speeches. At numerous tabs there are papers describing the country and the leaders with whom the president will meet, the issues he wishes to raise and those that might be raised with him, and talkers with suggested points he might make during the discussion of each issue, as well as the texts of suggested arrival and departure statements and toasts for the inevitable formal luncheons and dinners.*

---

* Every September the secretary of state must go to New York for a week or so to endure a grueling series of meetings with other foreign ministers gathered for the opening of the UN General Assembly session. There may be ten or more of these meetings a day, at intervals of as little as a half hour, and the talkers must be very brief. There is a story, perhaps by now embellished, that a secretary of state not noted for his work habits asked for a set of index cards, with the points he should make on one side and, on the other, the issues he could expect the other foreign minister to raise. At a meeting with the representative of a small Asian nation that wanted the United States to build it a costly and superfluous airfield, our secretary glanced down at the wrong side of his index card and to the horror of his aides committed the American government to constructing an airfield that the astonished foreign minister had not yet mentioned.

Although these briefing books and the State Department memoranda for the president on his meetings in Washington with foreign leaders could almost always use some pruning, Brzezinski's NSC staff made it a practice not to rewrite memos from the agencies to the White House. *Drafts* of letters and speeches, yes; but the agencies would object if their direct communications with the president were altered. Instead, the NSC staff would write its own, much briefer summary and strategy memorandum and place it on top of the agency's work. The president could then wade through the full material or use the shorter version. Carter, a voracious reader with an extraordinarily retentive mind, usually read the whole thing — and then made his points the way he wanted to, following neither the State nor the NSC script.

At almost every meeting of a president with a foreign visitor, an NSC staff member has had another duty, unless it could be fobbed off on an officer from State. By ancient custom, at most diplomatic meetings (save the most formal of negotiating sessions) a junior officer on each side takes notes of what is said, later summarizing it or as closely as possible providing a transcript. This report is called a Memorandum of Conversation, unaffectionately known as a MemCon. Few junior officials know how to take shorthand, and it is a struggle to achieve an accurate MemCon — especially when the junior official is also discreetly trying to pass helpful notes to his superior or when the senior official tells the notetaker to stop writing while he makes a confidential point (though he will nonetheless want the point remembered and recorded later). It helps when there is an interpreter whose notes can be consulted before the MemCon is drafted, but a MemCon is at best a boring chore.

Why do modern diplomats not take advantage of such twentieth-century devices as tape recorders (which in any case may be in surreptitious use at some meetings abroad) or even have stenographers present? Perhaps it is out of vestigial politeness: the notetakers are customarily discreet, shielding their little pads behind uncomfortably crossed knees, preserving the fiction that the words of Gentlemen need not be recorded. Maybe it is because machines or stenographers would have an inhibiting effect and spoil the attempt to create a personal tone in these professional meetings. It may also be that this laborious practice allows each side to record the meeting in a favorable light. This may not advance precise international understanding, but it allows both sides a useful diplomatic ambiguity. And within governments, it is not unusual at all for a junior officer to discover, upon receiving a corrected MemCon from the senior participant, that his superior's remarks have become a tad more precise and eloquent when recorded for posterity.

At least note-taking and preparing for presidential visits and press conferences and the like involved interesting substantive matters. The worst of the daily chores for Pastor and other NSC staffers was dealing with the flood of White House correspondence. Most responses to letters from members of Congress or the public were routine, requiring only a check of the State Department draft reply. But some required thought. All took up time a staffer would rather spend on other duties. Consider the Case of the Purple Letter. On July 13, 1978, Nicaraguan ambassador Guillermo Sevilla-Sacasa, Somoza's effusive brother-in-law, wrote Brzezinski "to congratulate you again on your intelligent and characterized actuations for the good of your great nation . . . on your judgments that the United States of America and Europe, not excluding other nations of the free world, need to 'jointly confront the Cuban-Soviet penetration in Africa.' . . . It was expected of your recognized talent. . . . Hoping to see you again soon, and with the renewed assurance of my high esteem and cordial friendship, I remain, Sincerely yours . . ."

The NSC secretariat, in charge of routing paper and enforcing deadlines, assigned Pastor the job of drafting a reply to this missive. As he was getting at it, a routine draft letter to Sevilla-Sacasa from the president arrived from the State Department. It congratulated the Nicaraguan on his thirty-fifth year as ambassador and twentieth year as dean (i.e., senior member) of the Washington diplomatic corps. On August 1, Pastor sent a memorandum to Brzezinski recommending against a presidential letter "because no one takes Sevilla-Sacasa seriously, and because he papers his walls with letters from his 'good friends' in the White House, over five administrations." Vaky, Pastor wrote, concurred.

Brzezinski's staff assistant disagreed, noting that Sevilla-Sacasa was, after all, an accredited ambassador, whatever people thought of him. Brzezinski, however, sided with Pastor, and on August 2 wrote the ambassador himself, conveying the president's congratulations and thanking him for "your kind comments about my work in your letter to me of July 13." Brzezinski's letter was, of course, drafted by Pastor. So while "no one took Sevilla-Sacasa seriously," a minor piece of business concerning him had required that Pastor draft a memo and a letter, review a draft by State, and make a call to Vaky. And every day there were many such items.

Work on the next of Pastor's list of duties — interagency coordination — was less time-consuming and more important. It involved trying to identify emerging policy problems and moving them into the formal interagency process; working on existing crises through further meetings; helping shape the interagency papers that preceded formal policy meetings and following up with the agencies involved to try to make sure the president's decisions were implemented; and trying to keep track of the agencies' daily work, clearing any items with important policy implications. In all of this, Pastor tried to be both advocate and adjudicator, arguing for his own views but trying also to see that the president received a fair picture of the positions of all the agencies involved on any particular issue. There were never any complaints about Pastor's ability to be both, although there have often been times in the Carter and other administrations when officials in the departments were mistrustful of national security assistants and certain of their staff members.

Beyond this agenda, there were usually several visitors to his office every day (including perhaps a friend who had recently visited Latin America, a reporter, a congressman, a representative of a public interest lobbying group, or, most often, an official from another department). A bachelor for his first few years on the staff, Pastor typically worked from 7:30 A.M. to 10 P.M. or later, six days a week. He never ate at his apartment. Cables and memos constantly accumulated and had to be read; and if he sensed that State hadn't shared an important cable, it had to be tracked down, sometimes through two or three telephone calls. (Like other officials, he almost never had time to read a newspaper, except for articles directly relevant to his work, much less a book or a scholarly journal.)

Most wearing of all was the telephone. Pastor tried to keep the first hour or so of every morning free to read and to plan his day, but even then, the phone would start ringing. It might be Brzezinski with an instruction, or Mark Schneider from the human rights bureau, who knew that Pastor was likely to be in his office then and unprotected by a secretary. Pastor received and placed about half his telephone calls himself, but during the busiest times, he needed the screen his secretary could provide.

This filtering of calls is necessary for most government officials. What began as convenience, however, has become an irritating ritual in which the telephone is a barometer of power. In many societies and languages, various forms of the word *you* convey degrees of respect or polite disdain. Democratic English has no such convention, but in the society of official Washington, telephone manners provide a nearly infallible indicator of rank. The junior official defers to the senior by coming on the line first, so the latter is not kept waiting. This requires very nice judgment by the secretaries who initially place and receive most calls: "Good morning. Deputy Assistant Secretary Pooh-Bah is calling Deputy Assistant Administrator Pish-Tush. Would you please put him on?" This may place Pish-Tush's secretary in a quandary. If she buzzes her boss on the intercom and suggests he take the call before Pooh-Bah is on the line, she is accepting his inferior status and may well incur his irritation. If she refuses and insists to Mr. P-B's secretary that *her* boss get on first, there may be an impasse. What to do? Perhaps best simply to finesse and say that Pish-Tush is not in.

It would be better if everyone did his own dialing, but this wastes time. It would be better still if the caller always picked up the telephone first when told that the respondent was available, whatever his respective rank. But few officials do so. After all, Washington is about power, and one form of power is making someone else pick up a receiver before you do.

During each day, it seemed to Pastor, the telephone calls increased exponentially. Every call led to three more, "so by the third call of the day, I had nine more to make. And as I started in on them, there would be a new call from Brzezinski's office asking for an urgent memo on something or other. And then my mother would call or the garage would need guidance on repairs on my car. And by then there were twelve other calls to make. As I wrote notes on all the matters that had come up, I would try to keep in some corner of my mind a picture of what it was that *I* had wanted to accomplish that day, to remember the first notes I had written to myself that morning. But they were at the top of the note pad, and by noon three more pages had been turned over."

So Pastor began to reserve Sundays for the third category of NSC work: thinking about new initiatives and policy innovations. Both Carter and Brzezinski loved new ideas, even if most had to be discarded as unwise or unworkable. It was Brzezinski's ability to come up with new concepts that made him Carter's favorite airplane companion. New initiatives were especially welcome if the president was giving a speech and needed a specific proposal to balance the general rhetoric. Pastor is especially proud of two of his ideas that became reality: the "Humphrey" scholarships for Third World students in the United States, and the Caribbean Group for Cooperation and Economic Development.

Pastor's most important job was to make sure the president had a chance to shape policy rather than having it simply evolve within the bureaucracy. On Nicaragua, he was absolutely sure that Carter did not want the United States to intervene to remove Somoza. So at the end of Vaky's informal meeting on August 29, after the argument had clarified the difference between Vaky and his questioners, Pastor suggested that the discussion be moved into formal channels: State should draft a paper laying out the options, which would be considered at a formal interagency meeting. Vaky agreed to this, and scheduled a meeting under his own chairmanship for

Labor Day, September 4, 1978. When Brzezinski learned of the meeting, he switched it from the State Department to the White House, where it would be chaired by his deputy, David Aaron.[5] The president had asked that an urgent recommendation on what to do about the deteriorating situation in Nicaragua be sent to him at Camp David, where he was about to begin his brilliant personal diplomacy on the Middle East.

Vaky was pleased neither by the shift in venue nor by the course of the Labor Day discussion. At the meeting, David Newsom, under secretary of state for political affairs, first presented a point upon which all the State participants agreed: that ultimately, Somoza had to go. The question was how. The first step in that direction should be to stimulate efforts by other Central American nations to mediate the dispute between Somoza and his internal enemies. The meeting soon turned, however, to the same difference of opinion between Vaky and Pastor that had appeared at the discussion of August 31. Vaky argued that only the United States had the influence to remove Somoza, while Pastor and I responded that Washington should not act alone in a mediation effort that might have that result. In the end, there was agreement that President Rodrigo Carazo of Costa Rica, who had offered to play the role of mediator, should be encouraged to step in. After the meeting, Pastor and Richard Feinberg of the policy planning staff drafted a letter from Carter to Carazo, and Pastor summarized the discussion in a memorandum for the president. The following morning, Carter approved both the strategy and the letter.

Carazo's enthusiasm for becoming involved had waned, however, and he asked for American help in getting other Central American governments to support his effort. Vaky was not surprised. He remained convinced that only the United States could do what was necessary to resolve the matter. At another White House meeting on September 12, he and Under Secretary David Newsom argued that the United States must step in as a mediator, but Warren Christopher and all the other participants at the meeting thought it better to keep the Central Americans out front.

In a way, the policy of "Let the Central Americans mediate

Somoza out of office" was a new version of "Let's have our cake and eat it too." Washington wanted Somoza out of power, yet the Carter administration could not take the responsibility for removing him without prejudicing its ability to pursue other, apparently more important foreign policy concerns such as the SALT II negotiations. The insistence that there be a Central American initiative, with Washington prodding discreetly behind the scenes, reflected a genuine belief in the principle of multilateralism, but it also flowed from a calculation of American global interests. The dilemma was deepened by the likelihood that effective American involvement would have to come from a presidential decision. Somoza was unlikely to be moved so long as he thought American policy was being made by officials like Pastor and Mark Schneider, whom he considered human rights ideologues without serious political backing. It would take word from President Carter himself, either directly or through a personal representative, to convince Somoza that Washington was serious about his leaving. But invoking Carter in such a message would also be all the more damaging to the standing of the administration on Capitol Hill if Somoza fought back by publicizing the affair.

The problem with the multilateral approach was simply that Vaky was right in his estimate of Nicaraguan reality: the United States could not avoid deeper involvement if it wanted to attack the Nicaraguan problem. Vaky was not opposed to a multilateral approach per se; he doubted, however, that such an approach could work if the United States did not take the primary responsibility for organizing it and seeing it through.

Meanwhile, events during September seemed to require a more assertive role by Washington. First, there was growing opposition to Somoza and the continuing bloodshed in Nicaragua. The strike led by the business community continued until September 25. The fighting in Estelí and elsewhere left as many as three thousand dead, according to the Red Cross, and some thirty thousand homeless. American officials were also increasingly concerned about the behavior of the National Guard. On September 21, a cable to Ambassador Solaun instructed him to protest to Somoza the "mounting reports of alleged atrocities by GN [the government of Nicaragua] against civilians in urban areas." (The cable, written in the Latin American bureau, shows how Vaky had by then taken over the action on Nicaragua within the State Department. It was not cleared either by the human rights bureau or by the policy planning staff.)

As a consequence of the burgeoning violence, important voices in Nicaragua were calling for a direct American role. On September 3, Ambassador Solaun reported to Washington that he had met with business leaders in Managua and Archbishop Obando y Bravo. All of them had urged mediation by the United States. On September 15, the opposition front FAO had appealed for a Central American effort, but on the twentieth a number of FAO leaders joined the archbishop in a new appeal for the United States to take a leading role.

Unwittingly or not, Somoza himself also brought Washington into a deeper role than it wanted, by opposing the kind of Central American initiative it favored. On September 6, Solaun reported that Somoza had asked to see him, and had told him that his government "would neither request nor tolerate OAS [the Organization of American States] intervention." Washington was being "duped," he said, by Venezuela and its president, Carlos Andrés Pérez. "Because of your human rights policy, a bunch of imbeciles [in Nicaragua] have thought that you are going to overthrow me. Do not contribute more to the tragedy of this country." Somoza dismissed the notion of a compromise solution, including a foreign presence to guarantee elections: "Latins," he said, "don't know how to compromise and don't understand free elections." (He apparently had never examined the reality of his democratic regional neighbors, Costa Rica and Venezuela.) Then, perhaps in an effort to soften his remarks, he disclaimed the public remarks of a close associate that Pastor, Mark Schneider, and Patricia Derian were Communists. On September 1, however, Somoza himself had said in a press conference that the United States was "in the hands of leftists and Communists."

In another talk with Solaun on September 7, Somoza specifically criticized the Carazo initiative. And then on the twelfth — as it happened, just after the conclusion of the White House meeting — Somoza killed it. Nicaraguan planes strafed areas of the southern border with Costa Rica, injuring a number of Costa Rican students. President Carazo, who in any case was moving toward offering more support for the Pastora-led band of Sandinistas operating out of his territory, renounced his mediation offer.

At this point, leaders outside Nicaragua became instrumental in bringing the United States to a central diplomatic role. In a conversation with the American ambassador, Venezuelan President Pérez reacted to the death of the Central American initiative by threatening military intervention in Nicaragua. When Vaky called him on September 18 to urge moderation, Pérez replied that because of its refusal to take decisive action, he no longer trusted the United States. Pérez then called for a meeting of foreign ministers of the Organization of American States, to discuss the Nicaraguan situation and the border incidents. That same day, at another meeting at the White House chaired by David Aaron, Christopher agreed that the United States would have to take another step: it should get OAS support for a mediation effort — still multilateral — that the United States would join and even lead. It was immediately clear from the OAS deliberations that while the organization might endorse a mediation effort, it would not carry one out. To do so would put it in the position of intervening in the internal affairs of one of its members. However, after a few days' discussion, the OAS did endorse the notion of multilateral mediation if any governments wished to undertake such an effort. The ball was in Washington's court.

On the evening of September 21, as the first day of the OAS meeting concluded, General Omar Torrijos, the flamboyant ruler of Panama who disliked Somoza almost as much as did Pérez, played his part in forcing the American hand. He sent word to Washington that the following morning Venezuelan planes stationed in Panama would be used to bomb Somoza's headquarters in Managua. This led, during the next two days and nights, to a series of emergency meetings in Washington and telephone conversations between American officials (including Carter) and Panamanian officials (including Torrijos). Finally, Torrijos and Pérez were persuaded to sheathe their swords. In the process, however, Carter assured Torrijos that the United States would participate in a mediation effort, and Brzezinski told the Panamanian foreign minister that Washington would consider actions affecting the composition of governments in the region "if it were a genuine collective effort."[6]

William Jorden, a former ambassador to Panama, had been dispatched to Central America on September 12 to consult with governments there about next steps. Now he was instructed to see Somoza. Following Washington's script, Jorden told the Nicaraguan that relations with the United States would be adversely affected if Somoza did not agree to an OAS-sponsored mediation. Jorden also told Somoza that in the American view, *he* was the cause of the polarization in Nicaragua, and the longer he stayed in power the more likely it was that Nicaragua would go Communist.[7]

The suggestion that Somoza leave office was strongly implied, but it fell short of Vaky's belief that Washington had to *insist* on his leaving — in his often reiterated phrase, that the American government must "talk turkey" with Somoza. Still, the Nicaraguan leader was hardly thrilled by Jorden's message. He immediately rejected William D. Rogers as the American representative in a mediation. A respected Washington lawyer and former assistant secretary of state, Rogers had been the one to tell Somoza that the Ford administration was going to be neutral in disputes between Somoza and his political opponents — and was going to keep a particularly close eye on how American foreign assistance was used in Nicaragua. Still, Somoza did not reject a mediation effort. A few days later he told Jorden that he would go along, although he preferred to call it an exercise in "friendly cooperation." The phrase seemed more respectful of Nicaraguan sovereignty.

This left the question of which governments should do the mediating. Somoza proposed that Argentina, Brazil, El Salvador, and Guatemala — all thought to be relatively friendly to him — join the United States in this effort, rather than the Dominican Republic, Colombia, and Honduras, as had been suggested. Vaky and other

American officials were not amused, and the next day, September 26, Vaky drafted a stiff reply. "Jorden should tell Somoza we will not continue this 'bargaining,'" the cable said. "Must construct a panel of four, two from each slate, plus U.S. If he doesn't agree, we cannot participate. Tell him, 'We are deadly serious about this effort. We do not wish to engage in games.'" The next day Somoza agreed to the United States, the Dominican Republic, Colombia, Guatemala, and El Salvador as the mediators. When Colombia proceeded to publicly condemn Somoza, he insisted that it be dropped. This was agreed to, but to balance the mediating team, one of Somoza's candidates, El Salvador, was dropped as well. On September 30, the OAS announced the formation of the International Commission of Friendly Cooperation and Conciliation. Somoza and the FAO, the coalition of his opponents, duly called for the mediation effort.

By mid-September 1978, American policy had come a long way: from distancing to support for a Central American initiative and then to willingness to join a mediation effort whose implied purpose was Somoza's removal. The policy still fell well short of Vaky's prescription of a determined American effort to remove Somoza, but an important bridge had been crossed. The United States was engaged in the affair.

EIGHT

Mediation in Managua

THE FIRST ORDER OF BUSINESS WAS TO SELECT THE AMERI-
can mediator. The administration chose one of its most skilled
and experienced career diplomats, William G. Bowdler, a former
ambassador to El Salvador, Guatemala, and South Africa, and a
participant in the negotiations that ended the 1965 crisis in the
Dominican Republic. Bowdler had a great deal of negotiating experience. He also knew Washington: a veteran of the NSC staff, Bowdler
was serving in 1978 as the assistant secretary of state for intelligence
and research. The son of missionaries serving in Latin America,
Bowdler spoke fluent Spanish. A tall, heavyset man, he conveyed
to all his associates an extraordinary sense of solid dignity, of
old-fashioned integrity. Despite his ready sense of humor and personal friendliness, Bowdler always spoke thoughtfully in official
settings, the sobriety of his words reinforced by his horn-rimmed
glasses and the dark suits he favored.

Vaky recalls that President Carazo of Costa Rica referred admir-
ingly to Bowdler as a man with *sangre fria* — literally, "cold blood,"
but better translated less literally as cool, or steady nerves. Bowdler
was by no means cold-blooded or indifferent; he was already following events in Nicaragua. As he read the background files and talked
to Vaky, Pastor, and others working on the problem, he — like
Vaky — was struck by the parallels to Cuba in the late 1950s.

Bowdler had spent four years in Cuba as a junior officer and had watched Castro take power with the collapse of the corrupt, unpopular Fulgencio Batista. Bowdler recalls that in 1958, after the miserable failure of a military offensive by Batista's forces against Castro's guerrillas in the hills, he drafted a dispatch to Washington that argued that Batista's policies and position were hopeless, that Castro would come to power unless something were done, and that the only hope was for Washington to push Batista out in favor of more effective, moderate leaders. The American ambassador in Cuba approved those parts of the dispatch that analyzed Batista's situation, but Bowdler's prescription of removing Batista went too far for him, and he deleted the recommendation. Elections were to be held in Cuba, and the ambassador said he believed too much in the electoral process to suggest ousting Batista. The November elections were held, Batista's party predictably found a way to win that would have made Chicago's Mayor Daley proud, the equally predictable angry popular reaction took place, and on January 1, 1959, Batista was on a plane out of Havana as Castro moved in to pick up the pieces. Now, in 1978, Somoza and the Sandinistas and a Washington unwilling to take firm action reminded Bowdler of those earlier days. "I lived through the Cuban thing," he recalls, "and I could smell it again." He became Vaky's strongest ally in pushing for an effort to get Somoza to quit.

Before he flew to Guatemala to meet with his colleagues on the mediation team, Bowdler and the two assistants assigned to him by the State Department, Malcolm Barnaby and James Cheek, drafted their negotiating instructions. (Most American negotiators help fashion their instructions; Bowdler did more of the actual drafting than is customary.) An action memorandum dated October 2, 1978, from Vaky and Bowdler to Warren Christopher (then the acting secretary) laid out these instructions and their rationale.

It is extremely rare for an American negotiator to act "uninstructed." Some other governments are less careful. At the United Nations, for example, it has not been uncommon to find representatives of some smaller nations taking positions at variance with those of their foreign ministries. It is also at the UN that American ambassadors are most likely to chafe under Washington's instructions. Henry Cabot Lodge, UN ambassador under President Eisenhower, took delight in recalling that he once refused to be instructed on a Security Council vote about which he thought he knew the president's mind better than the State Department did. When a State Department official called him to insist that he follow its instruction, Lodge heard him out, dismissed him with an Olympian, "I take note of the department's opinion," and voted the way he wanted.

In drafting his own instructions, Bowdler faced two issues. First, how detailed should they be? And second — the key issue, in his as well as Vaky's view — how much authority could he get to push Somoza toward resignation? He came up with very general instructions that set out his objectives — for example, that he should "work out between Somoza and the opposition the nature of the transition government which is to take the country to free and open elections" — while leaving him considerable flexibility in achieving them. This approach was appropriate for a situation in which he would be trying to mediate a freewheeling dispute among others rather than negotiating a careful bargain between the United States and another government. It was appropriate as well to the people with whom he would be working. When negotiating with the rather formal South Africans during his tour there as the American ambassador, he recalls, he had acted on the basis of detailed instructions from Washington. In Central America, the give and take was likely to be less structured, and he would need more room to respond spontaneously. He would, of course, stay in touch with Washington, through cables and telephone conversations with Vaky as the negotiations unfolded, and Vaky would keep Vance, Christopher, and the White House informed.

Thus, when approved by the Seventh Floor and the White House, Bowdler's instructions were not only general but very brief: six paragraphs in a cable barely more than a page long. This was in extraordinary contrast to the kinds of instructions given to our strategic arms control negotiators during the Carter administration, in which every point to be made by our representatives on every issue that might arise was hammered out in excruciating detail in a SALT working group chaired by an NSC staff member and in White House meetings chaired by David Aaron, Brzezinski's deputy. When these groups had defined the options (assisted by six lower-level interagency working groups and an informal strategy group), Cabinet-level meetings would argue the issues before sending them to the president. After the president had considered each detail of the positions to be taken, the Arms Control and Disarmament Agency would draft instructions for the negotiating team, including even the specific junctures at which it could compromise and move to its fallback positions.

Bowdler's instructions, approved by Christopher after clearance by Pastor at the NSC staff, remained essentially as Bowdler had drafted them, with a few changes made by Christopher and Pastor to ensure that there was no misunderstanding on the central question: the removal of Somoza. The instructions accepted the necessity of a transition, and stated that Bowdler could, "if necessary to assure [a peaceful and democratic] solution, persuade Somoza and his close relatives to step down in advance of 1981 and not run for office." But Christopher and Pastor wanted to be able to control how this goal was pursued: Bowdler was to "consult with Washington on what steps may be desirable and appropriate to achieve this result." Where the Bowdler and Vaky draft had described the basic objective of the mediation as seeking "an enduring peaceful solution," Christopher added the word *democratic* after *peaceful*. If necessary, we would seek Somoza's departure — but only through democratic means. And where Bowdler and Vaky had written that Somoza might have to be persuaded to "step down substantially in advance of 1981," Christopher removed the word *substantially*.

By October 4, when the instructions were approved and cabled to him, Bowdler had already left for Guatemala to meet with the other members of the mediation team. He already knew the two men with whom he would share the weeks of effort that lay ahead: Ramón Emilio Jiménez, a navy admiral and foreign minister of the Dominican Republic, and Alfredo Obiols Gómez, a former assistant foreign minister from Guatemala. Indeed, he recalls, "We were, in effect, friends."

Diplomatic friends enjoy a particular kind of relationship based on intermittent contact built through tours of duty that may overlap in various capitals or through negotiations that may bring them together for a few intense days, weeks, or months. Such friendships may achieve a kind of intimacy, but there are always boundaries in official lives: although diplomats may be honest, they can never be completely open with one another in discussing their work or even, perhaps, their personal lives. Such friendships reflect what is generally the diplomat's most important function: the ability to reconcile the differences among nations through careful bargaining. This depends more on accuracy and honesty than on wily maneuver. A diplomat should undoubtedly be flexible, able to understand the positions of others and to help design the arguments that will best advance the interests of his own nation, but it is interesting that in his classic *Diplomacy,* Harold Nicolson simply assumed the importance of high intelligence when listing the virtues of "the ideal diplomatist": truthfulness, precision, calm, good temper, patience, modesty, and loyalty.

Bowdler believes that the central ingredient of diplomatic friendships "is obviously trust." Diplomats may seek to charm each other into concessions, but in the end, charm is far less useful than a tactful honesty, especially if the object of the attention is modest and thus not susceptible to flattery. What matter in international negotiations are national interests, and the personal style of diplomats cannot alter them. What one diplomat wants to hear from another is an unemotional, authoritative statement of his government's position. A diplomat who lies, either because his superiors want him to or because he misrepresents his government's position, is a diplomat who will eventually be ineffective.

Bowdler and his associates trusted each other, which immediately helped establish an informal atmosphere for their talks about how best to proceed. Bowdler's instructions were broad, but his Dominican and Guatemalan colleagues had been given even greater freedom to maneuver, and they clearly were looking to him to provide direction. It was the United States, after all, that might have the pivotal influence in Managua.

But Bowdler did not want to get into such a position. When dealing with the Nicaraguans on both sides, and when presenting their work to other members of the OAS, the three men had to make it clear that this was a multilateral effort. So as the three talked the problem through, and later as they met with the various Nicaraguan parties, the American was always careful to listen as well as to speak, to let the others take the lead as often as he did, even if the crucial voice was his. The team easily agreed on a three-stage approach: "First, the achievement of a climate conducive to negotiations and identification of the position of the parties; second, evaluation of the situation and promotion of direct negotiations between the parties; and third, negotiation of a peaceful, democratic, and lasting solution."[1]

Immediately upon arrival in Managua, the team began meetings with a wide variety of Nicaraguans, including government officials and opposition leaders, representatives of labor and business, members of the press, church, and academic communities, and people on the street. After two weeks or so of such conversations it became clear that opposition to the government was very strong and widespread, and that neither the government nor the opposition was willing to think in terms of compromise. Not only had the fighting in September exacerbated the hatred between the two sides, but each thought it had emerged in the stronger position: Somoza because his forces had finally prevailed militarily, the opposition because it understood how weakened Somoza had become politically as a result of the bloodshed inflicted by the National Guard.

This was troublesome, because in any negotiation, a solution depends on each side's concluding that settlement will serve its interests better than continuation of the status quo: Will my government's security be better served by an arms race (can we win it?) than by the terms I can reasonably expect to negotiate in an arms control treaty? Is my party more likely to gain power through a fair election or through a continuation of the civil war? The key to success is not to be found in the genius of those designing compromise terms or in impassioned appeals to humanity and good feeling. In the end, it is the parties' calculation of interests and power — present and future — that decide whether a negotiation will succeed. The mediator's task is to develop fair terms and then to show the parties how those terms serve their interests. It may even be possible to affect calculations of self-interest through inducements (such as the massive aid programs promised to Israel and Egypt at the time of the Camp David Accords) or sanctions (as in the case of the settlement in Zimbabwe, in which a combination of fighting and an international economic embargo finally made the various parties prefer the uncertainties of an election to the certain pain they were all enduring). But it is usually impossible to predict when both sides will decide to settle. The mediator's patience here becomes essential, as he works and waits for the moment at which the various stars of peace come into alignment.

The mediators' aim in this case was to get both Somoza (represented by officials of his Nationalist Liberal Party, the PLN) and the moderate opposition (represented by the Broad Opposition Front, the FAO) to put their own settlement proposals in writing. At first, both refused. Each faction seemed to see in Bowdler's presence a return of the old American deus ex machina that could be made to serve its own political interests while confounding those of its enemies. Representatives of the FAO made clear their hope, probably encouraged by the attitudes of the mediators themselves, that Bowdler and his colleagues would resolve the crisis simply by forcing Somoza to step down. For his part, Somoza at least pretended to believe that the mediation would allow his opponents a face-saving way to surrender. On October 2, Ambassador Solaun reported to Washington that Somoza had remarked to him, "This outside presence will offer the opposition a chance to climb down the ladder from their extreme demands." On October 4, Somoza announced plans to double the size of the National Guard.

In refusing to make a written offer as a basis for negotiations, Somoza's position was that he should be allowed to complete his term in office. In 1981 the OAS could send observers to new national elections; meantime, Somoza's PLN would agree to hold direct negotiations with the FAO. But the FAO was already refusing to do this, for fear that such talks would divert attention from their central concern — Somoza's removal.

After a few weeks' urging by the mediators, the FAO at last offered a statement of its position. The terms were stiff: Somoza's immediate resignation and the removal from office of his various relatives, followed by the departure from Nicaragua of the whole Somoza family, the dismantling of his government, the reorganization of the National Guard, and the formation of a new government that would implement the FAO political program. This Government of National Unity would include a three-man junta, to be named by an advisory Council of State composed of two representatives from each of the sixteen organizations represented in the FAO and two representatives of Somoza's Liberals.

The immediate effect of the FAO proposal was not to move Somoza, but to split the Front itself. Sergio Ramírez, nominally the FAO representative of Los Doce (the group of twelve establishment backers of the Sandinistas), was actually under Sandinista orders. He was instructed by the FSLN to do something that might defeat the mediation: to "make a dramatic gesture — to resign and seek asylum." Ramírez did so, denouncing the FAO proposal as *Somocismo sin Somoza* and seeking refuge in the Mexican embassy. As Pastor notes, the Sandinistas had all along seen in the mediation a threat to their own prospects. The talks were obviously aimed at bringing moderates to power in a peaceful transition; the Sandinistas, who had more guns and fewer votes than the moderates in the FAO, needed a military struggle to take power. The FAO's participation even in an indirect dialogue with Somoza, especially through an American intermediary, had to be opposed, and in a way that would most damage the FAO itself.

Ramírez's action helped convince the mediating group that the key to a peaceful solution was Somoza's resignation: no settlement was possible without it. Bowdler already believed this; now his colleagues had come to the same conclusion. In Washington, Vaky supported a proposal cabled in by Bowdler that sanctions against Somoza would help bring about his departure. At an interagency meeting on October 31, however, Christopher and Brzezinski demurred and suggested a compromise: Bowdler, and his colleagues if they agreed, should tell Somoza that if he did not accept the FAO proposal, Washington would oppose a loan from the International Monetary Fund requested by the Nicaraguan government and would freeze remaining American aid to Nicaragua.

On November 6, Somoza's Liberal party spokesmen rejected the FAO proposal. The next day, the mediation team saw Somoza and delicately "inquired, with all the respect due his high office, whether for the sake of peace in Nicaragua, he would consider the possibility of resigning from the Presidency of the Republic." By directly, if tactfully, raising the issue of Somoza's departure, Bowdler was going farther than his instructions had contemplated, but his question reflected the consensus of the mediating team, and Bowdler was authorized to call for acceptance of the FAO proposal, which most certainly included Somoza's resignation.

When Bowdler met privately with Somoza on November 10 to repeat his request, Somoza refused even to consider resigning. Instead, he proposed an idea previously advanced by his Liberal representatives: a plebiscite to test the electoral strength of the various Nicaraguan parties. Bowdler was not attracted to the idea. The plebiscite would not address the issue of Somoza's remaining in office, and the FAO was opposed to the notion. For two generations, the Somoza family had used elections to ratify their rule rather than to provide a true choice to the people. Why would this be different?

Bowdler was skeptical about Somoza's real intentions in proposing a plebiscite, but he sensed that Washington's freeze on aid and its opposition to the IMF loan had shaken the Nicaraguan. He so informed Vaky, who asked for another interagency meeting to discuss full sanctions against Somoza, including new restrictions on trade and a threat that Somoza would be barred from entering the United States when he did leave office. Christopher and Pastor agreed that a meeting would be useful, and it was scheduled for Monday, November 13. It was to be the most important of the eleven interagency meetings held on the Nicaraguan problem in the fall of 1978 and January 1979.

*

Interagency coordination has generally been managed by committees that draw their authority from the NSC (a statutory body including the president and the most senior foreign policy officials); meetings of the NSC itself have become increasingly infrequent during the course of each presidency. Meetings of the whole Cabinet in which foreign policy has been decided have been as rare as the appearances of prothonotary warblers on the south lawn of the White House. Presidents do discuss international matters with the Cabinet, and may even pretend to listen to the views of, say, the postmaster general, but usually such discussions have been, in reality, a device to get the Cabinet behind some decision already made or planned.

Each president has organized the NSC interagency committee system in a different way — and indeed he should, in order to fit his own style of decision making and the roles he wishes his subordinates to play. Thus the foreign policy makers of each new administration first give thanks for their accession to power and then fall on each other as they battle over who will chair which committee in the interagency system.

Since the late 1960s there has been one constant in the interagency structure: the regional assistant secretaries at state have always chaired interagency groups that coordinate the implementation of policy and frame policy differences that might need resolution at higher levels. Above the interagency groups, however, each administration has designed its own committee structure. In the Carter administration, the structure rested on two Cabinet-level committees whose participants were approximately the same; the difference lay in who chaired them — and thus was in the best position to shape not only the discussions at the meetings but, more important, the papers to be discussed.

The Policy Review Committee (PRC) met to coordinate foreign, defense, and international economic policies; PRC meetings were chaired by Cabinet officers. Which Cabinet officer chaired which meeting depended on the issue. Since the PRC usually met over policy issues that were concerned more with foreign affairs than with defense or economic matters, the secretary of state or his deputy was usually in the chair, and State usually drafted the papers to be discussed, clearing them with the other agencies involved. The other interagency group was the Special Coordinating Committee (SCC), chaired by the National Security assistant. Its mandate included intelligence policy, arms control, and crisis management.*

Because of its ambiguities and flexibility, the Carter NSC system presented an invitation to bureaucratic struggle, depending as it did on a considerable degree of collegiality among the participants. At first the arrangement worked rather well, but by mid-1978 officials at State were becoming concerned at an emerging pattern: increasingly, Brzezinski and the NSC staff were calling SCC meetings, under their chairmanship, to discuss "crises" (an SCC matter) concerning issues that, it seemed to State, remained in the category of foreign policy.

Nicaragua had fallen into this pattern. The first meetings on the subject in September had been called by the NSC staff and chaired by David Aaron, Brzezinski's deputy, as "mini-SCC" meetings. As part of a general counteroffensive designed to restore the balance between SCC and PRC meetings, and because the issue on Nicaragua clearly turned now on devising a negotiating strategy rather than management of a crisis, State had insisted that the October 31 interagency meeting on Nicaragua be a PRC meeting under its own chairmanship. The pivotal November 13 discussion would be a PRC meeting as well.

After his unsatisfactory meeting with Somoza on Friday, November 10, Bowdler flew back to Washington. On Sunday evening, Vaky asked Bowdler, Pastor, Steven Oxman (Christopher's special assistant), and Brandon Grove (one of Vaky's deputies) to join him in his office to discuss the next day's PRC meeting. The first item of business was to hear from Bowdler on where matters stood. Bowdler had cabled a report on his Friday meeting with Somoza,

---

* According to *The Washington Post* of June 21, 1987, page B2, the Reagan administration had created by that year a spider's web of twenty-five senior indepartmental groups, fifty-five interdepartmental groups, and more than one hundred other task forces, working groups, and coordinating committees. Most, according to the *Post,* were "hollow shells."

but as Pastor listened to his fuller description of the Nicaraguan leader's remarks, he recognized for the first time the importance of the reference to a plebiscite. Might not this, he asked, be a device for resolving the issue? Could we turn the idea back on Somoza, making it a referendum on the dictator's continuing rule?

As Pastor recalls the meeting, Vaky and Bowdler dismissed the notion. The plebiscite idea was simply a "stalling tactic," Bowdler said. Vaky agreed: "He's throwing sand in our faces." A plebiscite would stretch out the negotiations, divide Somoza's opponents, and divert American public attention from the real issue: Somoza's departure. Further sanctions against him were now needed to tip the scales in favor of his leaving. Pastor agreed with this analysis of Somoza's motives, but both he and Oxman suggested that Washington could not simply reject out of hand a proposal for elections, arguing that a plebiscite on Somoza's continued rule would give the mediation a new legitimacy as the team negotiated the terms of a free and fair election. The move could also force the FAO to come together as a political party. Washington was already concerned about the FAO's ability to govern if Somoza were suddenly to step down. Wouldn't the experience of contesting an election serve the opposition well? Vaky and Bowdler were unconvinced. Somoza, they thought, would simply draw out negotiations over the form of a plebiscite, splitting the opposition in the process.[2]

The PRC meeting was scheduled for late the following afternoon, so time was short for writing the options papers. Usually, these papers were completed well in advance of the meetings. The NSC staff and the department chairing the meeting normally drafted a policy review memorandum calling for a study on the issue under discussion. The department then wrote the response: a memo, usually of twenty or so pages, that analyzed the problem, including its background and current status, and laid out the options that should be considered at the PRC meeting. In State, such a memorandum was always written jointly by the relevant bureau and the policy planning staff, in cooperation with the NSC staff and any other interested agencies, to make sure that everyone's preferred options were included and fairly described. The memorandum would make no recommendation; it was simply a basis for discussion.

Meantime, within each agency there would be arguments about the position it should take at the PRC meeting. In State, the argument would be contained in a memorandum to Vance or Christopher laying out the views of the bureaus and the planning staff, noting the arguments on each side if there were disagreement. A "prebrief" meeting would then be held so that Vance or Christopher could hear the arguments and make a final decision. The pre-brief usually took place just before the PRC meeting. Sometimes it continued in the car carrying Vance or Christopher and their accompanying officials to the White House, where PRC meetings were held.

In this case, there was no time for the formal process. The Sunday evening meeting was the first time Vaky, Pastor, and the others had discussed with Bowdler Somoza's latest position. Vaky quickly put together a discussion paper for the PRC, drawing on the work already done the previous week. The referendum idea, however, was new, and as Pastor recalls it, the paper did not make any substantial reference to pursuing it. So Pastor and Oxman wrote an options paper for Vance, Christopher, and Brzezinski that framed the issue the way the two wanted it considered. As Pastor recalls, there were three options: "(1) Transform the plebiscite idea into a vote on Somoza's staying in power and negotiate terms that would ensure a free election; (2) dismiss the plebiscite and apply pressure (a full list of sanctions) on Somoza to negotiate his departure in accordance with the FAO plan; or (3) discontinue mediation and walk away from the problem."[3]

Near midnight, Pastor returned to the White House to prepare a memorandum for Brzezinski, leaving it for Brzezinski's secretary to type and put on the national security assistant's pile of morning reading. (The office of the national security assistant generates so much work that one or more secretaries usually work a shift through the night.) Pastor's late-night work would allow Brzezinski to discuss the matter with the president the next morning, November 13, during the daily intelligence briefing.

At 5 P.M. on the thirteenth, Vance, Christopher, Bowdler, Vaky,

Brzezinski, Aaron, Admiral Stansfield Turner (then director of the CIA), David McGiffert (assistant secretary of defense for international security affairs), and General William Smith, representing the Joint Chiefs of Staff, took their places around the conference table in the White House Situation Room, in the basement of the West Wing. Vance, chairing the meeting, sat at one end; the others sat where they wished. Pastor and other aides sat near the wall, close by their superiors.

The problem posed for aides lining the wall in the Situation Room is not so much to be within whisper range of the participants' ears, should there be no time for scribbling a note, but to avoid kneeing their bosses in the back. The room is small, perhaps twenty by forty feet, and the table will seat fourteen or so, if they squeeze, with room for twenty or so wall sitters, if they squeeze even more. The table and chairs could well have been borrowed from the conference center of a Hilton hotel, except for the rarely used telephones secured under the table. The decor is simple. No Hollywood director would dream of so cramped and prosaic a setting. How could White House discussions, in which the brightly colored carnage of combat in a Vietnam or Nicaragua might be at stake, take place in an atmosphere whose hue, figuratively if not literally, is so gray?

Vaky recalls the argument as tense and very direct but never heated. It began with Bowdler's report on the status of the negotiations. This led to a debate in which Brzezinski played the lead in arguing for the revised plebiscite idea, with Vance and Christopher joining him, against Vaky's and Bowdler's pleas for sanctions (supported by Aaron and McGiffert). From time to time Admiral Turner interjected the CIA's analyses of the problem, but — as was proper for a representative of the intelligence community — he did not take a position on the policy decision. General Smith spoke little, but made clear the opposition of the Joint Chiefs to pulling the American military group out of Managua if sanctions were imposed.

As assistant secretary of defense for International Security Affairs, McGiffert was in charge of what is often called the Defense Department's State Department. He advised the secretary of defense on major foreign policy and international security issues, and represented him in the interagency policy process. International Security Affairs was not large in 1978 — McGiffert had some seventy officials working for him — and it had a large number of issues to cover. Its priorities did not include Central America. Indeed, the deputy assistant secretary whose duties included Latin America was also charged with Asian affairs, and gave priority to the latter, since the opening to China, negotiations on base rights in the Philippines, and talks on sharing defense burdens with the Japanese were matters of major importance. McGiffert himself was concentrating on such questions as NATO policy; arms control; relations with Japan; the Middle East and Persian Gulf; and military assistance programs around the world. Thus, the Defense Department did not play a central role on Nicaragua, which was still, in 1978, seen as a second-level security issue.

At the November 13 meeting, Vance, Brzezinski, and the other supporters of turning the plebiscite into a referendum on Somoza's rule focused primarily on the dangers of simply pushing Somoza into resigning. Was the democratic opposition cohesive enough to rule the country, or would there be a vacuum that would be filled by the Sandinistas? Who would lead the National Guard, and how would it be reformed? (Everyone at the PRC agreed that the future unity of a reformed Guard was important, to give a new government a military shield against the Sandinistas should the fighting continue.) What were the chances that Somoza would actually resign if we did impose sanctions? When Bowdler put the chances at a little better than fifty-fifty, Brzezinski leaped in: if there was such a strong chance that he would not leave despite U.S. pressure, Washington could easily end up embarrassed and without leverage in a deteriorating situation.

The proponents of a plebiscite had another set of concerns. How could the American government, especially under an administration dedicated to the promotion of human rights, oppose a democratic solution? To be accused on Capitol Hill and before the American public of overthrowing an anti-Communist friend of America would be bad enough, although the administration could at least point out Somoza's venality and loss of legitimacy with the Nicaraguan people. But to overthrow a government that was proclaiming its desire for elections would be still worse. How could the administration use Somoza's unpopularity as one justification for demanding his resignation if it refused to put his popularity to the test with his own people?

Vaky and Bowdler could not refute these points, but with their knowledge of Nicaraguan realities, they foresaw tremendous dangers in the plebiscite notion. The opposition FAO had already rejected a plebiscite; for Washington now to support it could leave the moderates isolated and vulnerable. The FAO had good reason to be cynical about Nicaraguan elections, and even if it went along with discussions on a referendum, Somoza would endlessly draw out such negotiations.

Vance and Brzezinski suggested that some of these dangers could be overcome: for example, we could promise the FAO that if they accepted the plebiscite idea, the United States would work to make it a fair one. (State Department planners had in mind such measures as assurances by Somoza that he would respect the results; the use of foreign observers at polling places; a strong OAS presence, perhaps accompanying any National Guard patrols allowed during the elections; and the temporary departure of Somoza during the electoral period.) If the FAO accepted a plebiscite and Somoza rejected it, Washington would come down on him with sanctions and support the FAO.

Vaky and Bowdler saw that this might meet some of the FAO's concerns, but it left two problems: as Brzezinski himself pointed out, if the FAO nonetheless rejected the plebiscite idea, Washington would be left on Somoza's side of the question with no place to go. And if the negotiations simply dragged on, with a new outbreak of fighting, the Sandinistas would gain at the expense of the moderates in the FAO as well as of Somoza.

As on most foreign policy decisions that rise to the level of a PRC meeting, the choice was neither obvious nor appetizing. A solution depended on conflicting calculations of politics in Managua and Washington, and on inevitably uncertain predictions about the future. Still, the debate that occurred was praiseworthy in a number of respects. For one thing, it clarified the positions of the participants and led them to focus on the future as best they could. Moreover, the group avoided what some models of bureaucratic behavior would predict: the participants did not act primarily on the basis of bureaucratic interests and ambitions. Both Vaky and Bowdler opposed their superiors at State; Aaron disagreed with Brzezinski; McGiffert supported a different option from the one favored by his Defense Department colleague, General Smith. And Vance and Brzezinski, then locked in struggle over the future course of policy toward the Soviet Union, agreed easily on Nicaragua.

After the meeting, Vaky turned to drafting a decision memorandum for the president. The fact that he rather than Pastor was writing it represented a minor bureaucratic victory for the State Department. In addition to trying to check the drift in 1977 and most of 1978 toward more and more meetings being held under NSC chairmanship, State had objected to the procedure in which an NSC staff member summarized for the president all choices emerging from interagency meetings. If State chaired a meeting, it wanted to summarize it as well, to be sure everyone's views were fully represented. The NSC staff would always see such memoranda; it was not clear to a suspicious State Department that it would always see the NSC staff's summaries before they went to the president.

In this case, however, Pastor was wired into the department through Vaky and through Oxman in Christopher's office, and he helped write the memorandum. Christopher thought Vaky's initial draft was too negative in its lengthy treatment of the plebiscite option -— he called it "advocacy rather than analysis" — and had Oxman work with Vaky to cut it back to a page and a half in what finally turned out to be an eight-page memo from Vance to Carter. Oxman and Pastor worked together in drafting the arguments for option one: the plebiscite. Vaky wrote the case for option two: a "démarche to Somoza and supporting measures, if necessary" (that is, sanctions). No one at the PRC meeting had spoken in favor of the third option — throwing up our hands and distancing ourselves from the problem — but it too was included.

The memorandum, dated November 14, was typical of such policy papers. Each option was described in practical terms: for the first option, the paper described how the negotiating group would propose a plebiscite and how it might respond to the possible reactions of Somoza and the FAO. The second option contained the talking points Bowdler would use in an approach to Somoza asking for his resignation and listed the sanctions to be taken if he refused. Following the description of each option was a concise list of the arguments for and against it.

When the memorandum arrived at the White House, Pastor covered it with a note from Brzezinski to the president recommending the plebiscite option. Vance had made no recommendation, perhaps out of respect for the position of his subordinates, Vaky and Bowdler. But when the president telephoned him to discuss the issue, he too supported the plebiscite. The president directed that Bowdler first try to convince his fellow mediators, and then the FAO and Somoza. In a brief meeting with Carter before returning to Nicaragua, a meeting that would strengthen his hand there by giving him the president's firsthand authority, Bowdler saw little point in trying to argue the president out of his decision.

Bowdler and Vaky were deeply discouraged by the road on which they had been set. Vaky considered resignation but like Bowdler decided to carry on. "It's the way you conduct business," Bowdler says. "If you're a good soldier you go ahead and carry out a decision the very best you can, within the limits of your instructions." They had done their best in arguing for an alternative. Now, if they resigned, would others do better at making the policy work? As Bowdler flew back to Managua, he had real doubts about his chances for putting all the pieces together. Even if he persuaded his fellow mediators to go along with the plebiscite idea, how could he deliver both the FAO, which already opposed it, and Somoza, when Washington insisted that the plebiscite be a referendum on his rule?

Yet during the next six weeks, Bowdler almost pulled it off. Less than a week after his return to Nicaragua, he had convinced the other members of the team that they should go along with revising Somoza's plebiscite idea. Working together, they produced the outline of a compromise proposal. Each side reacted at first with suspicion, but by December 6, after the mediators offered further clarifications and amplifications of their proposal, both accepted the proposed framework and agreed to negotiate the details of a plebiscite. Furthermore, Somoza lifted the state of siege and offered his opponents a general amnesty.

In Washington there was a mood of optimism. On December 7 and again on December 9, President Carter was upbeat in his public comments, referring to "remarkably good progress" and to the American role in helping "to shift the Nicaraguan circumstance from active and massive bloodshed and violence into a negotiation."[4] Both *The New York Times* and *The Washington Post* published editorials praising American diplomacy in Nicaragua.

In Havana the Sandinistas showed that they, too, were watching — and were worried by — the progress being made. At the urging of Fidel Castro, leaders of the three FSLN factions issued a "unity statement" and again rejected "the imperialist mediation." They were uniting, they said, "in order to guarantee that the heroic struggle of our people not be stolen by the machinations of Yankee imperialism."[5]

Somoza even seemed to be flirting with the idea of a negotiated solution. Through his cousin, Luis Pallais, Somoza asked Bowdler whether, if he were to leave Nicaragua, the American government would grant him asylum, assure him that he would not be extradited back to Nicaragua, and guarantee that his assets would not be seized. Bowdler sent an urgent query to Washington and in a few days received a reply: yes with regard to asylum, but only maybe concerning extradition and Somoza's assets. Couched in legal terms, the reply clearly had not been carefully thought through in terms of its political implications.

Vaky had made a rare mistake. He was later to wish that he had recognized the opportunity Somoza's inquiry presented to engage him in bargaining over the terms of his departure, playing on the dictator's most profound concern: his own physical and financial well-being. Vaky was preoccupied with the formal negotiations and other matters, and the noise level of other events led him to miss what he now concedes might have been a signal from Somoza. When he saw that the issue turned on questions of American law, he simply forwarded Bowdler's cable to the department's lawyers for a draft reply. Pastor was not told of the cable or its response.*

The FAO's decision to consider a plebiscite and to negotiate directly with Somoza's representatives had brought with it important political costs, however: four of its member groups, including Los Doce, had resigned. One critic said this left the Broad Opposition Front — the FAO — "neither a front, nor broad, nor opposed to imperialism."[6]

The first meeting between the committees representing the FAO and Somoza's PLN took place on December 8 at the Dominican Republic's embassy in Managua. It was followed by five more meetings during the next twelve days. At each session the mediators — usually one of Bowdler's two associates — would present an agenda and some kind of working document as a basis for discussion. For the last meeting, on December 20, they presented a more detailed *acta-compromiso,* which sought to bridge the differences between the two sides regarding the conditions under which a plebiscite might be held and — a more difficult problem — the actions to be taken by each side should it lose. The FAO insisted that if Somoza lost, he would have to quit the country. Somoza (through the PLN negotiators) was equally insistent that if he won, the FAO must join his government. The FAO, recognizing that this would be political suicide, refused to make such an unusual commitment. The mediators' compromise granted Somoza some of his points about the conditions under which a plebiscite might be held but suggested that in the event of the FAO's losing, it

---

*Bowdler's cable and the department's reply remain highly classified, and it is hard to determine exactly how the reply was drafted and authorized. Pallais has told Pastor that he flew to Washington to present Somoza's questions directly to Vaky. This does not square with Vaky's recollections or those of Bowdler and Vaky's deputy in the Latin American bureau, John Bushnell, who believe Pallais was confusing this with other trips he made to Washington.

would not have to join the government. It would instead play the role of a loyal opposition.

The meetings might not have been producing agreement, but that they were taking place at all was encouraging, a tribute to the skill and persistence of Bowdler and his colleagues. The mediators began their days at around 8:30 A.M., when they discussed the negotiating session for that day or, if there were none, began drafting the next paper to be presented to the two sides. Obiols, the Guatemalan, did much of the writing.

Negotiating sessions, first with each of the two sides, then with both, ran from about 10 to noon or so, then from around 2 until early evening. The October meetings with the FAO had taken place in a room provided by Archbishop Obando y Bravo; meetings with Somoza and his representatives had been held in Somoza's headquarters. Now, in December, the direct negotiations were held on neutral ground, at the mediators' embassies. As in most negotiations, there were opportunities for private talk before each formal meeting and during coffee breaks. It is often in such "corridor conversations" that one finds the hints dropped, the ostensibly personal thoughts revealed, that can lead to progress. The mediators chatted with the Nicaraguans about this and that in order to warm the atmosphere. If a member of the FAO was balking on a particular point, a mediator would draw him aside for a pep talk. The Dominican admiral was especially good at banter with the Nicaraguan military officers in Somoza's entourage.

A member of Bowdler's team — Cheek, Barnaby, or another — took notes at each negotiating session. In the evenings they repaired to the embassy to cable Washington. If they were at a particularly tricky point in the talks or if Bowdler thought he was pushing the limit of his broad instructions, he would call Vaky to discuss the problem.

Ambassador Solaun did not try to become part of the negotiations. Bowdler had discouraged this by pointing out that if Solaun were to attend, the Guatemalan and Dominican ambassadors would have to be invited as well. There is no set pattern for whether or not an American ambassador is included in talks being held by an envoy from Washington. When Henry Kissinger first met secretly with representatives of North Vietnam in Paris in 1969, the talks were arranged by the French government. The French knew about them, the Vietnamese knew, but Kissinger did not want the State Department to know, and so went to some lengths to keep the American embassy in Paris in the dark on what was said. On the other hand, Bowdler, when he had been American ambassador to South Africa, was included in most of the negotiating sessions over Namibia during the Carter administration. Now, Bowdler did not want to cut the embassy in Managua completely out, and so on most evenings he described the day's events to the ambassador and his senior staff and sought their advice on issues about which the embassy had particular information. Finally, after the reporting cable had been sent, any telephone call to Washington made, and the embassy briefed, Bowdler could return to his hotel for the night.

Every negotiation has its own rhythm. By December 20, Bowdler and Vaky knew that the talks between the FAO and PLN were coming to a head. If the *acta-compromiso* could not bridge the gap, the going would be very difficult. So when Bowdler took his seat at the sixth of the direct talks between the two sides, held at six P.M. that day at the American embassy, he did so with considerable anticipation. It was immediately clear, however, that all the work of the previous six weeks was imperiled.

First, the two sides could not agree on the minutes of the previous meeting. The mediators next moved on to the central business of the day, presentation of the *acta-compromiso,* which they had decided to present orally first, for emphasis. But as the Dominican, Admiral Jiménez, proceeded to read it aloud, Somoza's representatives began to interrupt with legalistic comments that were not only hostile but rude. (In its formal report, the mediation team was to put this more diplomatically, referring to the PLN representatives' "inconsiderate manner.") The session was adjourned without any serious give-and-take. The two sides took copies of the draft compromise and promised to respond in writing.

Bowdler was furious. Especially in diplomacy, genius is primarily patience, and it had taken all of Bowdler's considerable genius to bring the talks this far. Now, for the first time, he lost patience. The Nicaraguan foreign minister was leading the PLN delegation, and Bowdler spoke sharply to him, in a way he had never before used to address someone of that rank. The mediators and Washington were serious about the effort, he said, and it was about time the PLN stopped raising issues that seemed designed to defeat it.

Patience was wearing thin in Washington as well. It was time to take another run at Somoza, and General Dennis McAuliffe, the commander in chief of the U.S. Southern Command in Panama, was authorized to join Bowdler for a meeting with the dictator on December 21. Perhaps a military man could help impress the seriousness of the situation on Somoza, himself a former student at West Point. The authorizing cable from the State Department included talking points that suggested telling Somoza that there was no precedent anywhere for his demand that a defeated opposition join his government. Unless there were a rapid, successful conclusion to the talks, Bowdler could tell Somoza, "You can expect relations between our two governments will be strongly affected" — strong words for a diplomat.

At the meeting with Somoza, McAuliffe was blunt. "The reason that I'm here," he said, "is that we perceive that the cooperation you have given to the negotiating team is no longer evident. . . . We on the military side of the U.S. recognize . . . that peace will not come to Nicaragua until you have removed yourself from the presidency and the scene."[7] Somoza responded that there would be no problem if a plebiscite were organized along "traditional lines." And indeed, there never had been a problem with such "traditional" elections — at least insofar as the Somozas' hold on power was concerned.

What the Americans did not know was that after some weeks of indecision, Somoza had just decided not to go along with the revised plebiscite. His advisers had convinced him that he would lose a free election, and at a meeting with his cabinet the decision had been taken to string out the negotiations rather than simply reject the mediators' proposal.[8] So on December 21, the PLN sent the team a "preliminary response" attacking the *acta-compromiso* but promising a counterproposal. On the same day, the FAO notified the mediators of its acceptance of their plan.

The PLN behavior at the December 20 meeting had led Bowdler's colleagues to the same conclusion he had reached: the mediation had hit a wall. After receiving the PLN and FAO replies, the mediators went home for Christmas. The hopes of early December had nearly flickered out, and none of the negotiators really expected to return to Managua.

On December 26, Bowdler attended another PRC meeting in Washington at which the assumption, encouraged by Vaky and Bowdler, was that the mediation effort was finished. The discussion simply focused on how, not whether, to implement sanctions designed to force Somoza's acceptance of a fair plebiscite. On December 27, President Carter decided the sanctions should be phased so each succeeding step would have its maximum psychological effect. But the plan would only go into effect after Somoza had made his counterproposal.

As it happened, the cable reporting the new PLN position arrived that same day and went directly to the president, who found it more reasonable than did any of his advisers. Somoza objected to foreign supervision of the plebiscite as an infringement of Nicaraguan sovereignty. The president was sympathetic to this argument, and noted his reaction in the margin of the cable. Carter's advisers, more sensitive to the history of the Somozas' abuse of national elections, were not attracted by the PLN proposal of a national plebiscitary authority that could run the election. It was Pastor who came up with a way to try to finesse Somoza. Why not accept Somoza's idea, he suggested, but couple the national authority with an international group that would oversee the Nicaraguan body's work and mediate any problems that arose?

By January 5, Carter and Vance had agreed to this suggestion. The next day, Bowdler met with an FAO representative in Washington. When the Nicaraguan accepted the new formula, Bowdler asked the other mediators to join him in resuming the effort. The team met in the Dominican Republic to develop responses to Somoza's criticisms of their approach and to draft a paper (dated January 12) that presented the new compromise. Returning to Managua, they gave the proposal to Somoza and sent copies of their documents to the FAO. On January 18, Somoza's reply came in a note from the PLN. After once again attacking the *acta-compromiso*, the note concluded: "We reiterate the terms of our counterproposal of last December 26." As Vaky and Bowdler had surmised, Somoza had no intention of accepting a real compromise.

The mediation effort was clearly dead. The next day it was buried by an FAO statement that pronounced the negotiations closed. A frustrated William Bowdler made one last call on Somoza to tell him the team was prepared to return to Managua if the government decided to accept its proposal, and then he and his colleagues departed.

In Washington, Bowdler attended a January 26 meeting of the PRC at which the discussion was almost perfunctory. Christopher, Brzezinski, and the other senior officials were preoccupied by the crisis in Iran and the imminent visit to Washington of Deng Xiaoping, the Chinese vice-premier. There was agreement that sanctions must be imposed against Somoza, and that they should be both military and political. The economic aid program would be left relatively unscathed, largely because of the efforts of Congressman Charles Wilson. The Texas Democrat had informed the administration that if it further cut economic aid to Nicaragua, he would use his position on the House Appropriations Committee to attack the administration's foreign aid bill. There was also the fear that imposing full sanctions would remove future leverage with Somoza. So the meeting quickly concluded that the American military group in Managua would be withdrawn; that the already-suspended military assistance program would be terminated; that although current aid projects would be continued, the only new economic aid would go to projects that directly served the poor; that all Peace Corps volunteers would be brought home; and that the size of the embassy in Managua would be halved.

If the PRC meeting of November 13 had been a model of its kind, the meeting of January 26 was not. Everyone agreed with Secretary of Defense Harold Brown when he said that the longer Somoza stayed in power, the better were the chances that the Sandinistas would succeed him. But no one had much taste for trying to design a new strategy. The four options prepared for the meeting broke no new ground, and no bright ideas about Nicaragua leaped to minds now focused on other areas of the world. Nor did it seem urgent that a new policy be designed. Stansfield Turner, the CIA director, estimated that the chances were better than fifty-fifty that Somoza would remain in power until 1981. The National Guard, he said, had been strengthened; the Sandinistas were preparing for a long-term struggle.

And so, disappointed at the failure of the mediation and preoccupied with other issues, the Carter administration's senior policy makers used the sanctions against Somoza as a punctuation to their own attention to Nicaragua — at least for the next few months. The Nicaraguan whale was sounding again.

Pete Vaky was tired, disappointed, and rather angry. He agreed that sanctions against Somoza were the proper next step, but he knew they were little more than a statement of American disapproval. He saw trouble coming, but was not sure when it would come or how to prevent it. Even if the mediation effort had gotten further than Vaky had predicted in September, he could see that it had also produced one of the things he had most feared: the political exposure and weakening of the moderate opposition to Somoza. Yes, the mediation had brought together those moderates who participated, but as Vaky was later to argue in congressional hearings, "one of the agonizing things that the mediation process did was to bring people out whom you would not have thought would oppose the regime. People of the establishment, businessmen and the like, came out and declared their opposition. And they did it on our word that we were trying to resolve the problem."[9] The bitterness of the moderates was expressed by one of the FAO leaders, Alfonso Robelo, in March 1979: "First the U.S. came and told everyone that they would put pressure on Somoza to go. They created false expectations. When Somoza's reaction was to say, 'Come and do it physically,' they backed down. . . . It has a boomerang effect on the civil opposition, on the U.S. image."[10] In Nicaraguan eyes, the American *deus ex machina* had returned to the Nicaraguan scene in September but once again had not performed in godlike fashion. In addition, increased violence was likely, and now that the peace effort was sidetracked, it could spill over into neighboring countries.

Vaky was frustrated by the decisions of his superiors and by their refusal to accept his counsel. He knew they faced other, apparently larger, challenges in Iran and elsewhere (the Ayatollah Khomeini was returning to a turbulent Iran during this period) and he knew that senior officials had had legitimate reasons to oppose simply removing Somoza. Still, in his view they had failed to understand the realities of Nicaragua. He was particularly dismayed when, on January 31, President Carter made a notation on a letter from Congressman John Murphy that many of the New York Democrat's arguments in favor of Somoza's negotiating position seemed to make sense. Did the president not understand that the mediation was over? Robert Pastor quickly found a way to bring Carter up to date,[11] but for Vaky it was a frustrating reminder that an issue that meant so much to him was not near the top of the agenda at the highest levels of the government. And it was soon to subside further, almost completely out of sight.

NINE

State: The Press Briefing Room

WHEN THE NOON HOUR ARRIVED ON FEBRUARY 8, 1979, Hodding Carter III hurried to a windowless room on the second floor of New State to preside over the daily press corps briefing. As he walked, he thought about the items that might come up. One he knew about: today he would announce the sanctions the United States was imposing against Somoza for his refusal to compromise and allow a fair plebiscite to take place.

Every weekday, unless he was relieved by one of his deputies, Carter spent the midday hour playing matador with reporters, trying to guide them in certain directions and neatly sidestepping when they came too close to information he did not wish to share. On a bad day, a press spokesman could feel more as if he were running the streets of Pamplona than performing like Manolete. But Carter had very few bad days and was respected by the reporters for his willingness to work close to the horns of truth — to reveal as much as he could, to convey accurately the thinking of senior officials, and to engage in the give-and-take that could provide the snappy quotes so necessary to a good story. George Gedda, an Associated Press reporter who has been going to State Department briefings since 1968, calls Carter one of the truly excellent State Department spokesmen he has observed.

Carter's demeanor is one of contrasts. His bearing recalls his service as a Marine lieutenant in the late 1950s, yet his love of

political banter and storytelling is that of a Southern country gentle-
man–politician. His straight dark hair and prominent features give
his face a stern look — until one of his frequent hard laughs breaks
its planes. In 1977, a rookie, he was understandably cautious,
even stiff in his briefings. After graduating summa cum laude from
Princeton in 1957 and serving in the Marines, Carter had gone
to work for *The Delta Democrat-Times,* his family's newspaper
in Greenville, Mississippi.

During his eighteen years on the paper as reporter, editorial
writer, and editor, he received national attention for his journalism,
for his promotion of civil rights, and for his work for the Democratic
party. His participation in the 1976 presidential campaign of Jimmy
Carter (no relation) had led to an unexpected request from Cyrus
Vance that he become the spokesman for the new secretary of
state. It took a year or so for Carter to feel confident of his knowledge
of international issues, but he conducted his daily briefings firmly,
if cautiously. He knew it would be fatal to show fear or confusion
before the press. The key to the success of any spokesman, he
says, is that "you treat the reporters with the respect due to professionals doing their job and demand that they treat you with the
same respect. They can smell either contempt or fear."

By his second year in the job, Carter felt enough confidence to
let himself go, to be the Southern politician as well as the Marine.
He came to enjoy "the combat of give-and-take" and the banter
that could relieve a tense moment or suddenly put a reporter on
the defensive. The banter was effective but also dangerous. A hasty
remark could lead to disaster if taken by a reporter as a personal
attack. A bit of lighthearted irony, if printed as a serious remark,
could make Carter seem foolish. But Carter speaks for reporters
as well as for himself when he says that unless a spokesman is
prepared to mix it up a bit, briefings become sterile and serve
neither the press nor the department well. And George Gedda speaks
for most of his fellow reporters when he says that a good newsman's
only purpose is to get good stories, to push the spokesman but
not to embarrass him.

Carter bore an unusual responsibility for a State spokesman, but one that became a special strength for him. Secretary Vance did not enjoy dealing with the press and seldom provided the sharp-edged statements that make good copy. So during Vance's tenure, reporters were especially dependent on Carter to provide insights into the secretary's thinking. In private conversations with reporters and in formal briefings, Carter was keenly aware of his responsibility for portraying Vance's views and for defending the secretary from the oblique attacks that occasionally came his way from the NSC staff at the White House.

The February 8 briefing came at a particularly difficult time be-cause an unusually large number of stories were breaking that required comment by the State Department: the visit to Washington of Chinese Vice-Premier Deng Xiaoping; tensions on the Sino-Viet-namese border; the arrival in Teheran of the Ayatollah Khomeini and the imminent fall of the moderate Iranian premier Shahpour Bakhtiar; and a touchy argument with the Israelis over human rights in the occupied territories. In addition, reporters were in hot pursuit of a story, unhappily accurate, that President Carter had two days earlier called all of the department's assistant secretar-ies (including Hodding Carter) to the White House to berate them for recent leaks on Iran. The president had icily threatened to fire any assistant secretary whose bureau seemed responsible for future leaks, whether or not he or she was directly responsible.

So Hodding Carter knew this was going to be an especially tough session with the press. Even the small, airless briefing room seemed to reflect the tough neighborhood he worked. Although the televised pictures may show a spokesman discoursing authorita-tively in front of the seal of the department and a blue and gold map of the world, the off-camera reality is grubby. The worn yellow carpet in the room is badly stained, as are the walls. The fifty or so reporters sit at long semicircular tables of plastic wood veneer. A notice on the wall asks reporters not to remove chairs from the room. One wonders why they would want to do so, since the chairs too are plastic.

The February 8 briefing began, as Carter had feared it would, with almost acrimonious fencing about the president's meeting with the State Department officials. The reporters knew, of course, that the future of American relations with China was probably more important to the well-being of humankind than the president's relations with the State Department, but Washington turmoil makes news, and State–White House conflict is a traditional favorite. The irritated press spokesman did all he could to deflect the reporters from the story, calmly refusing to describe or comment on the meeting with the president yet unable to deny that it had taken place. The reporters persisted, and after about twenty minutes the briefing verged on the nasty when Carter was asked if he would be remaining in his job. (There had been some talk of resignations.) Like many of his colleagues, Carter had been infuriated by the president's threat, but he limited himself to a flat response: "I am going to be operating in this job."

It was a relief to be able to call on a UPI reporter, Juan Walte, because Carter knew the topic he would raise was Nicaragua. Ever since the January 26 interagency meeting on Nicaragua policy in the wake of the failed mediation, reporters had known the administration was working out the shape of the sanctions it would impose on Somoza. When reporters had asked Carter whether the final decision had been made, Carter had merely responded that various options were under review. Now Walte had been tipped off that Carter was prepared to announce which measures had been selected. The situation was somewhat unusual. Questions were seldom planted at the noon briefing; when the spokesman had something to announce, he normally made his announcement at the beginning of the session. But in this case the department apparently wanted to downplay the story by avoiding a formal announcement, perhaps to try to deflect new attacks on the administration by Somoza's supporters in Congress.

When Carter recognized him, Walte began: "Last week you said that the department was considering a series of options on Nicaragua, and I wonder if that study was completed, and if you have anything on that?"

"Yes," Carter responded as he flipped through a thick notebook, "I do." He went on to outline the measures to be taken — the termination of military aid (which had already been suspended), the suspension (rather than termination) of economic aid except for projects already well under way for aiding the Nicaraguan poor, and the withdrawal of the Peace Corps and a number of embassy personnel. Then, after reviewing the history of the mediation effort, Carter completed his lengthy announcement with a series of policy statements:

> The United States wants to note again its willingness to resume the conciliation efforts should conditions and circumstances warrant.
>
> We hope that efforts to negotiate a peaceful solution to the political crisis can be resumed, and we urge all Nicaraguans to avoid the temptation to seek violent solutions to problems that are best resolved through a national consensus.
>
> We would deplore any outbreak of terrorism or violence emanating from whatever source . . . which would only complicate the task of finding a peaceful solution.
>
> We call upon other governments in the region to avoid contributing to the continuation or spread of violence. We will continue to work closely with the OAS to the end that we can assist in promoting peace, democracy and full respect for human rights in Nicaragua. This has been conveyed to the government in Nicaragua.

"Should conditions and circumstances warrant . . . deplore . . . emanating . . ." — these were hardly words that typically tripped from Carter's tongue when making a point, nor were they phrases that lent themselves to quotes in lively newspaper stories. And they were not, of course, Carter's own words. He was reading his "guidance" on the topic, as the department's spokesman often must. Beside the podium stands a table on which reposes a fat notebook containing his guidances — prepared answers to the forty or so questions he is most likely to receive at the briefing. Tabs allow him to flip quickly to the relevant region or problem.

In his initial statement on Nicaragua, Carter was going to stick close to this particular guidance, not because of an attachment to the elegance of its language but because of his concern about the various audiences interested in what he said and the need to send

exactly the right message to each. The moderate opposition to
Somoza in Nicaragua and, even more, the leaders of Venezuela
and Panama had to be encouraged not to turn to violence now
that the mediation effort had collapsed. The hope, at least, of a
renewed diplomatic effort was therefore included in the statement.
And while the message to Somoza had to be firm, it could not
go so far as to demand his resignation, since that would offer
his friends in Congress ammunition against the administration.
Carter recalls that he had this congressional audience very much
in mind at the briefing, for he often had to answer critics of the administration's human rights policy who accused it of being more
opposed to the Somozas of the right than to the Castros of the
left.

Preparation of the spokesman's guidance is one of the most important and difficult daily State Department chores. It is of course
important for the bureaucrats involved, but it also has significance
for every American, since it is part of a process that decides what
is news, and thus which issues and portrayals of foreign events
will be printed in American newspapers and broadcast to millions
of viewers of television news. The daily news agenda in Washington
is shaped by both the government and the press, and there is much
debate as to which is more powerful. Some argue that the government is dominant, that it manipulates the Washington press corps
through leaks and "spin control." Others believe that television
now controls the process, as politicians and government spokesmen
fight for the exposure that can make them national figures and
dramatize their own special issues.

And yet, for the reporters covering the State Department and
for the officials who deal with them, by far the most important
arbiters of the news agenda are not the television reporters and
editors but *The New York Times* and *The Washington Post.* Although Hodding Carter reviewed a small mountain of articles every
morning, "It was the *Times* and the *Post* that were the real concern.
If they didn't give a story play, it didn't exist."

A reporter such as the AP's George Gedda knows he must pay

attention to any story on the first page of the *Times*. He admires
the *Times* but is also sometimes irritated by its power to shape
his own news agenda. "I sometimes wonder," he says, "why they
make the decisions they do as to what goes on page one. Sometimes
the AP could have the same story, written in the same way, and
not a single paper we serve would use it. But if the *Times* prints
a story on the first page — 'Goldfish sighted off Tierra del Fuego.
Both Chile and Argentina claim jurisdiction' — the AP assignments
editor will be sure to call to make sure I've seen it." Even if his
own editor does not call, Gedda knows that a *Times* or *Post* story
will be brought up by another reporter at the noon briefing and
thus become an issue. Of course, reporters and editors at these
two newspapers are themselves influenced by the wire service and
television stories that were carried the previous afternoon and evening, but a story in the *Times* or *Post* confirms its status as a
leading item.

When Hodding Carter and the public affairs officers for the
department's bureaus arrived at their offices every morning, they
turned first to the *Times* and the *Post,* and then to the wire services
and to summaries of other newspapers and television news broadcasts, scanning them for new items that might be brought up at
the noon briefing. By eight A.M. the spokesman's office had called
each bureau to discuss the preparation of the necessary guidances.
For some stories, the existing guidance would suffice; for others,
a revision or a completely new statement might be needed. In the
bureaus, the public affairs officers would go to the desk officers
for the necessary drafts while Carter proceeded to the Seventh
Floor for his daily 8:00 A.M. meeting with Secretary Vance. There
he would quickly run over the day's most important stories and
get Vance's initial views on how to handle them.

Carter's next few hours were usually taken up with further briefing preparations. He and his staff spent much of the time on the
telephone, pushing bureaus to come up with guidances faster and
trying to resolve disputes among them over questions — like human
rights — that involved more than one bureau. Often the bureaus
would address the easy questions, the ones to which there were

safe and obvious answers, and try to slip past the more controversial points (the guidances, naturally, that Carter most needed).

At midmorning Carter joined a conference call with the press officers at Defense, the CIA, the NSC staff, and the vice-president's office, with White House spokesman Jody Powell presiding. Those involved would compare notes on the day's stories and on their bosses' reactions to them. Powell would then decide which agency would take the lead on each story. Unless a foreign policy story was one on which the White House wanted to get credit for some good news, or unless there was a strong political angle, State generally took the lead and the others would refer reporters there. (Military stories, of course, went to Defense.)

Guidances from each bureau were due by 10:30. Sometimes they were on time; more often, Carter recalls, "There was a hell of a lot more last-minute writing and diddling with clauses and comments than anyone would believe. Which meant that sometimes I wasn't totally up to speed the way I should have been. There wasn't time, at the last minute, to absorb it the way I wanted to. And often, on tricky questions, the bureaus wanted simply to have me give a clenched-teeth answer, saying as little as possible." (In many guidances, the bureaus suggested two answers, the more forthcoming version for use only "if pressed" by reporters.) It was here that Carter did some of his most important work, fighting for more information that could be shared with the press and public, for answers that did not sound as if they were drawn from nineteenth-century diplomatic communiqués.

A later press spokesman, Bernard Kalb, objected also to the predictable style of the bureaus' guidances. He sometimes referred to the Latin American bureau press officer who often was pushing for new denunciations of the Sandinistas as "the representative of the firm of Wanton, Callous, and Cruel." The Near Eastern bureau's constant — and unwarranted — statements of optimism about the Arab-Israeli peace process earned from Kalb the title of "Movement, Motion, and Momentum."

At 11:30, with thirty minutes to go, Carter would meet with Vance or Christopher to review his guidance on the most troublesome questions or — if a guidance was unfinished or so defensive it was useless — to work out a new answer and to find out how far he could go in arguing policy points with reporters. From there it was off to the briefing, with a stop at his office to pick up any last-minute offerings from the bureaus.

The February 8, 1979, guidance on Nicaragua was somewhat unusual because it was the vehicle for initiating a story, though in a low key. The process is generally more reactive than aggressive, one of anticipating the questions reporters are likely to raise but seldom trying to shape the news. As Carter recalls, "Press guidance and press work consisted of *responses* to awkward, unpleasant, disquieting, explosive, unexpected events and attacks on our policies. In retrospect we might say we were trying to put a spin on the ball. But in truth, we were mostly just trying to *catch* it."

Press conferences held by presidents and secretaries of state are usually less defensive than their spokesmen's daily briefings. An effort is made to pick the two or three stories an administration would like to see emerge from such occasions and to prepare a new policy pronouncement or pithy remark for each. But even for press conferences by senior officials, the same sorts of guidances are prepared, usually consisting of a first paragraph designed to remind a president or secretary of the essential facts, followed by points to be made. For example, President Carter was armed with the following "Q and A" for a mid-February 1979 press conference:

Q: What does your administration hope to accomplish through the anti-Somoza measures announced last week?
A: We had hoped that the three-nation negotiating group would help forge an agreement between the Government and opposition forces as a means of reaching a peaceful and democratic solution to that country's political crisis. President Somoza refused to accept the essential elements of the mediators' most recent proposal for a fair plebiscite. Given the prospects for renewed violence and polarization and the deplorable human rights situation as reported by the Inter-American Commission on Human Rights we decided that our relationship with that government would have to change. Accordingly, we have decided to reduce our presence in Nicaragua.

*   *   *

— We hope that Nicaraguans will be able soon to resume efforts to find a peaceful solution to their crisis and that they will resist any temptation to resort to violence.

— We call on other governments to withhold any form of support which could be used to continue or spread violence in Nicaragua. In addition to its toll in human suffering, further violence would severely complicate the task of finding a peaceful solution to the crisis.

— We will continue to work closely with the members of the OAS to promote peace and democracy in Nicaragua and to avoid a widening conflict.

The prospect of a press conference concentrates the mind wonderfully, and senior officials pore over their briefing books no matter how turgid the Q's and A's produced by the bureaucracy. Their advisers know this, and see in the briefing books an opportunity for delicately promoting favored policy approaches. Press conferences are thus policy-making occasions not only in what is said but in the preparations for them.

No president, of course, would speak in the formal style of the Q and A above. President Carter would draw on the guidances to decide on the points he wanted to make but put the answers very much in his own words. Richard Nixon spent hours going over his briefing book, numbering the points he wanted to make in the margins of each guidance. (One could almost see him in his press conferences counting off these points as he made them.) The markings in the books, when returned to the NSC staff, became useful guides to his thinking. President Reagan reportedly practiced his answers with his advisers before going in front of the cameras.

When Hodding Carter finished reading his prepared statement on the sanctions against Somoza, the reporters leaped in. First came a series of questions by Lester Kinsolving, the conservative and contentious columnist whose attacks on the Carter administration and its human rights policies were a regular feature of the noon briefing. Other reporters were often irritated by the time he appropriated to engage Hodding Carter in policy debates, but Carter was not at all dismayed: "Les's early entry was, in some ways, a useful thing," he later noted. "It turned the exercise into a fencing match over ideology, which is always easier for a spokesman than hard questions over concrete particulars." Carter enjoyed the fencing, and had even used Kinsolving occasionally as a straight man. On two occasions he responded to the columnist's salvos by firing back at him a rubber chicken he'd hidden in the podium. Both times, Kinsolving joined the laughter.

"Are you punishing the people of Nicaragua [by suspending most economic aid] because of Somoza's lack of cooperation with the mediation effort?" Carter was asked. No, he replied, for three reasons: first, any economic programs that the United States might aid would depend for their implementation on the flawed Nicaraguan government; second, the situation in the countryside made such aid programs hard to implement in any case; and finally, the attitude of the government in Nicaragua "is in itself going to be or could be a major cause of suffering for the Nicaraguan people." The sanctions were designed to change the government's attitude, and thus help the Nicaraguan people.

But Kinsolving pursued his argument: How could a human rights policy lead to sanctions that cut off economic aid to human beings? "This is the human rights policy of the Carter administration in action, is that correct?" Carter did not want Kinsolving to put words in his mouth or to simplify his statement. And as he later noted, he knew that the best defense was offense: "No. I don't want you to . . . keep repeating what I said, Les. There are three factors in it . . . and you remember what they were, I'm sure."

Kinsolving then shifted the ground of his attack: "Will this same deep concern for human rights be applied to the three million dollars that you are asking the Congress to give to Mozambique, which the *Post* reported this morning has closed down fifteen Catholic, three Presbyterian churches, and the Anglican cathedral? Or is that something different?"

Carter would not be drawn: "The *Post* article obviously is more complex than you just mentioned. I have no comparison to offer you. We are talking about [Nicaragua] right now."

"You don't have any comparison, in other words?"

"No. Not at this time," Carter said, and having given Kinsolving his inning, turned to the other reporters.

At first the press corps tried to get him to go further into the nature of American discussions with Nicaragua's neighbors, or at least to specify which governments we had in mind when we called for restraint. To name them would have irritated the Panamanians and Venezuelans, so he initially deflected the questions by saying "I would not be able to go into that" or by simply repeating that his statement was a "generalized" call for restraint. He was using the passive technique that led one reporter, years later, to character-ize the noon briefings as like "swimming through molasses in search of news."[1]

After a time, however, Carter shifted back to the offense. When a reporter referred to the anti-Somoza activities of Panama and Venezuela, Carter responded: "What I am really interested in always is that superior intelligence and knowledge you have about the absolute actions of other governments. Do you want to claim that?" His questioner did not, and the reporters moved on to the details of the sanctions: How many Peace Corps volunteers would be withdrawn? What was the status of various aid programs? Carter had brought along Jeff Dieterich, the Latin American bureau's public affairs officer, to answer such questions. Twice, when neither Carter nor Dieterich could provide an obscure technical detail, they had to "take" the question, which meant they would provide the answer at a later briefing.

A reporter then tried to steer Carter in a policy direction he did not want to go, asking if his statements did not "call into question" the legitimacy of the Somoza government. With an eye on his pro-Somoza audience in Congress and the criticism that would follow a headline saying the administration was calling for Somoza's resignation, Carter cut him off: "I hope you read my statement very carefully before you run out of here and write a lead that in any way reflects what you just said."

After a few more questions on the nature of the sanctions, the briefing returned to the administration's human rights policy and an argument over whether it focused unfairly on smaller nations. Finally, when asked if the policy had not been "condemned," Carter reached for a concluding point: "The strange thing is the policy is rather universally accepted by people. Whether the governments always like it or not is not necessarily the same thing, unless we assume that all governments speak for the people." The reporters had heard the arguments on human rights before and knew that Carter would neither volunteer nor be trapped into giving them a one-liner on a Nicaraguan story he seemed determined to treat carefully. It was time to move on to a new topic, the dangerous situation along the northern border of Vietnam: "Before I came in here," a reporter said, "I read the UPI ticker, and as I read it, China has gone to war with Vietnam." "My God!" Carter replied, getting a tension-breaking laugh before taking up his next topic.

The discussion of Nicaragua had been rather "sterile," as Carter later put it, because he had wanted it to be. But the reporters had gotten what they most needed from the briefing: an authoritative statement of American policy and a sense of how important this and other news items might be when they decided on their lead stories for the day. For most stories, the briefing is only a starting point. The articles are put together during the afternoon as reporters check with their sources to get more facts and to pursue angles the spokesman refused to explore. As George Gedda puts it, "After the briefing you start calling people to get the between-the-lines version, because that's not the version you get from the podium."

A graduate of Southern Methodist University, where he majored in journalism, Gedda had become interested in Latin America during a stint in the Peace Corps. He went to Washington in 1968 to cover stories relating to the region, and was assigned to the State Department as a general reporter in 1975. Gedda was tremendously impressed by Secretary of State Henry Kissinger, by his ability to "explain the way the world works" and — especially — by the shrewd way he could make news. "When Kissinger gave a news conference," Gedda says, "it was a given that there would be an obvious story. Reporters get nervous when Ronald Reagan or

George Shultz holds a news conference and after forty-five minutes they still don't know what their lead is."

Gedda is moderately conservative on some issues, unlike most of his colleagues, who are probably moderately liberal or simply moderate. But as all reporters should be, Gedda is more a skeptic than a believer in ideologies. It is this pragmatic skepticism that made most of the State Department press corps unenthusiastic about ideological policy pronouncements in the early years of both the Carter and Reagan administrations. Gedda, however, would seldom argue policy with department officials. He wanted accurate stories, and to get them he needed sources, people who would either provide information or steer him in the right direction.

After lunch, Gedda would start making calls and visiting officials. (His lunch was usually eaten in the State Department cafeteria or at his desk. Stories of reporters regularly lunching at fancy French restaurants are, he says, for the most part "baloney, which is the kind of sandwich I usually brought to work.") The key to developing his sources was trust — trust that he knew an issue and would get the story straight, and more important, trust that he would protect his sources, revealing their names neither in his stories nor to other people.

Real leaks were rare, although occasionally a State Department official would slip a reporter a piece of classified or personal information — a hot cable, a draft policy paper, a negotiating position. Once, in 1978, an options paper on Nicaragua appeared in the newspapers within a few hours of its discussion at an interagency meeting in the department. Such leaks usually came from political appointees and the more ideological of Foreign Service officers locked in policy struggle with each other. Gedda found few of these leaks in the Carter administration — certainly fewer, he says, than in the administration that followed it. Much more often, he and his colleagues got their stories by calling officials and asking to drop in on them for twenty minutes or so to make sure an article was accurate. It was very rare that officials would give or show a reporter a classified document, but they would occasionally read passages from one, perhaps paraphrasing to skip over the most sensitive terms and to fuzz the origin of the reporter's information.

Some department officials simply refused to see reporters, fearing that if they were revealed as sources, they were likely to be excluded from meetings and in the long run would damage their careers.

Warren Christopher recalls that though he saw reporters, he was very careful in his dealings with them. He, however, had a different reason: he was concerned that if he was often quoted in the newspapers, he might seem to other officials to be trying to serve his own ego, and it was his job, as Vance's deputy, to serve the secretary with an unobtrusive public profile.

Most officials at the middle and top reaches of the department will try to be cautiously helpful to reporters, for important reasons. In the most elevated terms, it is their responsibility. As Frank McNeill, a former deputy assistant secretary in the Latin American bureau puts it, "Access to information is essential to a democratic American society." McNeill once was burned when he answered a reporter's call at 3 A.M. and sleepily used a phrase that, when printed, irritated a foreign government. But his mistake, he says, was in how he responded, not in taking the call.

Officials usually speak to reporters in order to explain, defend, and promote the policies on which they are working. For their part, many reporters are adept at pretending they already have more of a story than they actually do, dropping a fact here and there to imply knowledge of many more, and thus luring an official to go farther than he otherwise would in discussing details. Nevertheless, the official may wish to do this even when he suspects he is being led on, for it is in the interest of the government that the reporter not go off in an inaccurate, even damaging direction.

There are also personal reasons for officials to talk to reporters, motives the reporters can play on. To appear ignorant about a question is also to appear powerless. It suggests that you are not a part of the action, not a player, and in Washington, the perception of weakness can soon produce the reality. So some officials may unintentionally mislead reporters by trying to confirm or elaborate on stories about which they are not, in fact, well informed. In addition, reporters can sometimes stimulate a response from an official by quoting other, usually unnamed colleagues in an attack on the official's own views, performance, or institution. From the earliest days of the Carter administration, reporters carried barbed comments back and forth between political appointees at State and at the White House. "They are saying, at the NSC staff, that you at State are recommending a passive policy on X, that you are disregarding Soviet meddling on Y, that the success on Z was originally their idea and Vance opposed it." Or: "Over at State they are saying that you are going off half-cocked on X, that you are seeing Soviets under the bed on Y, which will only build up the Soviets in Third World eyes, that Z was State's idea." It was hard for officials on either side of the bureaucratic divide to resist defending themselves, and when some succumbed to this, the defensive comments by each side were seen as offensive by the other.

Who started the sniping? Each side believed it was the other, and at State, Vance tried unsuccessfully to put a stop to it. But reporters loved the conflict. It produced Washington gossip of the kind their editors and readers wanted, and it also provided a way for reporters to smoke out comments on the substance of an issue. At the White House, Brzezinski discouraged his staff from seeing reporters, and Pastor, for one, had his own reasons for worrying about his ability to remain anonymous. State Department officials, he thought, could speak more safely on background since there were many possible sources at State. But an article on Latin America that reflected the NSC's point of view would be blamed on him as the only staff member responsible for that region, especially since Brzezinski was not deeply involved in those issues.

Pastor paid a price for his reticence. He still recalls with some anger that after his first few months at the NSC staff, he started to get bad press. He was portrayed in some stories as a dangerous left-winger and in others as standing at the right end of the ideological spectrum, with Brzezinski. For this he blames the Latin American bureau (before Assistant Secretary Vaky took over). Instead of defending himself with reporters and giving them a sense of his views, he tried to get friendly officials at State to put a stop to it.

The response, he says, would be: "I talked to so-and-so, and he denies ever having said those things."

Did the bad press bother him? "Yes," Pastor says, "enormously. It always does hurt. And the worst part was how others at the NSC staff would do no more than laugh sympathetically about it if they themselves were not under attack. I would ask if I could respond to the charges, and Brzezinski would simply say I should shake it off. . . . More recently, I was telling a friend, a television newsman, how vulnerable one feels to the press. I said that one of the nice things about being out of government now is that I don't have to pick up *The Washington Post* in the morning, scared of finding my name and feeling like I'm going to throw up. He said that as a reporter, 'We *hoped* government officials would leaf through the papers and throw up.' "

By generally refusing to defend himself with reporters, Pastor missed an opportunity to get his side of the story across, and much more. It is a sad but not surprising fact that reporters are likely to be gentler with their sources than with those who do not talk to them. Indeed, it can be dangerous for an official to emerge too favorably in a hot story because his superiors may conclude that it was he who was the leaker. For the newspaper reader curious about the source of a story, the first question should be, Who will profit from it, either by being favorably portrayed or through the promotion of policies he favors?

There are many reasons, then, for officials to talk to newsmen, and most senior State Department officials saw reporters several times a week. The trick was to know — or learn — *how* to talk to them. First, in any talk with a reporter, it was important to establish ground rules. Few officials would speak on the record, which means that a reporter can use everything that is said and quote the source by name. This would be too dangerous and too inhibiting. (If all interviews were on the record, most officials would mouth mush and there would be few stories worth printing.) Reporters, on the other hand, do not like interviews off the record, because this means they cannot use the information given in the interview, much less cite a source, unless they can get it somewhere else. Nor will most reporters accept a ground rule once known as the

Lindley Rule for its inventor, Ernest K. Lindley, a former adviser to Secretary of State Dean Rusk. Under this rule, a reporter could use the information he was given but without attribution. This made the reporter highly vulnerable, since if he was misled it was only his own reputation for veracity that would suffer, a situation hardly likely to encourage scrupulous honesty among the officials he interviewed.

In general, therefore, officials and reporters meet under cover of some sort of "background." The reporter may use whatever information he is given in a background interview but may not name his source (or sources; on reputable newspapers, reporters must confirm their facts with more than one source). Instead of naming the source, the reporter describes him: "According to a State Department official . . ." The deeper the background, the more general the description: "According to a government official . . ." or "According to an informed American source . . ."

A second consideration for an official speaking with reporters was the audiences that would be reading his comments — foreign governments, members of Congress, interest groups, American voters, his own colleagues and superiors. What pleased one set of readers might well offend another, and responsible officials, especially in the ever-cautious State Department, try not to displease *anyone*. Hence the very careful nature of interviews, even on background, and the concomitant frustration of State Department correspondents.

There is also a problem in discussing potentially sensitive facts with a reporter. It is not always clear what is classified and what is not, since not all the information in a classified document is sensitive, and there may be a fine line between leaking new information and explaining facts the reporter already has. Most officials try not to cross the line of the permissible, however finely drawn it might be. For Paul Kreisberg, the deputy director of the policy planning staff, the rule was to explain what *had* happened and *why* a policy decision had been reached — the thinking that lay behind it — but not to get into current policy deliberations or intentions.

Finally, there was the tricky question of what to do when confronted by reporters with calumny from unnamed but probably identifiable colleagues. Many people at the Carter State Department and NSC staff refused to respond in kind to such attacks. Others could not resist. The former were probably the wiser, for in the end the internecine wars under Carter, like those of other administrations, grievously injured the participants and their president. In Walt Disney's *Bambi,* the mother of the rabbit Thumper was wise when she said, "If you can't say something nice, don't say anything at all." But she was, after all, only a rabbit, and a boring one at that.

Often, after the noon briefing had ended, Hodding Carter would go to the department cafeteria with a group of reporters for informal background discussions. He would then return to his office to attend to the chores of running the department's Bureau of Public Affairs, which churns out responses to most of the mail from the public, provides State Department speakers for groups requesting them, and organizes conferences on topics of departmental interest. Throughout the afternoon and into the evening he would get calls from reporters about stories they were pursuing, though at night most press inquiries could be handled by one of the bureau's duty officers.

For George Gedda and the other reporters covering the department, Hodding Carter was seldom the primary background source for a story. He knew about policy, but it was the desk officers and assistant secretaries who knew the details and who might go farther with trusted reporters than Carter did. Once Gedda had talked to such officials and was satisfied that he had his facts right, he would go to his desk in the State Department press room, a bullpen where the reporters sit in small cubicles to pound out their stories. Sitting at his computer, Gedda would call up from an information bank any related stories filed by AP in the last fifteen hours, in case his account was better as an insert to an existing piece than as a separate story. He would then write his copy, making sure the first paragraph could stand on its own and stringing out the succeeding paragraphs in descending order of importance, so that if an editor had to cut his story, it would stand up as a whole.

For television reporters such as Richard Valeriani of NBC News, the daily routine was much the same — the morning for reading and deciding on likely stories, with perhaps a call or two to sources; the noon briefing for policy statements and leads; the afternoon for checking sources. By midafternoon Valeriani would also check with his editor in NBC's Washington bureau and suggest the story he wanted to do. If the editor agreed, they would discuss how much airtime the story deserved, and Valeriani would write a script for, say, one and a quarter minutes to at most two and a quarter minutes. The script would be sent through the Washington bureau to the producer of the evening news program in New York. If it was approved there, Valeriani would memorize his remarks — which were never more than two pages long — and, standing in front of the department or in the lobby, with its flags as a backdrop, go before a videotape camera for a "standupper" that was fed directly to the NBC affiliate in Washington and from there to New York.

The taped report was used on the *NBC Nightly News,* but Valeriani remained at the camera site while the program was on the air in case there was a late-breaking development. In that event, he would update his piece or go live. Unlike some of his colleagues, he never taped his remarks in order to prompt himself through a little earphone while repeating the words on camera. For what would happen if a tape failed while he was on camera?

More and more, television news stories require "visuals." It is now usually not enough simply to have the correspondent on camera explaining the story; footage is also needed of the situation itself, either new reporting from abroad or tapes from the files. Half a minute of a government spokesman making a policy pronouncement will do, if nothing more exciting — someone shooting or screaming at someone else in an exotic foreign street — is available. That was why, if Hodding Carter failed to say in thirty usable seconds what the guidance had called for him to say in five minutes, he would be asked to go to the press room during the afternoon to film an appropriately brisk statement for television.

The presence of television cameras at the daily State Department press briefing has been a contentious issue among reporters. It was not until the Carter administration that cameras were allowed, after television correspondents had pressed Secretary Vance. Hodding Carter says that at least until the Iran hostage crisis in 1980, when his statements on the subject appeared almost every evening, he was not terribly aware of the cameras. Indeed, he wishes now that he had paid more attention to them, facing them directly from time to time to get his points across.

Gedda wishes the cameras were not there at all. He prefers the old days, when a spokesman could more easily slip into speaking on background or even off the record from time to time in order to explain the between-the-lines meaning of his guidance. It is difficult for a spokesman to do that when cameras are turning, although he will occasionally take the chance and trust that the footage will not be used, a trust only rarely violated. (Dignity forbids the logical solution — for the spokesman simply to throw his hands up over his face when going off the record.)

This is only one minor complaint among many about the impact of television news on the conduct of American foreign policy. The litany goes like this: Too often, television does not provide analysis of the issues it covers; it forces officials into making hasty statements and entices politicians into uttering simplistic stupidities; it washes dirty bureaucratic linen in public; it distorts the news agenda in Washington. Such charges are heard not only from print journalists, but from former and current government officials.

It is not surprising that television news should receive so much criticism, for it has become tremendously important. In 1984 *each* of the three network news programs reached some ten million to twelve million viewers, far more people than receive *The New York Times, The Washington Post,* and *The Los Angeles Times* combined. The potential of television news broadcasts for good or ill is obviously immense, yet much of the criticism directed at it merely represents the traditional complaints of government officials about the press as a whole. No law requires government officials to provide hasty answers to demanding television reporters, any more than they must rush to accommodate newspaper journalists who also have deadlines. No official is forced to go on *Meet the Press* to dispute his colleagues. To say that television distorts the daily news agenda is simply wrong: even for television reporters and editors, *The New York Times* and *The Washington Post* set the standard for what is news. Within the bureaucracy, although spokesmen have learned to tailor their statements to appeal to television news editors, the answer to the question always asked at government meetings on important issues — how will we deal with the press on this one? — would usually be the same whether or not television news existed.

Yet there *are* important differences between the impact of television news and the influence of newspapers, differences worth examining. First, television has a distorting effect on public debate about issues. To get access to television news (except for programs like *The MacNeil-Lehrer Report*), a political leader must at some point in a speech, press conference, or debate put his case into one short, dramatic "bite" for the cameras. "Bite" takes on a double meaning here, because he is most likely to get airtime if he is savaging an opponent. Nothing makes news like conflict and controversy. Television news broadcasters, then, in order to be fair — and they are extraordinarily careful to be evenhanded, more so than many newspapers — will show a similarly brief, hard-hitting rebuttal by the other side. The result is that the nuances of a middle way are lost: the public is encouraged to believe that the only choice is between two competing views. Just as bad, officials can be seduced into believing that their hard-edged view is an absolute truth. Some politicians who run for office without much foreign policy experience learn about international affairs during the campaign, as they and their advisers develop the pithy answers needed for television. They may then take office with thirty-second bites masquerading in their minds as policies.

Even more important than its effect on policy debates is the impact of television news on the public's perception of foreign realities. There is evidence that many viewers fog out when confronted with television news stories in which they have little interest.

A poll conducted one evening in 1979, just after a segment on a meeting between President Carter and German Chancellor Schmidt, showed that almost half the viewers did not remember seeing the story at all, and few of the others recalled the details.[2]

It is probably not a case, however, of in one eye and out the other. The *images* of the world conveyed in television news segments are almost certainly retained by the viewer. Those images, after all, are chosen for dramatic effect, and they are usually about people. Indeed, the people often seem to be speaking to each individual viewer, and the viewer responds with feelings of sympathy or hatred, admiration or contempt. Television engages the emotions of its viewers as newspapers seldom can, and thus indelibly paints the images of the world held by millions of Americans.

Though powerful, television faces some difficult problems in making its pictures of the world accurate. For example, it is hard for a television news program consisting only of short segments to make the important connections among issues. Thus, the images retained by the viewer can seem unrelated to each other, the world a still more fragmented and incomprehensible place than it actually is. Another problem is that without visuals, or footage, it is unlikely that a foreign news story will receive the attention it deserves on the evening news. Thus, the sporadic attention given to Soviet brutality in Afghanistan. Or consider the contrast between Vietnam and Laos, in the 1960s and early 1970s. American bombing in South Vietnam aroused the outrage of critics of the war: they could see the horribly burned little girl running down the road toward the camera. Yet the heavy civilian losses from the American bombing of the Plain of Jars in Laos, which produced no film, was never much of an issue. In the mid-1980s, anti-apartheid feeling swept the nation when American television cameras showed South African policemen shooting down black children. In 1986, when the South African government banned coverage of most violent incidents, stories still appeared in our newspapers, but without the visuals public interest in the issue waned.

All of this is exacerbated by the fact that a television picture may convey a single event, yet for the viewer the incident becomes a universal reality. In 1967, when three American C-130 transport planes were loaned to the Congolese government, their pictures filled the screen and made it look as if our whole air force was landing in Africa. The phenomenon can be found repeatedly: in the 1968 Tet attack on the American embassy in Saigon, in the pictures of the starving in Africa, in the images of Iranian or Palestinian thugs denouncing America. The specific is confused with the whole: the viewer comes away with an image of a Third World in which all Muslims are murderous anti-Americans and all Africans are starving mendicants. Yet in most of tragically torn Beirut, normal people go to work in normal jobs. And despite the horrors for Africans forced by drought and famine to rely on foreign relief efforts, most of the people of that continent work hard for a hard but life-sustaining living.

The television news pictures of an inchoate, dramatic, dangerous, even hostile world does not do much to draw American viewers into its affairs. Is it surprising that in 1980, when many of us saw and heard Iranians screaming abuse at America, their shouts seemed to be directed at us personally? The reaction was to want to scream back, to show them that America still could talk tough even if we could not get back at them in the safety of Teheran. And wasn't it natural also to be repelled by a world with such people? Too often, the contradictory impulses engendered by television's pictures of the more dramatic events in the world are bellicosity mixed with fear of involvement, or compassion for the starving tinged with a sense of helplessness.

Hodding Carter's policy statement about Nicaragua on February 8, 1979, was not particularly dramatic and received little television coverage. The next day, although his announcement made the front page of *The Washington Post,* the major headlines were devoted to the Sino-Vietnamese border dispute, events in Iran, and U.S. relations with China. *The New York Times* ran a short piece about the announcement on page seven. A number of newspaper reports on the subject noted that Panama and Venezuela would likely consider the sanctions against Somoza a mere slap on the wrist.

During that briefing on February 8, a reporter had expressed the same point of view, remarking to Hodding Carter that "in effect, you are just throwing in the towel." And in Nicaragua, Somoza may have thought he was in a strong position to shake off the moderate sanctions Washington had imposed. The National Guard had been considerably strengthened since the fighting of the previous autumn, both in its numbers and through large shipments of arms from Argentina, Guatemala, and Israel. Somoza sneered when asked by the Voice of America for his reaction to Washington's sanctions: "Yeah," he said, "how about those jerks?"[3]

TEN

On Capitol Hill

IN WASHINGTON, SOMOZA RELIED ON HIS FRIENDS IN
Congress to moderate the evident hostility of the Carter administra-
tion. In the House of Representatives, he had a core group of
supporters, the self-proclaimed "Dirty Thirty." One of its leaders,
Republican George Hansen of Idaho, denounced the sanctions on
February 21, 1979, in language typical of the group's rhetoric:

> Bullying, intimidation, and coercion have become the tools of
> an immature foreign policy and an inept State Department. . . .
> The reduction of U.S. assistance programs and cutback of Ameri-
> can officials and personnel in Nicaragua may seem like a penalty
> to the disoriented masterminds of our current foreign policy, but
> it must have been a breath of fresh air for President Somoza and
> his people when those pushy gringos left.
> The trouble with Nicaragua, Taiwan, Rhodesia, and many other
> devoted friends of the United States is that they remain loyal and
> anti-Communist in a day when it is stylish to play the kangaroo
> version of Russian roulette called "jump in bed with a Red, Fred."[1]

A few days earlier, however, President Carter had received a letter
from five senators (Kennedy, Cranston, Javits, Sarbanes, and Hat-
field) supporting the sanctions and urging him to take further puni-
tive measures if Somoza remained obdurate.

Such conflicting messages about the sanctions were typical of the role played by Congress during the last years of Somoza's rule. A few dozen supporters of Somoza and a rather smaller number of his critics saw Nicaragua as an important issue and tried to wield what influence they could, but for most members of the Senate and House, the subject was of little concern. There was an occasional vote on Nicaragua in the context of foreign assistance legislation, but no "carrier legislation" forced attention to the issue. The Nicaragua dilemma was not like the Panama Canal treaties, which required every senator to ponder his vote on their ratification or the implementing legislation.

Besides, in these pre-contra days in which Nicaragua was only sporadically a national issue, most members of Congress seldom had to face questions about the issue from constituents or reporters. Indeed, despite the extraordinary proliferation of foreign policy experts on congressional staffs during the 1970s, only a handful of staffers followed the Nicaraguan problem in any detail. No senator or representative can be personally engaged or even knowledgeable about the full range of foreign policy and domestic issues facing the nation, although some — like Congressmen Lee Hamilton and Stephen Solarz — are leading authorities on the full range of American foreign policies. Most pick a few issues on which to try to be expert, and when required to vote on other issues tend to follow the lead of their best-informed ideological allies.

With neither legislation nor headlines forcing congressmen to pay much attention to Nicaragua, the field was left to the most committed of Somoza's enemies and friends. The result was that the administration was not driven by congressional pressures in a specific direction; rather, its own inclination to find the compromise course was reinforced by the pressures from left and right. Beyond all the arguments of substance, it was clear that going easy on Somoza would contradict the president's emphasis on human rights and alienate his foreign policy allies in the House and Senate — while overtly seeking his removal would give the pro-Somoza Dirty Thirty ammunition they could use with their congressional colleagues and the public.

The activities of lobbying groups reinforced this pattern. Except when a dramatic event in Nicaragua produced a brief flurry of press attention and editorials, the issue rarely engaged the public and its mainstream opinion leaders. The moderate middle in public opinion was largely uninterested, and major public interest groups such as Common Cause and the League of Women Voters were concentrating on other issues. Thus lobbying efforts on the Nicaraguan problem were left to a few fervently anti- or pro-Somoza groups and individuals. The most effective of those working for tougher anti-Somoza policies were the occasional Nicaraguan visitors like Miguel D'Escoto, a member of Los Doce (the exiled supporters of the Sandinistas) who was later to be foreign minister in the Sandinista government. He and other Nicaraguans who visited or wrote members of Congress and administration officials about the human rights abuses of the Somoza regime usually got a hearing. American groups such as the Washington Office on Latin America pushed for attention through letters, occasional meetings with officials, and statements at congressional hearings. Perhaps more effective were Catholic missionaries in Nicaragua who sent back information on National Guard atrocities and anti-Somoza sentiment in the countryside. Their appearances and letters had special weight with anti-Somoza congressmen because in 1977, Nicaragua was seen on most of Capitol Hill (as it was in the executive branch) as a "human rights problem" more than as an issue in its own right.

Administration officials who worked on Nicaragua, however, universally say their thinking was rarely affected by anti-Somoza lobbyists. Although they might sometimes pick up useful information from them, the lobbyists were so predictable in their views that such nuggets tended to be discounted. And the propensity of the anti-Somoza groups for attacking the administration for what it had not done, rather than offering support for what it actually did, simply irked administration officials.

Anti-Somoza congressmen and their staffs were somewhat more receptive to information about National Guard abuses of human rights, and often used the statements of the Nicaraguan opposition in their own speeches. But the anti-Somoza groups lacked the two

essential ingredients that give clout to Capitol Hill lobbyists: votes
and/or money. Members of Congress listen to groups like the American Israel Public Affairs Committee and Transafrica because they
represent large constituencies of voters. And the proliferation of
Political Action Committees, or PACs, which raise money to be
provided to the campaigns of friendly politicians, is unhappy evidence of the power of dollars in Washington.

Most lobbying efforts by business and other PACs go into promoting tax bills or trade legislation of direct benefit to member firms
or industries. It is rare that representatives of American companies
seek to influence the decisions of officials in the executive branch
on general policy directions. No official interviewed for this book,
for example, could recall a single approach by an American business
with interests in Nicaragua.

On the pro-Somoza side of the issue were a number of public
relations firms and lobbyists hired by the Nicaraguan government.[2]
Three public relations firms were paid some quarter of a million
dollars annually to improve Somoza's image in the United States
by setting up press interviews with the dictator; issuing newsletters,
press releases, and films on the wonders of his country; and, in
an embarrassing episode, hiring two lawyers from Georgia to conduct an "independent" human rights investigation in Nicaragua.
The two had no difficulty determining that the attacks on Somoza
were unfair, but found the spelling of *Nicaragua* hard going in
their report, which was never published.[3] In addition, Somoza hired
Washington lawyer William Cramer, a former congressman from
Florida, and received the voluntary assistance of Fred Korth, a
former secretary of the Navy, in lobbying Congress against cuts
in American aid to Nicaragua. In early 1978, Cramer was being
paid $150,000 a year by the Nicaraguan government.

Somoza's critics in Washington may have bristled at the work
of such agents, but in truth the guns were seldom worth their
hire. Cramer, for example, called on some forty former House
colleagues before a 1977 vote on aid to Nicaragua, and sent a
telegram to every representative reminding him that Somoza was
an anti-Communist friend of the United States. By concentrating

their efforts on their conservative friends, Cramer and Korth were preaching to the converted. This may have helped stimulate continuing efforts by such allies as the Dirty Thirty and the congressmen they approached (who in turn talked up the issue with other colleagues), but it's doubtful that they changed many votes on aid appropriations. And it's certain that neither they nor Somoza's public relations people were able to overcome the Nicaraguan leader's terrible image with most legislators.

Brian Atwood, at the time the deputy assistant secretary of state for congressional relations, recalls that "the lobbyists on Nicaragua were up there on the Hill. They were able to write their memos saying that 'I visited Congressman So-and-so today' and collect their paychecks. But they weren't effective at all."

The Bureau of Congressional Relations at State — known as H, for Hill — tried to keep track of such things. (Like most of the bureaus, it is almost invariably referred to within the department by its initial. "Ask H to look into it" trips from the tongue more easily, and perhaps more pleasingly, than "Ask the Bureau of Congressional Relations to . . .") The bureau's most important function was to work with the White House officials in charge of congressional liaison to design and coordinate administration efforts to win passage of key foreign policy legislation, including appropriations for foreign assistance. During 1977, 1978, and the first half of 1979, their efforts centered on gaining ratification of the Panama Canal treaties and their implementing legislation. If it was to influence Congress effectively, it was important that the administration know about new legislation as early as possible, so the officers at H spent much of their time on the Hill, developing and talking to their contacts there, acting as a kind of early warning system.

H also had officers working with each bureau at State to coordinate efforts to influence legislation (appearances, for instance, by assistant secretaries at congressional hearings) and to stay abreast of any bureau activity that might later involve Congress, from a proposed treaty negotiation to a controversial policy decision certain to arouse congressional opposition.

It was on H that much of the daily flood of congressional mail descended. Letters to the president were almost always referred to State for a draft reply, and H coordinated this drafting with the appropriate bureaus. When a member of Congress wrote the department to ask for information or regarding a minor matter, the assistant secretary for congressional relations himself would respond.

Most congressional communications consisted of constituent mail, letters from the public that congressmen referred to the State Department for reply. This is an especially useful device for a congressman unwilling to take a clear position on a controversial issue. Better to write the voter that he has forwarded the letter to the State Department and to let the executive branch take the heat. So H handled some six hundred pieces of congressional mail a week, most involving stock answers precleared by the assistant secretary and the relevant bureaus.

Mail from and statements by members of Congress may illuminate the American political landscape for the administration, but what gives a congressman real influence on policy is power — political power of the kind wielded by anti-Somoza legislators such as Edward Kennedy, or a leadership position on legislation wanted by the administration, or a swing vote on an important committee. Beyond their ability to make trouble by making noise, the Dirty Thirty wielded little real influence. The group's leaders were not widely respected by their colleagues. Indeed, the two most active — Congressman John Murphy, a New York Democrat, and George Hansen, an Iowa Republican — were soon to run afoul of the law in the Abscam scandal and over campaign irregularities, respectively. A third leading pro-Somoza figure, Congressman Larry McDonald of Georgia, played so deep in right field that he was an embarrassment to the cause. A leader of the John Birch Society, McDonald drove Warren Christopher to fury when he impugned the loyalty of some of the State Department officials working on Latin American affairs. Rejecting a firm but tactful letter to McDonald drafted for his signature, Christopher personally wrote a much tougher one.

Jack Murphy had been a classmate of Somoza at LaSalle Military

Academy, and both had attended West Point. Somoza spoke on the telephone with his old friend in the House several times a week, and Murphy often flew to Managua to buck up the beleaguered Nicaraguan and put in a plug for him with any American reporters he could find. Murphy was the most vociferous of Somoza's defenders in congressional debates, a man who would have none of the "Yes, but . . ." arguments some would make ("Yes, Somoza is a dictator, but he is our friend . . ."). In September 1978, for example, he stated, "President Somoza has brought to Nicaragua the most liberal, progressive, and democratic government it has enjoyed in its entire history." Referring to the capture of the National Palace by Edén Pastora's Sandinistas a few weeks earlier, Murphy argued:

> Nicaragua has a constitutional government, and Anastasio Somoza is its constitutionally elected President. In that respect, it is no different than the United States. Yet if the Black Panthers, Weathermen, or Symbionese Liberation Army were to invade the White House, take hostages on Capitol Hill, and begin executing residents of Foggy Bottom, the *Washington Post* would certainly cry out for the speedy containment of such a bizarre move to take over the U.S. Government. So far, the media have been distressingly silent on the comparative situation in Nicaragua.[4]

In making his comparison, Murphy failed to mention the crowds of Nicaraguans lining the streets to cheer Pastora as he and his band drove safely to the airport after their successful raid.

Unlike most of the Dirty Thirty, Murphy was in a position to wield influence beyond rhetoric. Because he chaired the House Merchant Marine and Fisheries Committee, which would review the legislation on implementation of the Panama Canal treaties, he could try to trade this piece of legislation, an item of great concern to the administration, for a soft American stand on Somoza. And indeed, during late 1978, reporters heard Murphy threatening to link the two issues. On January 19, 1979, as the mediation was in the final throes of failure, Murphy and his wife had lunch at the White House with the president and Mrs. Carter, an encounter that was to become the subject of some speculation. Both the Panama legislation and Nicaragua were discussed, and some have suspected that Carter agreed to limit sanctions against Somoza in return for Murphy's cooperation on Panama.

Murphy did indeed go on to help produce the Panama legislation, which was passed by the House on June 21, 1979. Though there were constant wrangles with Murphy over the amendments he wanted in order to put his stamp on the bill, he met his commitment to getting it through. And in early June, when the Panama Canal Subcommittee of Merchant Marine and Fisheries linked the Nicaraguan and Panamanian issues in a hearing on gun running to the Sandinistas from Panama, Murphy remained absent. A few days before the hearing, after Brian Atwood had met with him, the congressman wrote a statement to be read at the hearing reiterating his support for passage of the implementing legislation.

The hearing itself was wild. Two Nicaraguan officials arrived to level accusations against the Panamanians. A wall of the hearing room bore a huge display of weapons captured by the Nicaraguan National Guard, an irresistible visual for the television cameras. At the last minute Brian Atwood decided it would not be enough to send the scheduled State Department expert witnesses and testified himself as well, clearing his hastily written statement with Warren Christopher before rushing up to the Hill.

A pleasant, even-tempered man, Atwood on this occasion let himself go, accusing the committee of airing a dispute between two Latin American nations that should properly have been brought before the OAS. He got what the administration wanted, an appearance that night on the evening news making the case that a defeat of the implementing legislation would damage American security. The next day, Republican Representative Robert Bauman of Maryland, a strident critic of the State Department and a supporter of Somoza, said that Atwood had been "the most impudent and arrogant witness I have had before any committee." Atwood recalls being delighted at the comment.

So the facts are suggestive of a deal on Nicaragua. After the

Carter-Murphy lunch in January, the administration seemed to lose sight of the Nicaraguan issue, and Murphy broke with his customary allies on Central American issues in order to work for the Panama legislation. Yet such a deal is a myth. Carter and Murphy have both said that Carter refused to consider taking a more sympathetic stance toward Somoza, and argued strenuously with Murphy over the issue.[5] Some of those who worked with Murphy during this period believe that he supported the Panama legislation primarily because he knew that the treaties would legally go into effect with or without the implementing legislation.

According to Brian Atwood, Murphy also knew that if he didn't play ball, jurisdiction over the legislation could be removed from his committee and given to others with a claim on it. And there was a question of ego. Both the president and the Speaker of the House had asked him to see the bill through, and he had agreed to do so. Especially after it included those of his amendments to which the administration agreed, the bill was *his.*

Nor is there any evidence that the administration backed away on Nicaragua because of the congressman. Murphy's concerns were not discussed at the interagency meetings on the sanctions during January 1979, and during the spring of 1979 no middle-level official pressed for action on Nicaragua only to be denied by senior officials who knew of a deal. The unhappy truth is that Nicaragua subsided as an issue during those months because the situation there was deceptively quiet and men like Assistant Secretary Pete Vaky were sick of Nicaragua in the wake of the failed mediation.

While Murphy and the Dirty Thirty had little influence on the specifics of the administration's Nicaragua policies, one critic occasionally did have such an impact: Congressman Charles Wilson of Texas. Many members of Congress feel a tension between their attraction to the life of Washington and their roots at home, but Wilson, first elected to the House in 1972, displays no such ambivalence. A wooden sign in his office proclaims "just a country dog come to the city." There is undoubtedly some artifice in his playing the role of the flamboyant Texan, yet the first thing that those around him say about Charlie Wilson is that he is a natural. He does and says what he wants, they say. "He's a man who will never have an ulcer."

On the wall of his reception area hangs a picture of Wilson with some Afghan freedom fighters. The photograph was not taken across the border in Pakistan, in the safety of the refugee camps where Zbigniew Brzezinski once brandished a rifle and where a stream of American officials and politicians have followed. No, this picture was taken inside Afghanistan, where Wilson had traveled in 1987 without the blessing of the State Department. Elsewhere on the walls, in addition to pictures of John F. Kennedy, Winston Churchill, Abraham Lincoln, and Tom Selleck as Magnum, P.I., are three Texas flags and a mounted Stinger missile launching tube that was used to shoot down a Soviet aircraft in Afghanistan.

The offices of members of the House are located in three buildings to the south of the Capitol: the Rayburn, Cannon, and Longworth buildings. To the north, for senators, their staffs, and their committees, are the Dirksen, Russell, and Hart buildings. Except for the martial ambience and the renowned good looks of the many women he hires for his staff, Wilson's offices are typical of rooms in these buildings.

To one side of the reception area is Wilson's own office, generously proportioned although smaller than those allotted to senators. To the other side is one of his staff offices. It is in staff offices all over the Hill that most of the work is done, at desks crammed five or six to a room, desks pushed in front of defunct fireplaces, desks so close to each other that the huge flow of paper — newspapers, clippings, books, thick transcripts of committee hearings, proposed legislation, drafts of speeches, reports from the Congressional Research Service, telephone messages — threatens to spill from one desk to another. Here the telephones are seldom quiet. For the "lege" staff of legislative assistants, or LAs, the paper lies in deep drifts. Over this chaos an administrative assistant presides, usually from his own small office; the congressman's personal secretary is also often given a separate space. (The press secretary usually can be found with the LAs.)

In the 1977–1979 period, it was in such an office in the Longworth building that Noel Holmes, Wilson's legislative assistant for foreign policy, helped Wilson do battle with the Carter administration over its approach to Somoza. A graduate of the University of California at Santa Barbara, Holmes had started out in Washington, as many do, on the administrative side of a committee staff. She then worked on domestic legislation before joining Wilson's office in 1977. Holmes's work days started rather late, around 9:30 A.M., but usually ran well into the evening. Her husband, a State Department official, also worked late, and both were fortunately drawn to the kinds of semi-official parties at which foreign policy matters make up what passes in Washington for small talk.

Holmes enjoyed the work of an LA. Some of it was routine, for instance drafting stock responses on foreign policy issues for other staff members who replied to the constituent mail. She herself worked on letters that posed particular difficulties and referred some to the State Department. More interesting were her calls to contacts in the executive branch (Wilson had some very good ones in the State Department) to get early word on forthcoming legislation or on policy decisions of interest, and her work with the LAs on the staffs of friendly congressmen to coordinate strategy and draft legislation they might jointly sponsor. She also enjoyed trying to persuade other offices to support bills of interest to Wilson, checking such legislation for legal clarity with the counsel of the appropriate committee and talking to reporters when a bill or hearing was drawing their attention. In addition, she helped prepare Wilson for hearings, usually scheduled for 10 A.M. Just as their staffs provide senior officials in the executive branch with talkers and Q's and A's for important meetings, press conferences, and congressional hearings, so members of Congress are given opening statements and a series of questions to which there may be particularly illuminating or embarrassing answers by witnesses appearing before their committees.

Holmes recalls that Wilson became involved on Nicaragua almost by accident. The Texan was an influential member of the important Foreign Operations Subcommittee of the House Appropriations

Committee. His was a swing vote on the committee. A conservative Democrat, he generally supported appropriations for foreign assistance programs but he was skeptical of the liberal foreign policy approach of the Carter administration and of the liberals who had been appointed to many of its leadership positions. This skepticism reflected both his genuine beliefs and his political position. As Brian Atwood points out, "Wilson is a Southern Democrat, and when the more liberal national Democrats achieve power in the White House, men like Wilson can become politically vulnerable at home over the policies of their party's president. As the tall cowboy from Texas, he wanted to demonstrate to his voters that he was a hard-nosed guy who could be distinguished from the Carter administration."

Nicaragua would be the principal issue on which he would do so. Because of his position on the appropriations committee, it was natural that lobbyists such as Fred Korth raised the issue of Nicaragua with Wilson, as did Congressman Jack Murphy. Ironically, however, it was the Carter administration that most effectively solicited his interest. During the spring of 1977, when the foreign assistance bill for fiscal 1978 was working its way through the legislative maze, Congressman Edward Koch of New York led a group of liberals determined to remove from it all military assistance to Nicaragua.* While Koch and his allies were opposed to such aid on human rights grounds, the administration decided at the last moment that it did not want to see the whole military aid program for Nicaragua killed. Keeping the program alive while actually withholding the appropriated funds until the human rights

---

* Foreign assistance legislation for the following fiscal year is submitted to Congress every January, together with the rest of an administration's proposed budget. The committees on foreign relations in the Senate and House then hold hearings and write authorizing legislation for submission to the full bodies of Congress. Since the power of the purse is the most useful of congressional powers, and since foreign assistance bills include the funds of most interest to foreign nations, it is through amendments to foreign aid authorizing legislation that congressional efforts to direct American foreign policy most often occur. The Senate and House appropriations committees then recommend the actual levels of funding for these bills; hence their extraordinary power.

situation in Nicaragua improved, it argued, would offer the maximum leverage with Somoza.

Noel Holmes recalls that Lawrence Pezzullo, then a deputy assistant secretary of state for congressional relations and later to be ambassador to Nicaragua, called on Wilson to seek help in preventing a victory by Koch. Wilson was only too glad to do so. Initially he lost to Koch in the appropriations committee, but he led a successful fight on the floor of the House to reverse the committee's deletion of the military aid. Some of the votes for Wilson's position came from anti-Somoza representatives who did not want to tie the administration's hands in its relations with Nicaragua.[6]

Once involved on the Nicaraguan issue, Wilson soon soured on the administration's approach. It was not that, like Murphy, he admired Somoza. He had not met the Nicaraguan at the time, and when he later visited the dictator in Managua, he was not impressed. Indeed, Holmes recalls that Wilson "felt it was a shame that Somoza could not have been a little more respectable. If Somoza hadn't been the person he was, it would have been easier to get a little more support for efforts to get more aid for Nicaragua."

In the autumn of 1977, as the administration moved to cut off economic aid to Nicaragua, Wilson became the most strenuous opponent of its policy. Yet he avoided the kinds of credulous statements about Somoza that had opened Murphy to ridicule. For Wilson, the question was not whether Somoza was a "son of a bitch," to recall FDR's probably apocryphal remark about the senior Somoza; he was ours, an anti-Communist ally. To lose him would be damaging to American interests. Wilson especially objected to what he saw as the administration's inconsistency in attacking Somoza with cuts in aid while continuing to provide assistance, for example, to Duvalier's Haiti. He found the denial of rifle swivels for the Nicaraguan National Guard incredible.

Wilson strenuously opposed the cancellation in October 1977 of two proposed Nicaraguan aid projects for nutrition and rural education, arguing not unreasonably that the decision penalized poor people for Somoza's sins. It was Wilson's threat to attack the whole aid bill that led the administration in the spring of 1978 to restore these $10.5 million programs in the fiscal year 1979 aid bill, although it refused to actually expend the funds. This did not satisfy Wilson, and at hearings he continued to rip into administration witnesses about their inconsistency in treating Nicaragua more harshly than they did some other nations whose human rights violations were obviously worse. He was not swayed by the argument that when other factors, such as American security interests, were taken into account, there would inevitably be inconsistency in any administration's human rights policies. In Wilson's view, though Nicaragua might be less important than the oil rich states in the Middle East, its strategic significance was no less than that of Haiti.

By late 1978, Wilson's denunciations of the administration's Nicaraguan policies had become as purple as those of any member of the Dirty Thirty. Visiting Managua at a crucial juncture in the mediation effort, Wilson told reporters that the State Department was being run by "a bunch of adolescent anarchists." American policy, he said, "was encouraging communism in the Caribbean."

The State Department seldom replies officially to congressional criticism of this sort, but Wilson's attack was unusually vehement. American policy, the department's spokesman responded, was to seek a "peaceful, democratic resolution" of the Nicaraguan crisis. Such efforts "are not helped, nor is public understanding of the situation improved by statements and charges such as those by Congressman Wilson." Wilson's remarks were "wrong in their assumptions and irresponsible in their phraseology."[7]

Wilson's mail on Nicaragua ran heavily in his favor, but his statements infuriated officials at State. On both sides of the argument, feelings had become personal. For more than a year, Wilson had been sniping at the human rights bureau and at Warren Christopher and his interagency group on human rights. He was especially critical of Mark Schneider, the bureau's deputy assistant secretary, perhaps because Schneider had already developed a reputation for his anti-Somoza views while working on the Hill in the early and mid-1970s. At one point the congressman summoned Schneider to his office for a confrontation over the administration's human rights policies. According to Noel Holmes, Wilson was not merely interested in pressuring Schneider, "he wanted to *meet* Mark Schneider. He felt it was very important to see what other people are like, particularly when they are that much of an influence on what you are doing."

Wilson welcomed a good face-to-face argument. Brian Atwood recalls that when Wilson sent him a nasty note in response to a State Department letter on Nicaragua, Atwood went to see this man he'd never met. After tossing the offending note on Wilson's desk, Atwood had it out with the congressman in an argument that both recall they rather enjoyed. And in early December 1978, when Warren Christopher met with Wilson to discuss his statements in Managua, the congressman unabashedly told a reporter the next day that "Christopher chewed me out."

The deputy secretary was angry not only about Wilson's activities and abusive statements. There was also his claim that the administration had made a commitment actually to disburse the funds for the two Nicaraguan aid projects he had preserved the previous spring. Now, Wilson claimed, the administration was going back on its word. He was publicly impugning the administration's and Warren Christopher's integrity. Christopher valued his relationships with many members of Congress and had been an effective worker for the Panama Canal treaties through intense yet calm advocacy. But in attacking his reputation for honesty Wilson had gone too far, and Christopher let himself go.

For his part, Wilson was angered that the State Department, which had originally sought his help on the Nicaraguan issue — and would again, for he was later to be helpful in passing appropriations for American aid to Nicaragua just after Somoza fell — would not be more flexible. According to Holmes, "He felt he was just hitting his head against the State Department's brick wall. Everyone he talked to there was so set on the policy, so sure that they were right, that they wouldn't think of compromising."

It was more than a clash over policy, she thinks. Wilson expected that State would do business the way it was done in Congress, through very personal dealings and compromise. In Congress, you try to "work out some kind of solution so that everybody, even though they are not totally happy, feels they've got some kind of stake in the game," Holmes says. When officials at State were angered by Wilson's tactics and refused to make a deal with him, they were in effect saying he was not a "player." On foreign aid questions, Wilson wanted that recognition.

At the White House, however, the congressman found someone who would listen to him, who was prepared to deal. Henry Owen had been brought into the White House to coordinate work on international economic summit meetings. (He and his opposite numbers in the other Western industrial nations were known as Sherpas for their work in preparing the way to the summits.) A skilled bureaucratic organizer, Owen had soon expanded his role to become the key White House figure on foreign economic policy. He was committed to a strong foreign assistance program and had a particular interest in aid to India and in the creation and funding of an Institute for Scientific and Technological Cooperation.

In the spring of 1978, when Wilson had told Owen that he would work to hold up the whole aid bill if the two loans to Nicaragua were not included, Owen had convinced Warren Christopher to go along. Now, in January 1979, as the administration considered its sanctions against Somoza, Wilson again called Owen with the same threat. According to Robert Pastor:

> The day before a PRC meeting to decide how to respond to the failure of the mediation, Henry Owen called to tell me of a conversation he had just had with Charles Wilson. Wilson told him that as a graduate of Annapolis, he had originally joined the House Appropriations Committee to work on the Military Affairs Subcommittee, but he had to accept a position on the Foreign Operations Subcommittee until there was an opening on Military Affairs. He had just been offered the position he coveted on Military Affairs, but rejected it so he could continue to oversee the Administration's policy on Nicaragua. Wilson told Owen that the aid bill would encounter serious problems if the Administration reduced aid to Nicaragua any further. "He can single-handedly eliminate Latin America from

the aid program this year," Owen said. A few hours later, Owen's Deputy, Rutherford Poats called me to say that Vice President Mondale had received a similar call from Wilson.[8]

At the January 26 PRC meeting, Owen argued for limiting the sanctions to military and political measures. Brzezinski agreed, on the grounds that the sanctions would be primarily symbolic in any case, and that some measures should be left in reserve for the sake of future leverage.

Unlike Congressmen Murphy, Hansen, and McDonald, Wilson had succeeded in influencing the administration in specific decisions. Yet Wilson did not consider this a notable triumph. The aid projects remained unimplemented and the hostility of the State Department to Somoza seemed unabated, though the Nicaraguan issue was of less interest to State as the spring of 1979 wore on.

Both Pete Vaky and Brian Atwood were displeased that Wilson had received as much consideration as he had. They believed that by giving in to him at all, the administration had bolstered his reputation for influence — and thus his actual power. He could have been beaten, they believe, in votes on the Appropriations Committee and by rallying the administration's allies on the floor of the House. But for Henry Owen and other senior officials, possible damage to the aid bill was too great a risk to run for the sake of marginal strengthening of the sanctions against Somoza.

In the end, the influence of Congress on the Nicaraguan issue in the 1977–1979 era had less to do with specific policy decisions than with the political context of the issue. When Senators Kennedy and Cranston or Congressman Koch pushed for action on Nicaragua, a president and administration that put human rights at the center of its foreign policy had to act or suffer political embarrassment. But if the administration went too far in attacking Somoza, vociferous opponents such as Wilson and Murphy would be sure to call public attention to Carter's destabilization of an anti-Communist leader and the rhetoric of the right about the radicalism of the Carter administration might seem more believable. By January 1979 not even Kennedy and his Senate allies were calling for Somoza's removal, so there would be no political cover for Carter if he engineered such an event.

The result was to reinforce the natural inclination of most officials to find a middle way, to encourage Somoza's departure from office but only in a way that could not be seen as American bullying. Out of both belief and political necessity, the president and his senior advisers insisted that there be a democratic process in Nicaragua through which to effect a change in governments. And American diplomacy, they believed, could only succeed with the participation of other governments in the region.

Pete Vaky rebelled against this moderate approach because he did not believe it could produce the one outcome that would head off disaster: the removal of the dictator. For this reason he was exasperated with Wilson, Murphy, and the Dirty Thirty. He was especially grateful for the support, even if quietly offered, of senators such as Jacob Javits, the influential New York Republican, who shared his estimate of the situation.

Despite his frustration at the way the congressmen managed to reinforce the policies of compromise, Vaky and others at the State Department understood that competition in Washington over policy is fair enough. Indeed, the Constitution implicitly calls for constant political tests between the executive branch and Congress in the making of foreign policy. To consider congressional efforts to influence policy illegitimate would be to leave the field to the executive branch and ultimately to deny democracy. But there is a distinction between a fight over policy and efforts to defeat that policy once it is made. What angered Vaky and others was the influence of Murphy, Hansen, McDonald, and Wilson not in Washington but in Managua. It was hard enough to convince Somoza to bend through the limited pressures approved in Washington. But when American congressmen appeared in Nicaragua to encourage Somoza, publicly and privately, to hold firm; when they appeared at a press conference there with captured Sandinista weapons, as they did in mid-November 1978; and when Somoza's air force dropped leaflets over the countryside with the pictures of the Americans and their endorsement of Somoza's version of a plebiscite — then, they thought, the congressmen had crossed that line.

ELEVEN

Slow Intelligence

WHEN CHARLES WILSON THREATENED TO DERAIL THE foreign aid bill and thus "wreck the whole train" during a conversation with Robert Pastor in the early spring of 1979, he seemed to be assuming that the administration was contemplating further action against Somoza. But Pastor knew that neither Wilson's threats nor his own counterarguments were necessary. After announcing the sanctions against Somoza in mid-February, the administration had no intention of taking any further action. In bureaucratic parlance, the issue was on the back burner as far as Washington was concerned.

In Nicaragua, however, the situation was heating up and Somoza was slipping — while Washington was very slow to recognize it. Tons of military supplies were being shipped from Europe and Cuba through Venezuela and Panama to the Sandinistas in Nicaragua and Costa Rica. Once President Pérez left office in March, Venezuelan support for the Sandinistas declined, but the governments of Cuba, Panama, and Costa Rica remained actively involved. Rodrigo Carazo in Costa Rica and Omar Torrijos in Panama hated Somoza more than they worried about who might replace him, and in any case they felt their support for the Sandinistas would buy them important influence in Managua should the revolution succeed. Some American reports also suggested that here and there bribery smoothed the way with Costa Rican officials who might otherwise have slowed these supplies.

In Nicaragua, military recruitment for the Sandinistas picked up during the spring, while desertions from the National Guard grew. On April 7 a few hundred guerrillas seized the city of Estelí and held out for a week of heavy fighting against a National Guard force twice their size before slipping back into the mountains. The Sandinistas were making political gains as well. In March leaders of the three Sandinista factions met in Havana and formed a unified National Directorate. As the Sandinistas banded together, Somoza's hitherto moderate opponents were fragmenting and drifting to the left. After the collapse of the mediation in January, the FAO, Somoza's mainstream opposition, joined with the Sandinistas' United People's Movement to form the National Patriotic Front.

Vice-President Mondale, Assistant Secretary of State Vaky, and Robert Pastor of the NSC staff met in March with President Pérez of Venezuela, who was then completing his term in office. As he had done so often before, the Venezuelan asked how the United States would get rid of Somoza. When Mondale expressed American distaste for Somoza but said that we had no intention of overthrowing him, "Pérez lost control over his poker face. You could see the dismay," Vaky says. "Pérez replied: 'In that case, blood will flow.' "

But Pérez's warning went unheeded in Washington. The scope of the arms shipments to the Sandinistas went unnoticed. Even Somoza's public assertions that he would soon defeat the Sandinistas went unchallenged within the American government.

In mid-May 1979, Richard Feinberg, the Latin American specialist on the policy planning staff at State, found himself sitting next to an analyst from the Central Intelligence Agency on a flight to San José, Costa Rica. Both were on their way to a Chiefs of Mission Conference, at which the American ambassadors in the region would get together with senior policy makers from Washington, including Assistant Secretary Vaky and Robert Pastor. (Such conferences are held regularly by the regional assistant secretaries.) As Feinberg spoke with the CIA official, he was struck by the analyst's confidence that Somoza would be able to remain in office until his constitutional term ended in 1981. Indeed, on May 2 the CIA had issued a secret intelligence analysis stating that Cuba had adopted a selective, "low-key" approach to revolutionary movements in the region to avoid provoking an American response.[1]

The two dozen or so participants at the Chiefs of Mission meeting sat around a large conference table for two days of discussion of American policy in Central America. Vaky's Latin American bureau and the policy planning staff were drafting an interagency study on Central American policy, and most of the officials from Washington were interested in discussing the region as a whole. Little attention was given to Somoza's future in Nicaragua, the assumption being that no crisis was imminent.

Yet within a week Mexico would sever diplomatic relations with Nicaragua and encourage other nations to do likewise. A week after that, on May 29, the Sandinistas proclaimed what they called their "final offensive." Hundreds of guerrillas crossed the Nicaraguan border from Costa Rica and engaged the National Guard, while the Sandinista radio proclaimed the "hour of the overthrow." There was only sporadic gunfire in the principal cities of Nicaragua, but in a quickly written intelligence brief, the CIA recognized that the Sandinista announcement presaged a new wave of fighting. The brief concluded, however, that the new offensive would not be powerful enough to defeat Somoza. Even a week later, as fighting intensified, Lieutenant General Dennis P. McAuliffe, Commander in Chief of the U.S. Southern Command in Panama, told a congressional committee that the FSLN "hit and run" attacks were "not very significant." Somoza's forces, he said, "are reacting, in my judgment, adequately to the situation and are able to regain control in the contested areas fairly quickly."

Feinberg's companion on the airplane to San José in mid-May was an analyst in the CIA's Directorate for Intelligence. He had neither cloak nor dagger. He and other CIA intelligence analysts did their work at desks in crowded rooms at CIA headquarters in Langley, Virginia, a seven-story building completed in 1963. Set in an area that was once Virginia countryside and retains pockets of bucolic resistance to suburbia, the building is more attractive than its New State counterpart. Indeed, Allen W. Dulles, the director of Central Intelligence who presided over the CIA headquarters design, saw it as conveying the atmosphere of a college campus.

The Directorate of Intelligence, which receives about ten percent of the agency's budget,[2] is divided into eleven offices. Five cover regional affairs (the Soviet Union; Europe; the Near East and South Asia; East Asia; and Africa and Latin America). The other six perform various functional tasks: scientific weapons research; global issues; information resources (a kind of intelligence library for the government); imagery analysis (the study of satellite and other photographic information); publications; and leadership analysis. The leadership analysts produce profiles of foreign leaders. State Department officials recall that in late 1978, the CIA wrote for the White House an extraordinarily detailed look at Somoza, including the most intimate details of his life with his mistress in Managua.

Intelligence directorate analysts draw on information from other sections of the CIA and also from the National Security Agency (the vast entity that collects electronic intelligence), from the State Department and its embassies, from the Defense Intelligence Agency and its military attachés abroad, and also from newspapers, journals, and scholarly books. Their work seldom receives much attention outside the government, but it is tremendously important.

For most Americans, CIA means spies and scandals, the Bay of Pigs and "assassination manuals." Although the agency's covert action — the secret manipulation of foreign events by American agents — is, ironically, the most visible to the public, the most controversial to its critics, and perhaps the most important to its public supporters, such dramatic activities take up only a very small part of the CIA's budget and efforts. The Directorate for Operations, which is responsible for clandestine operations abroad, puts far more effort into the collection of information than into covert action. It is then up to the intelligence analysts at their desks to try to make sense of the facts available — to turn this information into intelligence useful to our policy makers.

Carved into the wall of the main lobby at CIA headquarters is the biblical injunction "And ye shall know the truth, and the truth shall make you free." To the CIA intelligence analyst wrestling with a mass of contradictory facts and fragmentary information, there are times when another wise saying might come to mind, one most often ascribed by scholars to Samuel Goldwyn of Hollywood, California: "Only a fool would make predictions — especially about the future." For that is what the analyst must do: produce a succinct statement not only about a current situation but also about its implications for the future. To provide the policy maker only with the facts is to give him what's called a data dump. Such a report, like a lengthy, unfocused term paper by a college sophomore, may demonstrate how much the analyst knows and may even seem more objective than a predictive analysis. But a data dump creates only the illusion of objectivity, because the analyst inevitably has to choose certain facts while discarding others. Worse, because the policy maker must judge the consequences of alternative courses of action, he will have to make such predictions even if the analyst does not. Since the analyst is in a position to be more objective than a senior official who has a personal stake in the existing policy, it is wiser for the intelligence officer to take the first plunge into the murkiness of the future.

When the CIA's efforts at prognostication have failed, the results have sometimes been disastrous. But over the years the intelligence produced by the CIA has been very good. CIA analysts — probably the best in the American government, perhaps even in our society — think clearly and write well. And while no human being can be truly objective, CIA analysts are trained to ask the hard questions and to resist pressures to come up with the estimates of reality that the policy makers want to see. (Hence the heat the CIA received from the White House under Lyndon Johnson for its pessimistic estimates of enemy strength in Vietnam and from the Nixon White House for its analyses of Soviet missile deployments. Hence also the disgraceful way in which William Casey reportedly insisted in 1981 that the agency's analyses of international terrorism be altered to match the rhetoric of the Reagan administration.)

All Americans have a tremendous stake in the intelligence analysts' work, for when they are wrong, costly policy errors or military setbacks may follow. Their importance also flows from the fact that prudent planners base their calculations of military spending on "worst-case assumptions." For any nation, building defense forces inferior to those that a potential adversary *might* be creating is to risk a failure in deterrence and a military defeat. Thus, the more each side knows about the actual growth in military force levels of the other, the less its worst-case assumptions will lead it to unnecessary and provocative military spending of its own. Good intelligence on both sides can slow an arms race.

The CIA failed in its predictions about Nicaragua in the spring of 1979, and the analysts must bear a portion of the blame for extrapolating the shape of the future from the patterns of the past. Somoza had always survived before, and he had weathered the fighting of the previous September. Why, they concluded, should he not do so again?

Nevertheless, the blame for the miscalculation belongs not only to the intelligence directorate. The information at the disposal of its analysts was shockingly poor. In the mid-1970s the CIA cut back on its clandestine activities abroad. Public revelations during the previous two decades led to a national reaction against covert actions run amok, against assassination attempts worthy of the Borgias and ideas as ludicrous as the plan to provide doctored cigars for Castro that would make his beard fall out. Instead, technical sources of intelligence — satellite photography and the like — would be emphasized.

Even though the covert action programs run amok were what repelled the public and Congress, basic intelligence gathering, which is different from dirty tricks, was constricted as well. The cuts were heavy in Central America. As Robert Pastor notes, "The intelligence agencies, like the State Department, tend to believe that since we have the biggest stake in our relations with the larger nations abroad, cuts in personnel should fall first on our missions in the smaller countries. And they often send their best people to the bigger American missions. This is a mistake, since our influence is more important in the smaller places." There is also more information already available about a nation like France than about a Nicaragua. *Le Monde* supplies as much reliable information about French politics as our embassy and CIA station can provide. But in the smaller nations of the world, especially where the press is controlled by the government, reporting by our intelligence sources becomes vital to Washington's understanding.

Cuts in the number and size of CIA stations in the region contributed to the 1979 intelligence failure in Nicaragua, as did a hesitancy, at both State and the CIA, to have any contact with the Sandinistas. Though the embassy in Managua had started by the mid-1970s to develop contacts with the moderate opponents of the Somoza regime, it still avoided the Sandinistas lest it signal that it considered the revolutionaries to be legitimate contenders for power. Worse, as security in the countryside deteriorated in 1978, embassy officers were discouraged from traveling beyond Managua. Patricia Haigh was informally reprimanded for her adventure in the September 1978 fighting. It is no wonder that the embassy missed the build-up in Sandinista capabilities during the spring of 1979. And the CIA? Incredibly enough, a number of officials say the CIA had no sources of information within the ranks of the Sandinistas throughout this period. Nor did the CIA and our embassies in the region send personnel to the areas through which arms were moving into Nicaragua in order to report on the flow.

Fault for the intelligence failure must also be found with the consumers of the CIA's analyses: the policy makers and planners. Why did they not insist on better information? Requests were made for more information on the arms flows and other aspects of the situation, but there was no insistence that the CIA or embassies send people to dig more deeply. And there was no challenge to the prevailing wisdom that Somoza would hold on until 1981. The problem was that the CIA estimates nicely matched the mood and views of those who read them. As Pete Vaky recalls, the CIA view was "comforting" because it suggested the absence of imminent crisis.

Such intelligence estimates put any official who wanted to force urgent action concerning Nicaragua into a nearly impossible position. By May 1979 the White House and the Seventh Floor at the State Department were preoccupied with the final negotiations on the SALT II treaty, with preparations for upcoming summit meetings with the Soviets and then with allied nations, and with the president's plummeting popularity (which led to his retreat to Camp David, in early July, for two weeks' reflection). It would have been tough going to convince senior officials that they should precipitate a crisis by moving against Somoza when intelligence analysts were saying that Somoza could weather a new storm.

In early June, as the fighting in Nicaragua intensified, James Buchanan, a Latin American analyst in State's Bureau of Intelligence and Research, worked closely with Vaky in tracking the course of the battles. It proved difficult to convince most officials at State of the scope of the problem. When, for example, he presented incomplete but suggestive evidence of the growing flow of supplies to the Sandinistas, he found considerable resistance to his portrayal of a Cuban connection. Today, he recalls that one senior official was finally convinced; another, however, concluded a briefing by saying simply, "I don't believe you." And most officials seemed more receptive to any evidence that Somoza's moderate opponents remained a viable political force than they were to growing indications to the contrary. It was natural for them to do so: if the middle withered, the policy choices for Washington became much more difficult.

On June 9, 1979, although Somoza's forces in the south claimed victory over the guerrilla force entering Nicaragua from Costa Rica, the fighting was spreading elsewhere in the country. By June 11 there was heavy firing along the highway just north of Managua itself. On the same day, a working group was established at the State Department Operations Center for around-the-clock monitoring of events in Nicaragua.

On June 12 a FLASH message from Managua reported that a convoy of sixty official and private American dependents was setting out for the airport under the protection of a National Guard unit.

The message warned about press leaks, lest the Sandinistas interdict the convoy. A subsequent message reported a second convoy. The embassy was advising American citizens in León — where the Sandinistas had gained control and were fighting off National Guard counterattacks — and other contested cities to "remain in their homes in the safest posture possible." To Americans already crouching below window level, the advice probably seemed gratuitous.

Suddenly Nicaragua had emerged again as a crisis. On June 11, at an interagency meeting on Central American policy, the intelligence assessment was that Somoza would weather the current offensive but would not retain power into 1981. The next day the CIA again revised its estimate: Somoza would be able to hold on only for a short time. On June 19 it gave Somoza little more than a week.[3]

The pressures on the regime were coming from beyond as well as within Nicaragua's borders. Arms shipments to the Sandinistas via Nicaragua's neighbors continued, although a visit to General Torrijos by Robert Pastor on June 4 produced a statement by the general that Panama "will not intervene in the internal affairs of any country" and the shipments through that nation were probably reduced. Washington was to make a number of efforts to get the suppliers of arms to both sides to desist, but the attempts generally failed to reduce the arms flows. An exception was an approach to the Israelis in mid-June that apparently led them to recall a ship bound for Nicaragua with arms purchased by the National Guard.

On June 16 the nations of the Andean Pact — Bolivia, Colombia, Ecuador, Peru, and Venezuela — called on all nations to assist in "the installation of a truly representative, democratic regime" in Managua and recognized the Sandinistas as "legitimate combatants" in a "state of belligerency" with Somoza's government. At the same time, a provisional government for Nicaragua was announced in Costa Rica, under a junta including Daniel Ortega Saavedra, another Sandinista leader, and Sergio Ramírez of Los Doce; Alfonso Robelo, a Nicaraguan businessman; and Violeta de Chamorro, widow of Pedro Joaquín Chamorro, who had inherited control of the opposition paper *La Prensa* from her husband. In late May she had fled Managua for Costa Rica, and the newspaper had been closed shortly thereafter, when Somoza reimposed a state of emergency and censorship. On June 11, during fighting in the area, a National Guard tank had fired repeatedly into the *La Prensa* building, doing heavy damage. Now, on June 16, Doña Violeta became at least a nominal leader of the forces opposing Somoza. Meanwhile, Edén Pastora led three hundred more Sandinista fighters into Nicaragua from their base in Costa Rica.

These events forced a June 11 meeting of the interagency Policy Review Committee to go beyond its scheduled discussion of general approaches to Central America. The situation in Nicaragua demanded a new American course of action. Zbigniew Brzezinski proposed an idea discussed at interagency meetings the previous fall: linking Somoza's resignation to the establishment of an inter-American peace-keeping force to fill the vacuum until free elections could be held and a non-Somocista National Guard organized.

Although the State Department representatives at this interagency meeting agreed that Brzezinski's idea should be quietly explored with Latin American governments, at a White House meeting on June 19 to discuss what had now become a full-scale Nicaraguan crisis, the State Department expressed second thoughts. Secretary of State Vance reported that initial soundings suggested that the chances of gaining support for an inter-American peace-keeping force were slim. The problem was that the force would have to rely heavily on an American contribution, and memories of earlier American interventions were so vivid throughout the region that Washington's proposing such an idea was likely to backfire.

The State Department suggested instead a plan for the formation of a post-Somoza "Government of National Reconciliation" which could then invite the support of the United States. Brzezinski had doubts that such a government could hold together. It was essential, he argued, that the post-Somoza vacuum be filled either by an effective National Guard or by an international peace-keeping force. After some argument, a compromise was reached. Further consultations would be held with other governments in the hemisphere on a five-point plan that would include (1) a cease-fire, (2) a halt to arms flows for both sides, (3) establishment of a government of national reconciliation, (4) humanitarian assistance, and (5) some means, including the idea of a peace-keeping force, for keeping law and order during the immediate period after Somoza's departure.[4]

Brzezinski's argument was unusual in that he made explicit a concern that is often on the minds of senior policy makers but seldom stated: the domestic political implications of the decisions they face. Robert Pastor recalls that "Brzezinski said there was no interest in creating a crisis-like atmosphere after the summit [just concluded in Vienna between President Carter and President Leonid Brezhnev], but events in Nicaragua would impact on U.S.-Soviet relations and on the President's domestic political standing, particularly in the South and West." Mention of domestic politics at such meetings is generally considered bad form; issues should be decided on their merits. Statesmen worry about the interests of the nation; mere politicians think in terms of partisan political advantage. And since the authors of memoirs write as statesmen rather than as politicians, former presidents seldom mention their own political concerns in reviewing the history of their administrations. But even if unmentioned in most policy meetings and unrecalled in most memoirs, domestic political considerations inevitably play a role.

As the fighting intensified in Nicaragua, congressional supporters of Somoza launched an offensive on the battleground of American public opinion. On June 18 five senators and one hundred members of the House placed an advertisement in *The New York Times* warning of another Cuba and calling on the president to support Somoza. Two days later, however, a shocking event in Nicaragua created an overwhelming backlash: at a roadblock near Managua, a young member of the National Guard stopped an American television reporter, Bill Stewart of ABC News, calmly forced him to his knees, then made him lie on his stomach, and as television cameras recorded the scene for an outraged American public, shot the newsman in cold blood. The casual way the young man fired was a chilling demonstration of the diminishing value of human life in the civil conflict and the growing brutality of the Guard. The next day the White House and Congress were flooded with angry messages of opposition to Somoza and a stream of congressmen quickly issued statements condemning the Nicaraguan regime.

The event relieved the pressure from the right over Carter's Nicaraguan policies, but it is not necessarily immediate public opinion that is of greatest concern to officials worried about the political implications of a foreign policy decision. American military interventions abroad have almost always been popular at the time, yet if they are not quickly successful, people forget their initial enthusiasm and blame their presidents for undertaking such adventures. (Consider Korea, Vietnam, and the American experience in Nicaragua in the 1920s.) Similarly, the withdrawal of American support for a discredited dictator may at first be welcomed, but if the alternative to the dictator proves unattractive, the president will be open to political attacks for having "lost the country" (China, Cuba, Iran — or Nicaragua).

The argument between the State Department and Brzezinski over the wisdom of proposing a peace-keeping force for Nicaragua might well have dragged on for some time while State carried out its hesitant "consultations" with other governments. But a decision was forced by the fact that the United States had already called for a meeting of OAS foreign ministers to discuss the Nicaraguan crisis. This meeting was scheduled for June 21, and Secretary of State Vance was expected to deliver a statement on Washington's policy.

Policy speeches by a president or a secretary of state are tremendously important, not only in making public policy commitments but, within the government, in forcing decisions. At the June 19 interagency meeting, State and the NSC could agree to disagree about the peace-keeping force by leaving the issue to further consultations, but in Vance's speech the issue had to be faced: the idea of such a force would either appear or it would not.

At State, speeches by the secretary were usually drafted by the policy planning staff, working with the relevant bureaus. The first draft of the OAS speech was based on a text by the Latin American bureau, with contributions from the office in charge of OAS affairs and the human rights bureau. There was little time, and a draft was not completed until June 20, the day before the speech was to be delivered. Both Assistant Secretary Vaky and Secretary Vance reviewed it before sending it on to President Carter, who had asked to see it.

The draft statement followed the decisions of the June 19 interagency meeting and included a specific call for Somoza's resignation. But it made no reference to an OAS peace-keeping force, and it offered no criticism of Cuban support for the Sandinistas, even though the president had attacked the Cubans in a speech a few days before. Vance and Vaky were certain that public mention of a peace-keeping force would only irritate the Latin American audience, and any attack on Cuba would smack of propaganda and undercut the American proposals.

With less than twenty-four hours before the speech was to be delivered, the president went over it carefully. Presidents seldom like the way State Department speeches are written: the careful language of diplomacy does not lend itself to the rhetorical flourishes that keep an audience engaged. Teddy Roosevelt spoke for all presidents when he returned a State Department draft of a speech with this rebuke: "I did not deliver it as handed to me because it was fatuous and absurd. . . . There should be some sort of effort to write a speech that shall be simple and that shall say something, or, if that is deemed inexpedient, that shall not at least be of a fatuity so great that it is humiliating to read it."[5] Similarly, in March 1947, the State Department wrote the first draft of the famous "Truman Doctrine" speech calling for assistance to Greece. It was, Truman would recall, "not at all to my liking. The writers had filled the speech with all sorts of background data and statistical figures about Greece and made the whole thing sound like an investment prospectus."[6]

Since Vance would be giving the address, the president did not turn the draft over to his White House speechwriters to give it more flash. (It was not, in any case, as bland as the efforts that so offended Roosevelt and Truman.) Still, with his extraordinary concern for detail, Carter could not resist editing the words Vance would use. For example, where the draft speech warned that the Nicaraguan conflict was on the verge of becoming a war of national destruction, the president struck out the phrase *threatens to become* and substituted, in his strong, clear handwriting, *is becoming.*

Carter's main concern was with the omission of any references to Cuba and to the OAS peace-keeping proposal. After checking with Brzezinski, he added a paragraph referring to "mounting evidence" of Cuban involvement in Nicaragua's internal affairs that could transform those affairs into "international and ideological issues." Another insert in the president's hand stated that "all of the member nations of this organization must consider on an urgent basis the establishment of a peace-keeping force, to restore order and to permit the will of Nicaraguan citizens to be implemented in the establishment of a democratic and representative government."[7]

The following morning, Vance met with Vaky and others to go over a final draft of the statement. There is an unwritten law in the government that work on all speeches goes down to the last possible hour. Technology decides when that hour has arrived. Today, through the miracle of word processing, tinkering with a speech can continue almost until its delivery; in 1979 an hour or two were needed to get a speech typed and reproduced for release to the press. (Perhaps, if Lincoln had had a second envelope in his pocket on the way to Gettysburg, he would have been tempted to fiddle with perfection.)

At the meeting, Vaky objected strongly to including the OAS peace-keeping proposal in the speech. Vance agreed, and phoned Brzezinski. When the National Security assistant confirmed that it was the president's decision to go ahead, further protesting was useless. Vance and his advisers could, however, seek ways to make the proposal more palatable to the Latin Americans. It was the word *force* that was most likely to offend the secretary's audience at the OAS and thus divert attention from the other American proposals. The term appeared twice, once where the president had inserted it in the body of the statement and once in the summary of the American proposals. The president's first insertion was left as written, but for the summary, Vance, Vaky, and the others at the meeting sought a softer word. "An OAS peace-keeping *presence?*" Maybe. "*Endeavor?*" No. "*Mechanism?*" No. "*Effort?*" Too tentative. In the end, Vance came back to *presence,* which implied an actual OAS group in Nicaragua but was less specific and provocative than *force.* After making a few more stylistic changes, Vance approved the speech and it was rushed to a typist for final transcription.

At his appearance before the OAS foreign ministers, Vance called for Somoza's resignation and for the formation of an interim Government of National Reconciliation; a cease-fire with a cessation of arms shipments; an OAS peace-keeping "force" or "presence"; and an international relief and reconstruction effort. Recalling a prayer for peace in Nicaragua by Pope John Paul II a few days earlier, Vance concluded, "Our objective could not be more important: the restoration of peace to a stricken land."

Reaction to the speech was as Vaky had predicted. While the American press headlined the call for Somoza's resignation, the focus in Latin America was on the peace-keeping force — and the reaction was overwhelmingly negative. The Mexican foreign minister was instructed by his president to block this manifestation of American interventionism. He and other ministers began to urge an OAS resolution that would call for Somoza's resignation but would fail to mention most other aspects of the American proposal.

Finally, after considerable lobbying by Deputy Secretary of State Warren Christopher, Vaky, and Robert Pastor, the OAS passed a resolution that called in general terms for steps to promote a peaceful solution to the crisis while also urging the replacement of the Somoza regime. Some useful general language had been gained — the OAS resolution would be helpful in putting pressure on Somoza — but in failing to come up with concrete language that could be used with the Sandinistas and those supplying them with arms, American diplomacy had hardly triumphed.

Pastor recalls that when he returned to the White House he found Brzezinski "in a very different world, contemplating military intervention" in Nicaragua. Brzezinski felt that Carter's credibility with the Soviets required an American willingness to use force. Concerned more about regional realities than global signaling, Pastor argued that "if we intervened unilaterally, we would justify Soviet action and provoke a strong reaction in Latin America."

Nonetheless, on June 22, at the Friday morning breakfast the president regularly held with his senior foreign policy advisers, Brzezinski urged direct military action. It would prevent a Castroite victory in Nicaragua, he argued, demonstrate American power in our own backyard, and prevent a defeat in Central America that would damage the president's ability to win ratification of the SALT II treaty in the Senate. But the president and the others at the meeting — Vice-President Mondale, Secretary Vance, Secretary of Defense Harold Brown, and White House Chief of Staff Hamilton Jordan — did not respond with any enthusiasm. Vance pointed to the negative Latin American reaction to an OAS peace-keeping force, and the president made it clear that he was opposed to any unilateral intervention.[8]

It was clear that with the demise of the American notion of an OAS peace-keeping force and with an accelerating trend among Latin American governments to throw their support behind the Sandinistas, a new American strategy was desperately needed. At interagency meetings on June 23 and June 25, a response was developed that again reflected a compromise between the views of the State Department and those of the White House. Vaky and other State officials argued primarily for building bridges to the Sandinistas' provisional government, trying to moderate its outlook and strengthen the position of the non-Sandinista members on the junta. Brzezinski concentrated on the political and military structure that would be left when Somoza departed. The compromise, suggested by Warren Christopher, was to try to do both.

William Bowdler, who had returned to his duties as assistant secretary of state for Intelligence and Research following the failure of the mediation effort, would be sent back to Central America to establish contact with the junta in San José, urging it to negotiate a peaceful reconciliation in Nicaragua after Somoza's departure. At the same time, the United States would quietly seek the creation by Nicaraguan moderates of a post-Somoza executive committee. Backed by a reformed National Guard, this executive committee could negotiate a reconciliation with the junta while the Sandinista military commanders and new leaders of the National Guard could form a new Nicaraguan military integrating the opposing forces. No one thought all this would be easy. The junta had immediately rejected the proposals Vance had presented at the OAS meeting, and it was unlikely to give Bowdler a warm reception. Nor was it clear how many moderates were willing to join an executive committee in Managua. In addition, a new, non-Somocista leader for a reformed National Guard had to be found.

Bowdler immediately ran into trouble in San José. By June 28, before he had a chance to speak with members of the junta, the entire American plan was leaked to *The New York Times*. In New York, William Wipfler, head of the Human Rights Office of the National Council of Churches, read the *Times* story and called Sergio Ramírez in San José. Ramírez, a member of the junta and a closet Sandinista, was shocked and angry when Wipfler read the article to him and asked for his opinion.[9] The next day, the junta rejected the U.S. proposals. It was leading a provisional government that it considered the proper successor to Somoza. Why negotiate an alternative?

In subsequent days, as Bowdler met with members of the junta, he sought to persuade them at least to broaden their membership by including more non-Sandinistas. This, too, proved impossible. Oddly enough, his opposition did not come from the Sandinistas and their representatives on the junta. The Sandinista leaders consulted with Fidel Castro, who told them to go ahead and let the junta be expanded. (Castro knew the junta really did not matter, since the Sandinistas controlled the military forces opposing Somoza, and their guns would convey political power after the revolution succeeded.) No, it was the non-Sandinista *moderates* who were most opposed to increasing their own numbers on the junta. Alfonso Robelo — later a leader of the contras opposing the Sandinistas — and Violeta de Chamorro were apparently reluctant to see their own influence (such as it was) within the junta decreased or to appear less militant than their Sandinista colleagues.[10]

Clearly, the United States could gain influence with the junta only by shaking the confidence of the Sandinistas in their inevitable triumph. Only to the degree that there was the prospect of a reformed National Guard and some kind of interim moderate leadership when Somoza left would the junta be likely to see its own interests as served by negotiation of a compromise solution. But could such arrangements be made? A new American ambassador would have to try.

TWELVE

End Game in Managua

AMBASSADOR SOLAUN HAD RESIGNED DURING THE EARLY
spring. In April, Lawrence Pezzullo, our ambassador to Uruguay,
received an urgent telephone call from Harry Barnes, director general of the Foreign Service in charge of personnel. Would Pezzullo
go to Managua as the new American ambassador? Pezzullo replied
that he wanted to consult with his wife. She told him he would
be crazy to accept, that the job in Managua was a no-win situation.
In a subsequent conversation Pezzullo hesitated, Barnes persisted,
and our new man in Managua finally agreed to go.

His mission would be extremely difficult: creating a viable transition mechanism in Managua. Vance, Vaky, and Barnes had chosen
Pezzullo because they believed he had the strength of character
and personal force to deal firmly with Somoza, to speak to him
in his own strong language. A tall, athletic man with strong features
and a salty manner of speaking, Pezzullo was known as an intelligent
and tenacious scrapper. He had little taste for diplomatic indirec-
tion; he was friendly, but very direct.

A native of the Bronx, Pezzullo had joined the Foreign Service
in 1957, after having worked as a schoolteacher. His first assignments had been to consular and administrative posts, including a
tour at the embassy in Saigon in the early 1960s. His talent and
taste for politics gained him a series of appointments to political
sections at various embassies in Latin America, interspersed with

assignments in the State Department, including work on congressional relations. As the American representative in Uruguay since 1977, he had been a forceful ambassador, urging human rights reforms on the military regime there.

After his confirmation by the Senate as ambassador to Nicaragua, Pezzullo attended the mid-May Chiefs of Mission meeting in Costa Rica and then flew to Washington to work closely with Vaky and Bowdler as the new American strategy was developed during June. He attended the interagency meetings at the White House and understood very clearly the priority Brzezinski assigned to developing an interim structure that would be in place when Somoza left. "The White House," Pezzullo recalls, "was obsessed with the 'vacuum' that Somoza would leave behind him. 'What do we do about the vacuum? How do we fill it?' Half the time, I thought I was being sent off to clean a house."

Actually, housecleaning was not a bad metaphor for the first part of the new ambassador's task, which was to persuade Somoza to resign. On June 18, Pezzullo had met at a Washington hotel with Luis Pallais Debayle, Somoza's cousin and confidant. Carefully following approved talking points, the American asked Pallais to convey an important message to Somoza: the United States wanted to see him resign in a statesmanlike fashion, leaving behind him a government of national reconciliation and a reformed National Guard. Pallais had flown to Managua with the message and had conveyed the dictator's response to the American embassy there. Somoza would resign if there was an orderly transfer of power under OAS auspices and if he was allowed to live in exile in the United States without fear of extradition to Nicaragua.

On June 26, Pezzullo left for Central America to discuss the matter directly with Somoza and to work at filling the vacuum. He flew on an official jet to Panama, and the next morning boarded a small airplane for Nicaragua. The main airport outside Managua was temporarily closed because of the fighting, so Pezzullo landed at a small airfield on a farm near the Pacific coast. The drive to Managua reflected the deteriorating situation: fighting was widespread throughout the country and the outskirts of Managua had become a war zone. The ambassador's limousine had to be escorted by a National Guard armored car, and a bodyguard rode shotgun for Pezzullo. "We drove like hell all the way," he recalls. "That was my introduction to my new job." As soon as he reached the embassy, the ambassador called Somoza and asked to see him. A meeting was scheduled for that afternoon.

For obvious reasons, Pezzullo had decided to forgo the traditional formality of presenting his credentials to the Nicaraguan president. At 4:30 he drove from the embassy to Somoza's "Bunker," the military headquarters in the center of Managua. The little ranch house on a hill just above the Bunker reminded Pezzullo of the houses beside a California golf course. In the living room he found a tense but composed Somoza dressed in a business suit. Also present were Somoza's cousin, Luis Pallais; Foreign Minister Quintana — and, sitting on a corner of a desk, the dictator's old friend, Representative Jack Murphy. Pezzullo had met Murphy in Washington and was not completely surprised to see him now. But he hid his reaction and paid no attention to the congressman.

Murphy's presence made the meeting seem slightly unreal from the start, and Somoza's opening remarks did little to change the impression. "I brought the Foreign Minister with me," Somoza said. ". . . I had rather listen to you in English; me being a Latin from Manhattan, I had rather listen to the things in your language because I can understand them just as well as in Spanish. I have asked Congressman Murphy to be here because I believe that it is necessary . . . for him to witness to this — I welcome you, Mr. Ambassador, to Nicaragua."[1]

"Thank you," Pezzullo replied. "We met a long time ago, in '73, after the earthquake. I came down for a short visit and we had breakfast together; you were gracious enough to invite me for breakfast."

Somoza responded that he did not remember the occasion, and Pezzullo had no interest in refreshing his memory. Pezzullo had been deputy director of State's Office of Central American Affairs at the time, and had been appalled at what he had seen both of Somoza's rule and of the obsequious performance of Ambassador

Turner Shelton. On his return to Washington, Pezzullo had recommended to the director general of the Foreign Service that Shelton be replaced, only to be told that the State Department was powerless to do so; Shelton enjoyed too much support from Nixon's White House. Indeed, Pezzullo was warned to be very discreet in his comments about the ambassador.

Now, Pezzullo decided to come quickly to the point. Following the talking points he had used with Luis Pallais in Washington, he delivered Washington's message, emphasizing that he was speaking for President Carter, lest Somoza think the message came only from the State Department:

> Well, let me state the positions my government has taken after very serious and thoughtful consideration. It is nothing we take lightly, it was done at the top. . . . It was all done on the basis of our long relationship; a long feeling of friendship with you, the government, the people. . . . The conclusion we drew up after [careful study] and after the experience . . . of the mediation effort of last year, is that we have come to a point here which obeys certain priorities; and, as we have stated, and the Secretary stated yesterday before the Congress, we don't see a solution without your departure. We don't see the *beginning* of a solution without your departure.

Pezzullo went on to outline the plan to appoint a constitutional successor to Somoza who could arrange a cease-fire and negotiate a peaceful settlement. "We don't want to see chaos in this country and we don't want to see something we will all be unhappy with. We think that . . . without a statesmanlike act on your part, we are going to be caught in something which is going down. . . . That's essentially where we come out, and it is done without rancor . . ."

"I don't see it in your face, Mr. Pezzullo," Somoza interjected.

"You don't see what?"

"Rancor in your face."

Pezzullo confirmed that there was none, and said that the United States hoped the Nicaraguan would leave "with dignity." He was surprised by Somoza's response. Speaking dramatically, the dictator said he had been told there would be no room for negotiation, but that his "point of view would be listened to" — and asked for permission to present his views. Taken aback, Pezzullo said, "Sure; that's what I am here for." Somoza then got to his feet and left the room, saying he had to meet with his associates. Quintana and Murphy followed him.

On reentering the room, Somoza made the two principal points on his mind. First, he said, "We want certain guarantees that will insure that this country will not be taken over by the Communists — that's the most practical thing. . . . What are you going to do with the National Guard of Nicaragua? I don't need to know, but after you have spent thirty years educating all of these officers, I don't think it is fair for them to be thrown to the wolves."

Somoza's second concern, his own future, was at first expressed in indirect terms: "The other thing is that since we are good friends — because today we heard on a news station a report that was adverse to me, to my name, my family, my tradition, nevertheless that is part of life — we are good friends with the United States, and we should be treated as such."

Pezzullo responded first about the future of Nicaragua, saying that the prevention of a Communist victory depended on there being a clean break with the past. The United States would do what it could to preserve the Guard, but the Guard must be made into a "professional" force. More important was the political context; a military takeover or superficial change would only be perceived as *Somocismo* without Somoza, and then the United States could do nothing to help save the situation.

Somoza then asked about the political transition after his departure. He was told that the idea was for him to turn over power to someone in the Nicaraguan congress who would in turn be followed by a political arrangement that represented a "break" with the past. Somoza wondered whom the Americans had in mind to serve in a new transitional government. Pezzullo's answer was awkward: "We haven't been able to pull all that together yet." "Oh," said Somoza. "But we will," the American continued. And then, more honestly: "I don't know if it will work. I really don't know if it will work."

Despite this not terribly reassuring reply, Somoza offered his cooperation in trying to ease the transition and, at Pezzullo's request, promised to offer his thoughts at a subsequent meeting on how to build and preserve a reformed National Guard.

The conversation was interspersed with the Nicaraguan's rehearsal of his bitterness at the Carter administration for its treatment of him. For all these years, he insisted, he had been America's friend: "I threw a goddam Communist out of Guatemala in 1964," he said, referring to his 1954 assistance in the successful CIA effort to overthrow Jacobo Arbenz. "I personally worked on that. I do the same thing with the Cuban Bay of Pigs. . . . The U.S. called me and I agreed to have the bombers leave here and knock the hell out of the installations in Cuba, like a Pearl Harbor deal. . . ." Now, he complained, the Communists were coming back to destroy him, and the Carter administration seemed to be helping them do it.

Pezzullo suggested that the reasons for the revolution had more to do with internal events in Nicaragua than with the administration's policies but he did not press his points. He did not want to provoke Somoza into reversing his decision to resign.

With a sad smile, Somoza went on to say that he was a realist and a politician. He knew he had to go:

> So, let's not bullshit ourselves, Mr. Ambassador. I am talking to a professional. You have to do your dirty work, and I have to do mine. . . . So let's not, shall we say, try to hide. . . . I don't want to get into an argument with you because, my dear friend, I was practically brought up in the U.S., I have nothing against the people of the U.S.

It was the Carter administration, he concluded, that "has done the most to do me in."

This led to Somoza's second major point: the terms of his entry into the United States. "Don't force me to resign and walk through the bush. Because if you don't give me an alternative to go where I think my other country is, the U.S., my alternative is to resign and go to the bush. And then you have a Sandino again, all over again, and this poor goddam country will never have peace." Pezzullo let pass the terrible irony: that the son of Anastasio Somoza García, who was responsible for the murder of the anti-American guerrilla of the 1920s, should now entertain the extraordinary flight of fancy of becoming another Sandino.

Pezzullo made it clear that Somoza would have a visa and could come to the United States if he wished to. The Nicaraguan was amused when told that his priority immigrant status came from his relationship to an American citizen: his estranged wife, Hope. But the ambassador offered no guarantees against extradition, and in a later conversation the Nicaraguan was told that he could not have diplomatic immunity, only the normal protections of American law.

The ambassador then moved to some indirect blackmail. Much depended, Pezzullo said, on how Somoza behaved when he left:

> The point is, if you left with a certain amount of dignity . . . If you walked out of here and went after the States and after the Carter Administration, talked to Reagan and [cozied] up to the Reagan campaign, it might make you feel better but it wouldn't help you. And I am not speaking as a partisan, because I don't give a damn if it is a Republican or a Democrat in there because I am going to retire in a couple of years anyway. It doesn't matter to me, but [what I say to you is] the truth . . .

Somoza responded: "They shouldn't make me mix into their internal politics."

But Pezzullo reiterated the point: "I think if you walked in [to the United States] with a nice tone to your approach . . ."

Now Somoza seemed to understand. "My dear friend," he said, "I am a giant to be talking to you right after I have had the Hemisphere clobber me [at the OAS meeting]." He would behave. Pezzullo hastily humored him: "I don't know how you keep [the situation] going," he said. "I admire you."

As the meeting concluded, Somoza reiterated that he was willing to leave, and asked how soon he should go. Pezzullo thought that it should be speedily: within a week.

"Supposing I leave tomorrow?" Somoza asked.

"I don't want you to leave tomorrow," the American quickly responded. "I've just got to get things organized a little bit . . . Talk to a few people. . . . Please don't move too precipitously."

As Pezzullo rose to leave, Somoza concluded the meeting on a typically dramatic note: "My dear friend, we have been victorious. We have gotten licked a couple of times, but this time I am not going to move without having my back protected, so you are my protection."

"Let's do it with grace," Pezzullo reminded him.

"Right!" said Somoza.

It was 7:30 when Pezzullo finally left the Bunker. He hurried back to the embassy and dashed off a FLASH NODIS SPECIAL ENCRYPTION reporting cable to Washington, with a copy for Bowdler in San José. At the end of the three-page message, he expressed uncertainty about how the dictator would behave: "Although Somoza promised to plan the final days together, his character and past performance leaves much doubt. At least he got the message that there are no easy ways out. He clearly wants safehaven in the United States."

Pezzullo wrote also that although Congressman Murphy had never offered a comment at the meeting, his "presence may be useful; he was a party to this understanding." A later cable on July 14 was less positive about Murphy: "Murphy is marginally interested in the National Guard and Liberal Party, but very, very interested in the Somoza business. Somoza referred to Murphy in our first meeting as the associate; business partner would have been more accurate." It had been a bizarre meeting, but at least the first step had been completed. The vacuum had been created, at least in principle. Now came the harder part: creating an arrangement to fill the vacuum before Somoza actually left.

For the preceding few days, at Washington's instruction, the embassy had started consulting with moderate Nicaraguan leaders about participating in a transition government after Somoza's departure. While the reaction had been encouraging, the embassy had encountered considerable skepticism about whether the OAS and the United States would act with sufficient determination to ensure both Somoza's removal and a peaceful transition to a popularly elected government. The memory of the failed mediation effort was vivid. Why now believe that a new American effort would be any more successful? Why link their political fortunes, and perhaps their lives, to an American plan that might not succeed, and thus be exposed to the wrath of the Sandinistas?

Embassy officers were thus bearish about the possibility of putting together an interim executive committee of moderates. As Pezzullo listened to them express their views on his first day as ambassador, he found that what they said made sense. He was not impressed, however, by the overall quality of the embassy staff he had inherited.

In mid-May, at the Chiefs of Mission conference, he had met a political officer from the embassy and had asked him to prepare a background analysis of Nicaraguan politics. It was now the end of June, and nothing had been done. What the same officer *had* done, in the midst of the important consultations with Nicaraguan moderates and meetings with Somoza, was to send Washington a lengthy cable conveying, in its original Spanish, a statement delivered to the embassy by a minor Nicaraguan political party. When Pezzullo asked why he had bothered sending it, the officer replied that he thought someone in Washington might be interested. If you thought it might have some interest, Pezzullo asked, why not translate the passages that mattered into English and write your own paragraph explaining their significance? *He missed his chance to make a difference,* Pezzullo thought, resolving not to offer the young diplomat any important new chores.

In the midst of a crisis there was no time to try to train inexperienced Foreign Service officers or to wait for the work of more senior embassy officials who could not, he thought, "step lively." Nor did the new ambassador trust the discretion of the military attaché; he feared that what was said at embassy meetings might find its way through him to the National Guard and to Somoza.

That evening, when he went for the first time to the stately ambassador's residence high on a hill overlooking Managua, Pezzullo found further evidence for his view of the embassy's past performance. It was already plain to him that embassy officers had been circumspect, to put it charitably, about venturing into dangerous areas of the country, and this had limited the embassy's ability to report accurately on events. Now, when he climbed the stairs and entered his bedroom, he found new evidence of this preoccupation with security. Even though both the hill on which the residence was located and the building itself were well guarded, the ambassador's bedroom was nevertheless fitted out with bullet-proof doors and shutters. There was also a machine in the room that Pezzullo at first took for a fancy radio with a large plastic console. Further investigation revealed that it was a device for monitoring adjacent hallways and stairs by means of closed-circuit television cameras. The device was rigged to trigger tear gas canisters at strategic points. Pezzullo was appalled that embassy security officers had suggested to the previous ambassador that such a system was either necessary or useful, and he ordered it removed.

The new ambassador had brought with him Malcolm Barnaby, an experienced officer from Washington, who remained in Managua for the next few days. And in two weeks Tom O'Donnell, a good-humored, unflappable professional with whom Pezzullo had worked in the past, would arrive in Managua as his new deputy chief of mission. Pezzullo could rely on both of them. Inclined in any case to work on his own, Pezzullo wrote off the rest of the embassy staff as not being of much help. It was, Pezzullo recalls wryly, "a strange assignment. I was walking into a country I had been to twice in my life for visits of only three or four days. I was being asked to tell a president to resign in the middle of a civil war. And I was then to fill the vacuum he left, though I barely knew the names of anyone except the major Nicaraguan actors. . . . And I didn't have an embassy I could trust. It was a very funny feeling."

The embassy's skepticism about putting together an executive committee was reinforced when, on the same day Pezzullo arrived in Managua, the moderate FAO issued a communiqué supporting the junta in Costa Rica: "The Junta, on which the FAO is represented, and which the FAO has supported and continues to support, constitutes the beginning of that democratic and pluralistic régime which must accede to power upon the fall of the Somocista government."[2]

The next day, June 28, Pezzullo cabled Washington that there was little chance of forming an executive committee of any size. Instead, he argued, Somoza should be persuaded to turn over power to a member of the Nicaraguan congress or of his cabinet, who could then negotiate with the junta. Pezzullo thought this should be done quickly, before the situation deteriorated further, and recommended that he be authorized to tell Somoza to resign by the third of July.

At the State Department, Vaky did not think the executive committee idea would work, and he agreed with the ambassador's recommendation. American efforts, he thought, should now be directed at trying to gain influence with the junta. The Sandinistas were now in such a strong position that they would inevitably come to power. Trying to create an alternative political structure in Managua would only deepen the Sandinistas' hostility to the United States and make it harder to deal with them later.

At the White House, however, officials had read reports of conversations Pezzullo had just held with the Catholic archbishop and the president of the Nicaraguan Red Cross. Both thought the idea of an executive committee was a good one, and the archbishop offered to supply names of possible members. So the NSC refused to accept the State Department's view that the notion was dead.

At interagency meetings on June 28 and June 29, State and NSC officials argued to no conclusion. There was no way to resolve the dispute at once, because Carter, Brzezinski, and Vance were all in Tokyo at an economic summit. After their inconclusive meetings, officials at both State and the NSC wrote private cables to Vance and Brzezinski in Japan, making their cases and suggesting that the issue go to the president. But when confronted with the dispute, Carter — who was deeply involved in a wrangle with the allies on a joint response to the energy crisis — refused to decide. He wanted to know what the leaders of other Central American nations thought, and asked that President Torrijos of Panama be secretly invited to Washington after Carter's return, to consult on next steps.

Meanwhile, on June 29 and again on June 30, Pezzullo sent additional cables to Washington expressing his view that the executive committee idea was "a dead letter." On June 28, the same story in *The New York Times* that had led the junta to reject the American plan also caused the FAO and Nicaraguan business leaders to denounce it publicly. Nor did Pezzullo's continuing conversations with the few moderates he could find in Managua offer much hope. "Fear of reprisal by the [Sandinista] FSLN," he cabled, "and the lack of any assured security and support base are the principal factors inhibiting the individuals we have contacted from becoming part of a caretaker Executive Committee. They see the Junta in San José supported by a FSLN force and [by] such countries as Panama and Costa Rica, while they would have nothing but helpful words from the US Government as of the moment. Realistically, we have little prospect of interesting any individuals to play this hero role without greater assurances . . ." The key, Pezzullo added, was to move quickly in establishing a reformed National Guard under new leadership. If it appeared that there would be an alternative force to the Sandinistas, then there might be more candidates for a caretaker body that could negotiate a moderate solution.

On Friday, June 29, Pezzullo went again to the Bunker to meet with Somoza, and again the Nicaraguan agreed to resign. In his reporting cable, Pezzullo suggested to Washington that the resignation take place soon, on the following Tuesday or Thursday, July 3 or July 5. Setting the date for July 4, he wrote, "seems a bit much." At another meeting the next day, June 30, Pezzullo gave Somoza and his entourage U.S. entry visas, but he could not yet give the Nicaraguan a date for his departure. The result was that Somoza began to panic.

Before the American ambassador could get back to the embassy and write up his report on the meeting of June 30, Congressman Murphy had already called Deputy Secretary of State Christopher to convey Somoza's version of the encounter. In addition to scooping

Pezzullo, the congressman complained that the American military attaché in Managua seemed to be trying to get the National Guard to carry out a coup. The State Department urgently informed Pezzullo of Murphy's call, and he responded with a FLASH message stating that Somoza was indeed jumpy and feared assassination. The military attaché, he wrote, had simply been consulting his contacts in the National Guard about possible new commanders.

The cable from the department irritated the harassed Pezzullo, but a subsequent cable from State truly disturbed him. An interagency meeting, he was told, had decided that he could not yet give Somoza a departure date because the repercussions were not yet clear enough. Before he left, there needed to be a credible, non-Somocista caretaker ready to replace him. A member of Somoza's cabinet would not be credible. In addition, Washington instructed, Pezzullo should keep working on preserving some kind of effective but reconstituted Guard presence.

Pezzullo was incensed. Why didn't Washington understand that there was no way to "fill the post-Somoza vacuum" satisfactorily? That the civil war was intensifying? That people were dying? That time was working against Washington? The sooner Somoza left, the more likely it was that whoever replaced him as caretaker would have something left with which to bargain. Every day the fighting continued there was less chance that a significant National Guard could be given new leadership. Once Managua was under siege, there could be no real negotiations because the Sandinistas would taste imminent victory.

As he flew back to Washington to attend an interagency meeting of the Special Coordinating Committee on Monday, July 2, Pezzullo thought he knew what needed to be done: "Get the goddam guy out. Stop the killing. The faster the knife goes in, the better." But in Washington, he felt as if he had entered a dream world. Before the meeting, Robert Pastor asked him a series of questions about post-Somoza arrangements and a tired Pezzullo exploded. Washington was out of its mind, he said, if it thought some elaborate structure could be created. That was harebrained. There was a goddam war going on down there. The place was coming apart.

At the meeting, Pezzullo repeated that Somoza was ready to go and needed only a date. The executive committee idea, he said, was dead. The only hope was that if Somoza left very soon, the power vacuum might be filled by the Guard under a new commander. However, he said, the Guard would need some "confidence-building measures" — training and assistance from the United States that would help its new leaders act on their own, out from under the shadow of Somoza. And this would take some time. You couldn't simply flip a switch and have a reformed National Guard.

Warren Christopher and Pete Vaky were leery of too close an association with the Guard, and returned to the point they had made at previous meetings about seeking to build American influence with the junta and the Sandinistas. Others, led by Brzezinski, feared that without our building up the Guard, there would simply be a post-Somoza collapse. In the end, a compromise was agreed upon. We would seek to create a *new* junta in which moderates held the balance of power. In return for our getting rid of Somoza, Torrijos would be asked to help out in two ways: by rallying support in Central America for whomever replaced Somoza and by discontinuing arms shipments to the Sandinistas. If he refused to go along with the latter, the United States would reserve the right to resupply the National Guard.

After the meeting, Pezzullo accompanied a number of the participants to a discussion with President Carter. The ambassador privately thought little of the Special Coordinating Committee's recommended strategy, and he was impressed by the way Carter immediately saw how unworkable the approach was. How, he asked, could the United States persuade the Sandinistas to change the junta in any meaningful way? Why should they agree to effectively giving up power? The president's participation in the making of policy toward Nicaragua had in the past been sporadic and sometimes unhelpful. To be sure, he had been perfectly consistent in insisting that America act in concert with others; that we respect Nicaraguan sovereignty; and that our policies be based on democratic principles. These general precepts had provided the basis for Robert Pastor's more specific views during the past two years.

But there had been trouble when the president dipped into the details. His idea of sending a letter to Somoza in the summer of 1978 had backfired. He had muddied the issue during the last days of the mediation effort. And his insertion, at Brzezinski's suggestion, of the peace-keeping idea in Vance's OAS speech had produced a diplomatic setback. The problem was that since Nicaragua had never emerged as a priority issue, Carter had sometimes acted on the basis of scraps of information: a paragraph in the Evening Notes from the State Department or an item in a general intelligence report. He had made all of the policy decisions, but on the basis of written summaries of the various interagency meetings. Issues with a higher priority were draining his time, so the most efficient way to deal with second-order problems like Nicaragua was on paper. Thus he never heard the give-and-take of the arguments and may have missed some of the nuances.

Now the crisis in Nicaragua called for more active involvement. As the president talked the issue through with his advisers, Pezzullo was impressed with his realism and intelligence. As much as anyone there, the president understood that there were severe limits to what the United States could accomplish, especially if it acted alone. Carter was right, Pezzullo thought, when he observed that a reconstituted National Guard could achieve legitimacy only if it was supported by other Central American governments. And without such a Guard, no successor to Somoza could hope to negotiate successfully with the junta.

To Pete Vaky, it was unlikely that a reformed Guard could survive, even with support from other Central American governments. The revolution, he knew, was not only against Somoza; it was aimed at the Guard as well. After almost fifty years of the Guard's identification with the Somoza regime, and after all the bloodshed and suffering of the past weeks — and years — it was almost inconceivable that the Guard, however reformed, could gain legitimacy with the Nicaraguan people. But at least, Vaky thought, the president and other officials had moved past the illusion of a post-Somoza executive committee.

The next morning, on July 3, the president presented a new plan to Torrijos. The United States would see to it that Somoza left; Torrijos would help in arranging a cease-fire, would consult on names to be suggested to the junta in order to broaden it, as well as on a new National Guard commander, and would halt the shipment of arms to the FSLN. In addition, the Panamanian would help gain the agreement of the junta to the following scenario for events in Managua: the Nicaraguan congress would name a successor to Somoza, who would step down shortly thereafter, turning over power to the junta. The junta would in turn organize elections, forgo reprisals, and merge the National Guard with its own forces.

The Panamanian's reaction to the president's proposal seemed to be all the Americans could have hoped for. Torrijos greatly admired Carter and, obviously delighted to be offered such a leading role by the American president, expressed enthusiasm. It would take him a few hours to sell the plan when he met with the Sandinistas, he said, but he thought they would go along. After the White House meeting, Pastor noted uneasily that Torrijos seemed vague about the details of what had been discussed, and he had taken no notes. Mostly he seemed excited about the prospect of Somoza's leaving. It was not the first time, Pastor thought, that Central American leaders supporting the Sandinistas had seemed fixed on the simple objective of removing Somoza, without considering very carefully what would follow. Still, the American plan might work: after all, Torrijos had assured Carter that he could do what needed to be done.[3]

Pete Vaky was immediately dispatched to Venezuela, Colombia, and the Dominican Republic to gain support for the Carter plan. Bowdler returned to Costa Rica to pursue his talks with the junta. And Pezzullo flew back to Managua, to try to identify a new, politically clean commander for the Guard and to work out with Somoza a procedure for naming a successor, a man who would assume Somoza's office and then, before even tasting power, relinquish it to the junta. Pezzullo thought the new scheme was makeshift but might somehow work. At least the strategy no longer required his trying to persuade frightened Nicaraguan moderates to risk their necks by joining a post-Somoza executive committee.

As he got back to work in Managua, Pezzullo was struck by how theatrical it all felt. If he had not been so aware that the fighting was real, the ambience would have seemed straight from a Hollywood movie — the blue lights of the police cars that escorted him back and forth between the embassy and the Bunker, the dialogues with Somoza, sitting in his little California ranch house, bombs dropped by Somoza's forces blasting the city, helicopters buzzing around. Tom O'Donnell, the new deputy chief of mission, arrived on July 7. He had served in Managua as chief of the embassy's economic section in the early 1970s and had seen the devastation of the earthquake. Now, as he was driven in from the airport, the destruction wrought by the fighting reminded him of those earlier scenes.

There was now an evening curfew, so the embassy was shut down in late afternoon to allow local employees to get home. Because of the dangers in the city, many members of the embassy staff had moved to the safety of the residence, and every evening, twenty or thirty people would join Pezzullo at dinner. Afterwards, he and O'Donnell usually escaped to a study at one end of the building, a large, handsome room with leather chairs and sofas, book-lined walls, and large doors opening onto a closed porch and thence to the gardens. Here they would talk over the day's events and write their evening cables to Washington.

There was no way to deliver the cables to the code room at the embassy offices half a mile away, so Pezzullo and O'Donnell communicated with the code clerks on walkie-talkies outfitted with scrambling devices. One evening, as he stood on a balcony, speaking to the embassy office building below, Pezzullo could hear shots at the base of the hill. Embassy security officers rushed out, shouting that he might get himself shot, that the gunfire was directed at him. Pezzullo doubted this, but agreed to interrupt his transmission until a quieter moment. The security men were obviously annoyed with him for being on the balcony at all.*

During the drama, the embassy deliberately cultivated a sense

* Years later, when the local employees were asked for their recollections of Pezzullo, they invariably recalled his seeming indifference to the dangers in Managua in early July 1979.

of calm. In times of crisis, the code of the Foreign Service requires something approaching a competition for Most Unruffled Demeanor. Besides, there were lighter moments to break the tension. ABC News reporters lent the embassy a videotape of the movie *Young Frankenstein,* and for days Mel Brooks provided the kinds of running gags that people embrace at times of stress. There was also enjoyment in recalling how, late one afternoon, a junior consular officer at the embassy had been astonished to see Bianca Jagger, the Nicaraguan wife of British rock star Mick Jagger, rolling into his office. Her car had suffered a flat tire near the embassy and she demanded urgent assistance in fixing it because the curfew was approaching. The young officer knew that the embassy had been asked by Senator Jacob Javits's office to keep an eye out for Mrs. Jagger, a friend of the Javits family. When he called the ambassador's office to request instructions, Pezzullo, deep in urgent work, responded succinctly. "Tell her," he said, "that we don't do tires."

At first Pezzullo refused to make time for meetings with the many American reporters who had arrived in Managua to cover the war, telling his press officer to put the media off with the message that he would see them when he had any news for them. Now, after a week or so on the job, this excuse would no longer do. The press officer urged Pezzullo at least to see the reporters from *The New York Times* and *The Washington Post,* and Pezzullo agreed. After he started meeting occasionally with reporters, usually "on background," Pezzullo quickly realized that the press officer had been right. The news people seemed almost universally sympathetic to the Sandinistas and not only hostile to Somoza but suspicious of the American government. Their suspicions were at least partially eased, he felt, by his talks with them.

Most of the reporters were housed next door to Somoza's Bunker at the Intercontinental Hotel, an oddly shaped edifice modeled on a Mayan temple. As the fighting worsened, more and more members of the government moved to this hotel as well, making it a useful hunting ground for official sources. Moreover, the hotel provided the telex and telephone services the reporters needed to transmit their stories back to the United States. At the end of the day, the reporters usually congregated in a bar at the "Intercon" to swap stories of the fighting and to discuss political trends. As is usual at such gatherings, a few of the most experienced foreign correspondents held court. (These are the reporters a wise embassy press officer will cultivate. They are useful sources of information and even wisdom. And if they have a clear understanding of the reasons behind American policy, they can help educate their junior colleagues in the course of these evening exchanges.) One stringer for an American newspaper (a stringer is paid by the story rather than on a regular salary) recalls that the conversation at the Intercon bar was almost invariably abusive of Somoza and supportive of his enemies. This was especially the case, of course, after the murder of Bill Stewart of ABC News by a National Guardsman.

But the reporters, like so many of the Nicaraguans with whom they were speaking, did not seem to be pro-Sandinista as a matter of politics. For them, the heroes of the unfolding story were not the Sandinista *commandantes*, but Los Muchachos, the young Nicaraguans doing battle with the unpopular National Guard. At a press conference in Managua during this period, pro-Somoza Congressman Larry McDonald accused American reporters of a bias for the Sandinistas and complained about the "unbelievable distortion of the news about Nicaragua in the media." An ABC correspondent, Tom Shell, spoke up and asked McDonald "to walk down here on the beach at the lake and look at the bodies with their hands tied that [the National Guard] is burning in the morning. And you come down here and accuse us of distorting? Where the hell have you been, sir?" Obviously unfazed, McDonald went on to address a group of Somoza supporters at the hotel, telling them to "take heart, keep your courage and stand firm . . . we are coming to your assistance."[4]

Having seen so much of the daily misery inflicted on the people of Nicaragua by the fighting, the reporters were understandably stunned when they discovered that Somoza had agreed to resign but had been asked by the American government to delay his departure. On July 7, the State Department cabled the embassy that

Karen De Young had published a story in *The Washington Post* reporting that Somoza was ready to go but that the United States was temporizing while negotiations were conducted with the junta in Costa Rica. Somoza told De Young that he had said to Pezzullo the previous week, "Alright, I'm ready." Now, Somoza said, he was a "tied donkey fighting with a tiger."[5]

The next morning, July 8, Pezzullo replied to the department in a FLASH message reporting that the De Young article had led COSEP, which represented anti-Somoza business leaders, to issue a statement accusing the United States of prolonging the bloodshed. The editorial staff of *La Prensa* had made the same case. Pezzullo suggested officials prepare a rather tortured press guidance noting the complexities of the situation and the importance of achieving a negotiated, democratic solution.

But the fact was that Pezzullo himself was highly impatient. It was clear from his own talks with Somoza that the dictator was extremely edgy. The tiger Somoza feared was not only the Sandinistas; it was also his own National Guard. Now that the word was out about his departure, Somoza's power over his military men was evaporating. If they turned on him, Somoza's life might be in danger. On July 5, Pezzullo had reported on Somoza's fears and his own concern that the transition process begin soon. In an urgent cable on July 6, the ambassador repeated his concern and reported that Sandinista forces were gaining momentum. "Time is not on our side," he warned.

In the wake of the De Young article, Pezzullo let his concern for quick action overcome his sense of realism. If the negotiations with the junta were to drag on much longer, he cabled Washington, and the strength of the National Guard continued to erode, it would be best simply to get Somoza to resign at once. Somoza could appoint his foreign minister as his successor. The minister could then publicly break with Somoza, release political prisoners, and appoint a non-Somocista commander of the National Guard. A "wave of public joy" at Somoza's departure would sap "an unknown, though perhaps considerable, amount of [Sandinista] support and thereby permit moderates to play a bigger role in forming a transition government."

Pezzullo would later say that in retrospect this cable did not "wear well." But at the time, he was becoming extremely frustrated with Washington, "which seemed to think it had time to burn" in making sure all the pieces were perfectly in place before setting a date for Somoza's departure. So Pezzullo had talked himself into an optimistic scenario that might encourage Washington to make a bold move.

Officials in Washington were not convinced by Pezzullo's vision, however, and continued to hope that Torrijos and Bowdler could gain the junta's agreement to compromise. Unfortunately, after leaving Washington on July 3 on wings of optimism, Torrijos had soon discovered that it would be no easy thing to get the junta to go along with the plan to which he and President Carter had agreed. The Panamanian's previous support for the Sandinistas had not purchased the leverage he had anticipated. In particular, as Vaky had foreseen, the junta balked at agreeing to any plan that might leave the National Guard intact, whatever its leadership. So after a few days, Torrijos stopped portraying the plan as a Panamanian initiative; it became the American proposal.

As Torrijos gradually backed away, Ambassador Bowdler picked up the talks with the junta. He, too, found the going difficult. But as instructed, Bowdler persisted — while Somoza panicked, Pezzullo fumed, and officials in Washington argued about what to do. Finally, on July 10, the administration had had enough, and Bowdler was told to issue an ultimatum. If the junta did not broaden its membership, call publicly for a cease-fire, and commit itself to free elections, the United States would consider "alternative steps."

Actually, no one in Washington was sure what those alternative steps might be, and the Sandinistas knew that although serious fighting might lie ahead, events were moving in their favor. So when Bowdler presented the American ultimatum on July 11, the Sandinistas simply responded with their own plan: power would be handed by the Nicaraguan congress directly to the Sandinistas' government of national reconciliation, led by the junta. The National Guard would be abolished; its members who had committed no crimes could either leave military service or be considered for membership in the Sandinista army. In a letter to the OAS the next day, the junta committed itself to "full respect for human rights" and to hold "the first free elections that our country will have in this century."

This assurance fell well short of Washington's desires, but it was better than nothing. On July 13, an interagency meeting decided to start playing the end game and to salvage what it could. Pezzullo was instructed to ask Somoza to leave soon, and to present to the dictator a list of men who might act as a new commander of the National Guard. The new commander would then negotiate the details of a cease-fire and some form of amalgamation of his forces with those of the enemy. Bowdler was directed to press the junta for assurances that the shift of political power would be as smooth and bloodless as possible.

While Washington was arriving at these decisions, Somoza decided on one last effort at preserving power. At 6:15 P.M. on July 13, acting at the suggestion of Congressman Murphy, he placed a telephone call to President Carter which was taken by Warren Christopher and Robert Pastor. Somoza said he wanted to come to Washington to explain to Carter how he could contribute to the national security of the United States. Christopher said he would pass the message along, but urged Somoza to talk to Pezzullo.[6]

Vaky then quickly drafted a letter from Vance to Somoza. Writing on behalf of the president, Vance reiterated the American view that a satisfactory military solution seemed impossible. The only hope of any kind of democratic outcome was through an immediate transition process. "I therefore urge you to arrange your departure without delay," the letter concluded. "We will receive you in the U.S., as Ambassador Pezzullo has indicated. Your continued delay will only prolong the conflict and bloodshed and compromise our ability to try to achieve a moderate outcome." The letter was flashed to Pezzullo.

In Managua, meanwhile, apparently sensing from his talk with Christopher and Pastor that Washington was indeed determined that he go, Somoza decided to see if he could rally support for the National Guard from friendly neighboring governments. Soon after speaking with Christopher, he flew to Guatemala to meet with President Romeo Lucas García and asked that the Guatemalan discuss with other military leaders in the region the possibility of their intervention in Nicaragua on behalf of the Guard. By now it was midnight, but word of the meeting quickly got to Washington. When officials there were asked by the Guatemalans if the United States would support such an intervention, the reply was negative. It probably didn't matter: the Guatemalans were not apparently inclined to act on Somoza's request.

The next day, July 14, Pezzullo handed Vance's letter to Somoza, suggesting that the Nicaraguan resign and leave the country in the next few days. The Sandinistas were now preparing a final military assault, and if it came before Somoza's departure, it would look as if he were fleeing in defeat. Also, if Somoza left sooner, the new National Guard commander would be in a stronger position politically. On the fifteenth, the American ambassador gave Somoza a short list of candidates for leadership of the Guard. It had not been easy to come up with good suggestions. Washington had been sending Pezzullo the names of men who had previously served in the Guard and now had strong non-Somocista credentials, but they either lacked sufficient command experience or had been out of the country so long that the Guard would never follow them.

Somoza had also made a few suggestions of his own. Pezzullo's deputy, Tom O'Donnell, who was now accompanying the ambassador to his meetings with Somoza, thought he remembered one of the men Somoza put forward, a former National Guard officer who was now a successful businessman. He checked with the embassy and confirmed that Somoza's candidate was one of the "fastest guys with a buck" in Nicaragua. At their next meeting, when they asked Somoza if he really thought his man had the kind of reputation a new National Guard commander would need, the dictator replied that he would be a very good negotiator but that it was true the man had a "sweet tooth."

In the end, with no acceptable suggestions either from Washington or from Somoza, Pezzullo had to rely on the embassy to come up with candidates. The military attaché could not do so: his own soundings with the National Guard had only produced a panicky reaction from Somoza about his activities. So the ambassador turned to the CIA station chief, who gave him six good names. Pezzullo questioned him closely to make sure that the six were not associated with the CIA and then presented the list to Somoza at their meeting on July 15. The Nicaraguan was impressed, telling Pezzullo he "knew his onions." Somoza's choice: Colonel Federico Mejía, a competent, apolitical engineer in the Guard. Pezzullo at once cabled the name to Bowdler in San José. The junta had insisted on seeing the list of possible candidates, and now wanted to interview Mejía. Bowdler arranged a secret meeting for members of the junta and Mejía in San José (which Bowdler did not attend).

Pezzullo had now worked out with Somoza a detailed plan for the transfer of power, and Bowdler had gone over it with the junta. The agreed scenario was this: as soon as Somoza and his entourage left for the United States, the Nicaraguan congress would appoint a new president. Somoza had chosen for this role the speaker of the lower house, Francisco Urcuyo Maliaños. To the degree that he was known for anything at all, Urcuyo, a physician, was known chiefly as a Somoza loyalist. According to the plan, at 8 A.M. the day after Somoza's departure, the new president, together with the new leader of the National Guard, would go out to a hotel at the airport. Meanwhile, a delegation from the junta would fly in from San José and go to the same hotel. There, Urcuyo would announce a cease-fire and the two delegations would meet, in the presence of Ambassador Bowdler and the Nicaraguan archbishop, to discuss the details of the cease-fire and a fusion of armed forces. Mejía would act as chief of staff of the Guard and would deal with his opposite number in the Sandinista forces. Power would formally be transferred to the junta within three days.

Now, on Monday, July 16, with a new National Guard leader named, the plan could be set in motion. Pezzullo and Bowdler were communicating directly and trying to keep Washington informed through cables and telephone talks with Vaky. As the main Sandinista forces were drawing closer to Managua, every hour counted, and it was decided that Somoza should leave late that very night. Pezzullo was tired but excited. Finally, after all the policy arguments and all the planning, they could bring the affair to a finish. He had only to see Somoza go and get Urcuyo and Mejía to the airport on time.

Soon, however, Somoza telephoned. It would be too dangerous, he argued, to bring a Sandinista military group to the airport for the meeting with Urcuyo and Colonel Mejía. Some young Guardsman might get "trigger-happy." Wouldn't it be better to fly Mejía to San José for military talks there? Pezzullo agreed and called Bowdler, who confirmed the new arrangement with the junta. An American aircraft was laid on for the flight. All that remained was to let Mejía know that the plane would take him to San José. Pezzullo tried to telephone Somoza, and then Urcuyo, to ask them to pass the message to Mejía, but he was not successful.

By now it was 10 P.M., only hours from Somoza's resignation and departure. Pezzullo called Mejía directly and, assuming that Somoza had told him of the plan that he go to San José, said that the plane would be waiting for him at the airport at seven the next morning. Mejía said nothing, which Pezzullo thought was odd. He dispatched the military attaché, who was to accompany Mejía to San José, to find the colonel and to confirm that he would make the flight.

Midnight passed. At 1 A.M. the Nicaraguan congress met at the Intercontinental hotel and accepted Somoza's resignation, naming Urcuyo as his successor. Somoza and his entourage departed soon afterward for their flight to Florida. Power had been transferred. So far, it seemed, so good. Next would come the morning trips to the airport, Mejía for his flight to San José and Urcuyo to the hotel there for his meeting with the junta.

Then everything began to go terribly wrong. Despite the late hour, "President" Urcuyo immediately gave a prepared radio address to the Nicaraguan nation. He declared an end to the Somoza era and called for a new dialogue with all democratic groups in Nicaragua. He made no reference to the junta, no call for a full cease-fire. What, Pezzullo wondered, is going on?[7] Soon his telephone

rang. It was the American military attaché reporting that he had
seen Mejía. The news was terrible. The new National Guard chief
of staff refused to fly to Costa Rica the next morning because he
had been ordered by "the president" to attend a 10 A.M. meeting
at the Bunker on the military situation. "*Which* president?" demanded Pezzullo, Somoza or Urcuyo? The attaché did not know.
Frantically, Pezzullo tried to telephone Mejía. He couldn't get
through.

At 4 A.M. the ambassador finally reached Urcuyo, who was settling
into the presidential office at the Bunker. The American reminded
Urcuyo that, according to the plan, he had agreed to meet with a
delegation from the junta that morning. Urcuyo said simply that
he would not. Pezzullo was dismayed. He called Vaky in Washington
to tell him that the American plan seemed to be falling apart.
Vaky said the only thing Pezzullo could do was to keep trying to
hold things together.

Pezzullo tried to sleep for a few hours. Then, just after dawn,
he went to the Bunker and insisted that Urcuyo be awakened to
meet with him. The encounter did not go well. Urcuyo said that
he would transfer power to a pluralistic junta but never to a Communist one. Pezzullo insisted: there is an agreement that you will
turn over power to the junta. "Like hell there is," said Urcuyo.
For a while the new president and the diplomat continued the
exchange in terms neither presidential nor diplomatic, and then
an outraged Pezzullo returned to the embassy. He called Vaky
again, who once more called for continued efforts to resuscitate
the plan. Meantime, in San José, Bowdler informed the junta that
there would be a delay, urging patience. But as soon as they heard
of Urcuyo's speech, the junta broke off all contact with Bowdler.

For Pezzullo, the long-awaited day of Somoza's departure had
become a nightmare. He went to see Mejía, who denied that either
Somoza or Urcuyo had ever told him of a plan to discuss a cease-
fire and a fusion of his forces with the Sandinistas. Mejía looked
at him, Pezzullo thought, as if he were a man from Mars. Clearly,
Mejía was speaking the truth. Mejía had been duped and so, Pezzullo
realized, had the Americans. What had happened?

Now, Pezzullo recalled how terrified Somoza had seemed — not only about the Sandinistas' advances, but about a coup by the National Guard. If word had gotten out that Somoza was going to leave and the junta would soon take power, the National Guard might either have collapsed or taken revenge on the dictator for his betrayal. Somoza therefore had needed to buy time to make a safe escape. Could he have pretended to Urcuyo and the Guard that although he was leaving, the struggle would continue? Could Somoza have told Mejía, in order to persuade him to accept his new assignment, that he would be taking command of a real fighting force with a decent chance at survival? Might he even, perhaps, have told the colonel that the Americans would support the Guard in their struggle?

But even if Mejía was in the dark, Urcuyo knew the plan — O'Donnell had carefully gone over it with him. Could Somoza have told Urcuyo to pay O'Donnell no mind, that *he,* Somoza, Urcuyo's lifelong leader, knew what the real plan was: that Urcuyo should stay on to put together an alternative to the Sandinistas? This seemed to Pezzullo the only possible explanation. Urcuyo was noted more for his vanity than for his intelligence, and Somoza could easily have made him believe that he could be the man of the new hour in Nicaragua. Maybe Urcuyo believed that if he forced the issue by acting as the real president, the United States would intervene to save him. He had indeed seemed puffed up with pride at his new office that morning, and this theory also fitted well with Mejía's comments. In his conversation with Pezzullo, Mejía had apparently expected that he would be receiving active American military support in an effort to prosecute the war against the Sandinistas.

Both Pezzullo and American policy in Nicaragua were now in an impossible position. With limited supplies of ammunition, the National Guard faced collapse, yet during that afternoon Urcuyo began appointing cabinet ministers as if organizing a normal administration. Incredibly, he even called on the Sandinistas to lay down their arms. To Pezzullo, he seemed to be in cloud-cuckoo-land. If the United States stood by and watched the debacle, the Sandinistas

would win a military victory and they would come to power convinced that Washington had been a party to Somoza's deception.
This would considerably reduce any chance of influencing them
in the future.

A way had to be found to dissociate the United States from
Urcuyo. So Pezzullo decided he should leave Managua, denouncing
Urcuyo's action as he left. It took a difficult telephone call to the
State Department to persuade Washington that he was right, but
Pezzullo succeeded in doing so. The next morning an exhausted
American ambassador gave a brief statement to the press at the
embassy and then, with twenty members of the staff, drove at
high speed to the military section of the airport. There they found
chaos. National Guardsmen were milling around, many seeking
escape from Nicaragua. The situation was so disorganized that
two relief aircraft used for transporting food and medical supplies
into the country were hijacked by members of the National Guard
for flight to Guatemala.

Pezzullo could see that an American C-130 transport plane, "The
Nashville," had somehow landed in the confusion and was waiting
on the apron with opened cargo door, surrounded by National
Guard jeeps with their machine guns trained on it. The pilot had
his engines running as Pezzullo and his party climbed aboard
through the rear ramp. With a roar, the aircraft lurched into the
air directly from the apron. In the cockpit, when Pezzullo thanked
the pilot for his good work, the young American could not conceal
his excitement. They had been forced to circle for a considerable
time above the airport, he said, and had barely found room to
land. "Where are you from?" Pezzullo asked. "I flew in from Panama," was the reply. "I was assigned there from Tennessee for
two weeks of National Guard duty." "Well," Pezzullo told the
airman, who suddenly looked very young indeed, "you can go
home now and write about this one."

In Washington, the State Department spokesman echoed Pezzullo's press statement criticizing Urcuyo's actions. But more would
be needed to dislodge the would-be leader. Warren Christopher
called Somoza in Florida and in diplomatic but firm words reminded

him that his status in the United States was part of a package deal. As Urcuyo himself was later to describe the event, Somoza then called the new Nicaraguan president. "Chico," Urcuyo recalled Somoza as saying, "I am lost. I am a prisoner of the State Department. I was just called by Warren Christopher, Assistant [*sic*] Secretary of State, to tell me that if you don't give up power to the junta . . . they will give me up to the Sandinista Front. That you can definitively not count on any class of aid from the North American government."[8]

In the meantime, Colonel Mejía had telephoned the Sandinista military commander, Humberto Ortega, in Costa Rica, to try to discuss the terms of a cease-fire in place. This would allow the remaining National Guard units to preserve their integrity for a while, at least. Ortega told Mejía that because Urcuyo had broken faith, there would be no standstill arrangement. Only an unconditional surrender would now be accepted. With this news, even Urcuyo knew it was over. At 8 P.M. he and a group of associates boarded airplanes sent by the government of Guatemala for his rescue. As he left, there was firing on the outskirts of the airfield.

Just before dawn the next morning, July 19, the last National Guard flight out of Managua took Colonel Mejía to safety. In a meeting with Tom O'Donnell before he left, Mejía acknowledged having been misled. But he remained loyal to his government and to the end refused the Sandinistas' demand for unconditional surrender.

At the American embassy, Tom O'Donnell and a skeleton crew stayed behind under very difficult conditions. The only remaining secretary refused to leave because the evacuation flight would not take animals, and she was too attached to her dog — a friendly, well-behaved mutt — to leave it behind. The code clerk simply took up residence in the code room, where he would sleep for the next week, until something like normalcy returned.

At around 4 A.M. on July 19, just as Mejía was leaving the airport, O'Donnell awoke at the residence. He turned on the radio and heard a new station calling on the Guardia to lay down their arms and go home — or, if they wished, to turn themselves in to the Red Cross or a local Catholic church. Later that morning, trucks began to roll into Managua carrying victorious Sandinista irregulars cheering and shooting their rifles in the air.

For weeks Managua had seemed like a ghost town, but now that the war was over, the Sandinistas seemed to bring with them the promise of fulfilled hopes. Rich or poor, radical or moderate, apolitical or committed, Managuans flooded the streets and squares of the capital. Each seemed convinced that the revolution would be good for him or her. One American reporter noticed a wealthy couple dressed in red shirts and black pants, the Sandinista colors. They had spray-painted "FSLN" on their Mercedes.[9]

In midafternoon, Tom O'Donnell was called by the embassy in San José to say that Bowdler was on his way to Managua with some of the junta leaders and OAS representatives. With a Marine guard and an Air Force officer riding shotgun in the ambassador's car, O'Donnell headed for the airport. As they passed central police headquarters, they saw weapons being passed out to twelve- and thirteen-year-old children, who were trying to figure out how to load the ammunition clips into the rifles. O'Donnell had decided to fly the American flag on the limousine, and at first regretted his decision when he saw all the rifles. But the crowds seemed happy to see the flag, flashing V signs to O'Donnell and his companions, who returned them.

At the airfield, however, the Americans had to talk their way past a tough young Sandinista soldier who at first insisted that they remove the flag, which O'Donnell refused to do. When he was informed that the Americans were there to meet the new government of Nicaragua, soon to arrive from Costa Rica, the soldier waved them through. Inside the terminal, all was confusion. The plane from Costa Rica was delayed. No one knew where it was or who was on it. Finally, at around 6:30, it arrived in the gathering dusk. Bowdler and the OAS representatives, who were to witness the inauguration of the new government, deplaned, but there were no senior members of the junta to be found. Some, it turned out, had been flown into Nicaragua at León the night before; others were elsewhere in the country. After waiting well into the evening, the OAS representatives were bedded down in a hotel near the airport and Bowdler and O'Donnell returned to the residence.

And so it was not until the next day, July 20, 1979, that Daniel Ortega, other Sandinista leaders, and the members of the junta, standing on a fire engine, finally drove into Managua. Fifty thousand Nicaraguans cheered wildly as the new government was sworn into office before the National Palace that Edén Pastora had seized with his small band of guerrillas eleven months before.

As William Bowdler watched the elated crowds in the streets, he thought back over the failure of the mediation effort and then found his memory taking him back farther still, to the early days of his career in the Foreign Service. "I've seen it before," he thought. "It's Cuba all over again."

THIRTEEN

Afterthoughts

YEARS LATER, IN RETIREMENT AT HIS HOME ON THE RAP-pahannock River in Sharps, Virginia, Ambassador Bowdler reflected on the parallels between Cuba and Nicaragua. He had witnessed the jubilant enthusiasm with which the overwhelming majority of the Cuban people had welcomed their revolution. In 1979, as the Sandinistas took power, he knew that the Nicaraguan revolution too would fail to meet the expectations it had engendered. How could it be otherwise, when so many people had so many different hopes for it? He knew also that when disappointment replaced enthusiasm, many Nicaraguans, as many Cubans had done before, would blame the United States for their predicament.

This was but one of the many extraordinary similarities between America's experiences with Cuba and with Nicaragua. Like the Carter administration in 1978–1979, the Eisenhower administration had tried first to reform an unpopular dictator friendly to the United States and then to disassociate itself from him. Neither Eisenhower nor Carter was successful in his modest efforts to build a workable relationship with the revolutionary regime that replaced the fallen dictator. The "loss" of Cuba, like that of Nicaragua, became an issue in the next presidential campaign in the United States. John F. Kennedy used Cuba as a weapon against the Eisenhower administration and Richard Nixon in 1960, just as Ronald Reagan and his supporters used Nicaragua, along with the fall of the shah in Iran, against Jimmy Carter in 1980. Both the Kennedy and Reagan administrations came to grief in their efforts to overthrow the revolution they had denounced. To Bowdler, as to others, the Reagan administration's support for the opposition contras seemed nothing more than a tragic, "slow-motion Bay of Pigs." Finally, the contras gave the Sandinistas a justification for their repressive behavior and military build-up at home and for their claims to assistance by the Soviet Union and other fraternal governments abroad — the same opportunity offered Castro by the Bay of Pigs.

To Bowdler, our Cuban experience offered clear lessons for dealing with post-Somoza Nicaragua. In 1987, as in 1979, Bowdler had little sympathy with the Sandinista revolution, but he also thought the United States had neither the blandishments nor the power — if exercised at an acceptable level of cost — to significantly influence the course of the revolution. To this former professional diplomat, it was a question of understanding the essential relationship between a goal and the power to achieve it. When Washington's reach exceeds its grasp, disaster is sure to follow.

"The sensible reaction to the Nicaraguan revolution," Bowdler said, "would have been to avoid open hostility to it. Then the Sandinistas could not use the United States as an excuse for their own mistakes. We should have maintained a correct relationship, initially offering them limited amounts of assistance until their new leaders defined their position on pluralism at home and alignment abroad. Instead of trying either to seduce or to overthrow them, we should have been watching very carefully to see that they did not act in ways that seriously affected the security of their neighbors or ourselves. Now we should be negotiating agreements with them that would limit both the Sandinistas' actions beyond their borders and the presence of the Soviets and Cubans within Nicaragua. Then we should make sure that they abide by them. These things could be done."

Sitting in his office at the Carnegie Endowment for International Peace in 1987, former Assistant Secretary of State Pete Vaky applied the same point about the relationship of power and goals to the

experiences of 1978 and 1979. He recalled that when Ambassador
Bowdler arrived in Managua to undertake his mediation effort,
he had been called the new Stimson. But Bowdler could not play
the same role. In 1927, Henry Stimson used American influence
to the fullest, even threatening the use of force, to gain an end to
the fighting among the Nicaraguan factions and their agreement
to national elections. In 1978, Vaky argued, Bowdler failed because
he had nothing like the same leverage. Washington wanted Somoza
to agree to the fair elections that would have resulted in his peaceful
removal — but was never willing to push him hard enough to win
his acquiescence. The result, said Vaky, was that by mid-1979,
all of Washington's choices had become more difficult.

Certainly, without a decision by the administration to intervene
far more deeply than it was willing to do, the strategy for dealing
with the crisis of June and July was doomed. This strategy had
three parts, each with its advocates in administration councils. At
least in retrospect, one can see that all three were centrally flawed.

In the first place, some argued that a last-minute political alternative to the Sandinistas could be created. The problem was that
unless the United States was willing and able to guarantee their
success, Nicaraguan moderates were not prepared to risk their
careers — and even their lives — by agreeing to serve on an executive
committee or to do anything else that would offend the Sandinistas.

Second, others urged that efforts be made to induce the Sandinistas
to compromise. In retrospect, this also seems to have been an unlikely proposition. It was an illusion to believe that the Sandinistas,
smelling success, would make any serious concessions unless forced
to do so. They had shown that they were prepared to make tactical
compromises — for example, in working with those moderates who
would join with them. But these were merely the compromises
they thought necessary for victory. Washington wanted more: a
settlement that represented a real sharing of power. Why should
the Sandinistas have agreed to this, when they were close to military
success? Serious compromise would have been a betrayal of their
ideology, the pain of their struggles, and their personal ambitions.

Finally, a third strand in the strategy had to succeed in order to encourage the moderates to act in defiance of the Sandinistas, or to push the Sandinistas towards moderation. This was the creation of a non-Somocista military force that could stand up to the Sandinistas. The NSC staff was correct in arguing the logic of this point. Only a reformed National Guard could have given Nicaraguan moderates the necessary confidence to take a stand while shaking the Sandinistas' conviction that no compromise was necessary. But was this view realistic? The possibility of creating a new National Guard, even with deep American involvement in buying the time necessary for its reconstitution, was very slim. The popular uprisings of 1978 and 1979 were directed not only against Somoza but against the Guard. Hatred of the Guard was broadened and exacerbated by its brutality in the fighting of 1978 and 1979. For many Nicaraguan families, this hatred had been building for two generations, since the time when Anastasio Somoza García rode the Guard to power. In giving its protection to the dynasty ever since, the Guard had become inseparably associated with it.

American officials who believed that an apolitical Guard could be created in 1979 had forgotten history and the illusions of the American officials who had created the Guard fifty years earlier. Merely naming a new commander and removing the worst of the organization's officers and units would not have made the Guard a legitimate force in Nicaragua, capable of keeping order through its command of popular respect as well as its use of force. By mid-1979 only an active American military presence and a large-scale training and supply effort could have brought about a reformed Guard. Could such an effort have succeeded? It seems most unlikely. Even if it had been feasible in American political terms, an intervention of this sort would have offended the nationalistic sensibilities of most Nicaraguans.

The fact is that when Nicaragua exploded in mid-1979, the Carter administration was caught with no good options. In retrospect, the policy debates in Washington during that period seem unreal. They appear now as desperate efforts to find a way to influence a flood of events that surged far ahead of Washington's real power or even understanding. As late as mid-1979 a Sandinista victory was not inevitable. But it could neither be prevented nor much delayed by the limited measures the administration considered.

The Carter administration was not the first to be caught short of options at such a moment. Time and again, when a radical revolution in the Third World has reached its flood stage, American policy makers have found themselves overwhelmed. In China in the 1940s, in Cuba a decade later, in Vietnam in the 1960s, and in Iran and Nicaragua a decade after that, American responses have differed in their particulars but have been consistent in their failure. In every case, the choice in the end has come down to acquiescence or intervention — with either coming at considerable cost both to the United States and to the president who was held accountable for failure.

Politically, it does not matter very much whether a crisis takes place in a large nation of obvious importance to us, like China in the late 1940s, or a small one of which few Americans had even been aware, like Vietnam in the late 1950s or Nicaragua twenty years later. Any president will come under attack for the "loss" of any nation to communism or any other revolutionary movement. From the 1930s to the mid-1970s, Central America was dismissed as a backwater. Many years ago, "Managua, Nicaragua" was a catchy phrase in a popular song but to most Americans meant little more. Or who would have argued in the 1960s that the future of Angola was a vital American interest? And in 1972, "Afghanistan, Bananastan" was a silly password in a popular movie. But after their revolutions, Nicaragua and Afghanistan were hardly amusing catch phrases. And in the mid-1970s, once there was a Marxist government in place, Angola became widely seen as strategically important because of its proximity to the South Atlantic sea lanes.

The lesson is clear. The political fortunes of our presidents are hostage to events in the farthest corners of the world, and influencing such events is as much a test of American foresight as it is of American power.

When fording a river, it's best to look upstream, to where the force of the water is probably less troublesome, the turbulence of the rapids less dangerous. Indeed, the source of a river may be a spring or small stream whose direction can easily be altered. A stream of events is similar, and in every crisis, the foreign policy maker is tempted to look back and say, If only . . . If only we had known a crisis was on the way and acted sooner, when our choices were easier, our influence greater . . .

Such foresight, however, requires two things: an understanding of the past causes of revolutionary explosions, and more career officials who are capable of analyzing foreign realities and then effectively portraying those realities to other branches of our government.

UNDERSTANDING THIRD WORLD REVOLUTIONS

The origins of revolutions are highly complex and uncertain, and our difficulty in understanding them is compounded by the way they are portrayed through competing myths in our political debates. These myths appear and reappear in our national debates over such matters as who lost China and why the Vietnam War happened.

Are revolutions the simple product of political repression and economic rapaciousness, as the left would have it? Do the peasants and urban poor rise in anger when they can no longer bear their lot? Only rarely. History and contemporary societies are filled with outrageous injustices that have produced no revolt. Poverty can as easily produce resignation as rebellion; all too often, repression succeeds.

Or are revolutions caused primarily by outside agitators spreading Marxist-Leninist doctrines and Czech rifles, as one hears from the right? Seldom, if ever. Foreign doctrines and smuggled rifles may play a role, but in every one of the revolutions that have bedeviled American foreign policy makers since World War II, the agitators were members of an indigenous elite. If the ground is not already fertile, no revolutionary seeds can be sown successfully — as Castro has discovered in South America.

Is the answer, then, to inoculate a society against revolution by encouraging economic progress, as liberal advocates of generous foreign aid have argued? It is not so simple. Indeed, economic growth often leads to political instability.

Understanding revolutions is more a matter of art than science, of intuition than deduction. And every revolution is different, rooted in a particular culture and time. Yet it is possible to see patterns in revolutions as dissimilar as those in China and Cuba, in Vietnam and Iran. The explosive formulas differed, but eight elements were present in each — as they were in Nicaragua in 1978 and 1979.

In each case, *economic progress had brought with it vast social changes.* People moving to the cities in search of new jobs, people buying radios and learning of different and better lives beyond their villages, people losing the sense of tradition that had explained their place in society and even in an orderly universe — such people are far more likely to rebel than are peasants whose misery differs little from that of their parents and ancestors. Moreover, economic progress is inequitable. There are always winners and losers, and the latter are likely to outnumber the former. For the majority who may be better off in absolute terms but are falling behind in a relative sense, economic growth has fallen short of heightened expectations. The result is anger.

The likelihood of an explosion is especially high during a period when economic growth levels off or is followed by decline. In Nicaragua, the gross domestic product more than doubled between 1960 and 1975, in part through infusions of American aid. But the earthquake in 1972 severely damaged some sectors of the economy, and a decline of foreign investment and a drop in coffee prices created more widespread economic deterioration in 1975–1976. There was some recovery by 1977–1978, but subsequent rapid inflation made even the economic winners fearful of the future.

In each case of revolutionary change, *access to political power was either severely limited or denied to all but a few favored by the regime.* Social changes, especially broadened educational opportunities, tend to make people more interested in the political life of their societies. When they sense that they are getting less than their fair share of an expanding economy, they turn to political action for redress. And when this drive for political participation is denied, the bravest and angriest will turn to armed action — to revolution. Before each revolution, political institutions had not evolved to accommodate the increased demands for political participation that come with economic and social change.

And so it is *the frustrated elite that stimulates and leads revolutions,* not the poor or the peasantry. It is the elite that has the highest expectation of economic gain and political participation. When the French built a modern educational system in Vietnam but reserved the best jobs and all real political power for themselves, they created a revolutionary tinderbox. Ho Chi Minh and his closest revolutionary comrades went to the best schools in the colony. In Nicaragua, opposition to Somoza in 1978 came not only from poor communities like the Indian barrio of Monimbó; it spread across every elite group in Nicaragua: businessmen, journalists, students, intellectuals. Some were jealous of the dictator's wealth; a few were disdainful of his personal style; but most were angered by Somoza's abuse of power and the political monopoly he and his cronies enjoyed. Leadership of the Sandinista movement came largely from those who were members of the elite, either by birth or education. Sandinista guerrilla leader Omar Cabezas, in his popular memoir *Fire from the Mountain,* does little to disguise the frustration and condescension he at first felt in dealing with the campesinos he sought to recruit. He himself came to the revolution as an idealistic student whose parents were members of the Conservative opposition to Somoza.

It is important to note that for many of the elite leaders of revolutions everywhere, Marxism and radical action became attractive only *after* they concluded that easier paths to reform were blocked. Even Tomás Borge, the hard-line Sandinista ideologue, was a member of the Independent Liberal party, which espoused "Keynesian economics, socialist economic reformism, and Jeffersonian democratic politics."[1] But in 1956, after the assassination of Anastasio Somoza García, the government arrested and tortured Borge, and thus helped radicalize him. In Cabezas's case, he joined the FSLN partly because he hated Somoza but also because he found the invitation to revolution a challenge to his manhood.

Commitment to the ideology followed rather than preceded commitment to the cause.[2]

Elite revolutionaries cannot succeed, of course, without mass support. Ironically, *support by the rural and even urban poor may be rooted more in tradition than in radicalism, and may flow more from a desire to conserve a way of life than to change it.* The Chinese and Vietnamese revolutions succeeded only after they played down their Marxism and wrapped their appeals in the traditions of their societies. As presented in traditional rural areas, their Marxism sounded as if it came more from Confucius than from Lenin. Especially important in such situations is the issue of land. To the peasant, a revolutionary call for the redistribution of land is not a radical departure from the past. The land was often taken from his family in an earlier time and is simply being restored to him. Many factors may have contributed to the loss of land. In Nicaragua as elsewhere, population growth combined with the rise of large landholders had contributed over the generations to widespread landlessness and rural unemployment. But population growth is a diffuse phenomenon; wealthy landowners are easier to recognize and to hate. Cabezas recalls that in approaching the campesinos, "the first thing we would ask is if they owned the land they lived on, and the answer was always no, it belonged to the 'rich folk'. . . The generation of campesinos we knew would tell us about how their great-grandfathers had owned land. And the story of what happened was passed down from great-grandfather to grandfather to father to son. They were now a generation without land."[3]

The FSLN was more explicit in its radical message than the Vietnamese and Chinese revolutionaries, franker even than Castro had been in the mid-1950s. But before 1978 the appeal of the FSLN, in those rural areas in which it made some headway, was based on traditional as well as radical approaches. Its position was greatly strengthened by the endorsement of Catholic priests who espoused "liberation theology." For the campesino, this meant that the most important of traditional institutions was behind the movement. Sandinista organizers also learned to conduct their recruiting through traditional family ties.

Throughout the world, *successful revolutionary movements have relied heavily on an appeal to nationalism, even when asserting that they were part of an international movement.* It is unlikely that Mao Zedong, Ho Chi Minh, and the Ayatollah Khomeini could have succeeded had not the Chinese, Vietnamese, and Iranian people perceived them as leading a popular reaction against a disliked foreigner. The Chinese Communists' fight against Japanese invaders gave Mao his patriotic mantle. For the Vietnamese Communists, the French and later the Americans provided the foil for Ho's nationalism. American officials entering a Vietnamese village after the local organizers of the National Liberation Front had left would find that the painted slogans the NLF left behind referred to social justice far less often than they attacked the government in Saigon for being an American puppet. In Nicaragua, the symbol of the revolution — and every revolution relies heavily on symbolic appeals — was a man who personified patriotic nationalism. César Augusto Sandino was remembered chiefly for his fight against the Yanquis. The efforts of FSLN theoreticians to give him a post hoc ideology were always rather lame.

Repression of its opponents may help a regime hold on to power, but it also helps the revolutionaries broaden their appeal. The jails of the South Vietnamese government provided one of the best recruiting grounds for the National Liberation Front. In Nicaragua, the growing brutality of the National Guard turned more and more Nicaraguans from passive dislike to active hatred for the Somoza regime. Sandinista bands that found little support in the countryside in the 1960s and early 1970s found much greater sympathy in 1975–1977 in areas where National Guard patrols had abused the people in the course of anti-FSLN campaigns. Similarly, repression of the Nicaraguan labor unions turned their leaders toward the revolution.

While not as important as internal factors, *the role played by outsiders in supporting or opposing a revolution can have significance.* Mao and Ho received important military assistance from the Soviet Union and other foreign supporters. Iran's Khomeini found refuge in France. American intelligence could find little evidence of meaningful military support by Cuba for the FSLN in

1978, but the Cubans were nevertheless providing safe haven, training, and political advice for some of the Sandinistas. Much more significant by 1978 was the growing opposition to Somoza, and the aid given to his enemies, by the governments of Costa Rica, Panama, and Venezuela. By 1979 Castro too was moving into high gear in his support for the Sandinistas.

Perhaps even more important than outside aid to revolutionaries is the role of external supporters of a regime under attack. In China, Vietnam, Cuba, and Iran, the patron of the defeated regimes — the United States — wavered in its support, usually for domestic political reasons, just before the final collapse. That support may have been a double-edged sword, since it raised xenophobic hackles and offered the revolutionaries an important issue. But when the support weakened, there is no question that these regimes lost heart while their opponents gained courage.

In Nicaragua, Somoza knew that the attacks on his human rights record by the Carter administration were sending a message to his opponents. It was that human rights policy, he said in early October 1978, that had convinced Nicaraguans that they "can overthrow my government."[4] Thus, as the State Department's Wade Matthews argued in 1978, the denial of military aid to the National Guard had more than a physical effect: it was a political statement, even if Washington was proclaiming its political neutrality among the various Nicaraguan factions.

In each case, Washington stepped back in part because of the crumbling of the regime, its growing inability to govern effectively, to command the political loyalty of even its traditional supporters, to lead an effective military establishment. As Hannah Arendt has written, "Revolutions are the consequences but never the causes of the downfall of political authority."[5] The point is clear in Nicaragua. By helping create conditions of violence in the countryside, the FSLN did contribute to the overthrow of Somoza, but to a larger extent it took advantage of his fall. In 1975 and 1976 the FSLN probably commanded no more than one hundred or two hundred guerrillas. By 1978 the Sandinistas were trying to capture the leadership of a largely spontaneous uprising against a regime that had alienated a whole society.

In the end, the collapse of a regime is usually military as well as political. To be sure, revolutionary leaders must gain a certain degree of political support. But revolutions are not elections; most rely on violence. When a regime loses its capacity to meet force with effective force, when it is able neither to inspire nor to coerce, it will fall. The regimes of Chiang Kai-shek, Ngo Dinh Diem, Nguyen Van Thieu, Shah Mohammad Reza Pahlevi, and Fulgencio Batista were notably similar in their corruption, inefficiency, and growing estrangement from their people. All either failed to maintain an efficient military force or in the end lost its loyalty. For the shah, there was also a loss of will, a hesitancy to use the power at hand.

Having once relied on repression for survival, a dictator who hesitates to use such measures is ready to become history. A little repression can be a dangerous thing. Every time Somoza loosened the repressive screws in a bow to international and especially American opinion, his action was insufficient to gain popular support. When he announced in February 1978 that he would leave office at the end of his constitutional term in 1981, the reaction was not relief but disappointment that his departure would not come more quickly. In September 1977, when he temporarily lifted the state of emergency, and again in June 1978, when he released political prisoners and gave promise of a liberalized approach, the actions merely did him double damage. Opponents felt freer to express their discontent, and at the same time rising political expectations set a trap. As John Booth notes, "On both occasions, Somoza raised hopes for an end to the violent excesses of the National Guard and for either the moderation of the regime or its negotiated demise — but both times he quickly frustrated those hopes."[6] Denied hope means deepened anger. Yet Somoza could not have fulfilled those hopes by abandoning repression altogether, for it was only the National Guard that kept him in power. Nicaraguans did not want a new Somoza; they wanted no Somoza — and soon.

The study of revolutions should discourage anyone who believes human behavior can be reduced to a science. Writings on the subject by social scientists should be coupled with a reading of Cabezas's memoir or *Man's Fate,* the magnificent novel of the Chinese revolution by André Malraux. Both are a humbling reminder of how idiosyncratic human behavior shapes history. As Robert Pastor wisely points out, predicting revolutions is not unlike forecasting seismological events: one may believe that a revolution or an earthquake is likely to occur along some political or geological fault line, but the crucial question of *when* it will take place remains mysterious.[7]

Still, successful rebellions generally occur on the lines of the pattern suggested above. Certain factors may be more important in one case than another, but these factors have been present in every case of revolutionary change in the Third World. If a policy maker finds himself dealing with a situation in which every item on the checklist seems present, it is probably time to prepare for some kind of crisis.

Unhappily, the complexity of the pattern plays into the hands of ideologues interested in scoring debating points by seizing on one aspect of the problem and proclaiming it to be *the* cause. It is all too easy to write a compelling article or speech showing that revolution follows economic injustice, or the denial of political rights, or support of revolutionaries by the Soviets or Cubans, or the denial of American aid to a beleaguered dictator. Many take this road. But to focus on some causes while dismissing others is not mere intellectual cheating; it leads to policy failure.

A conservative analysis, which focuses on the balance of military forces and the competing support offered to a regime or to the revolutionaries by Washington or Moscow, overlooks the underlying reasons for a political explosion. The Third World policies of the Reagan administration — increases in military assistance at the expense of economic aid, and promotion of economic growth without equivalent regard for economic equity — have probably done more to encourage than to prevent future revolutions.

Arguments by Jeane Kirkpatrick and others that the United States should support friendly tyrants in trouble because revolutionary regimes tend to be still more tyrannical may be right in their estimate of most revolutionary regimes.[8] But they are disingenuous, at best, in suggesting that our most troubled authoritarian friends can be reformed once the security threat is suppressed. A regime reduced to dependence on American military assistance is likely to be a regime, like Somoza's, that has lost its legitimacy. The governments of Chiang Kai-shek and the shah, of Batista and Somoza, were so widely opposed in their own countries that liberalizing reforms offered too late could only hasten their collapse. Thus, for a conservative administration in Washington, a policy of "support today, reform tomorrow" in dealing with such leaders is likely to become merely a perpetual statement of intentions. It will always be reform tomorrow, never reform today. America will be chained to a regime that dares not become anything but oppressive. And a regime chained to Washington further loses its legitimacy by offending the people's sense of national independence.

Although the traditional liberal prescription for political and economic reforms does focus on the root causes of revolution, it is, like the conservative view, incomplete. By the time a friendly despot has lost his legitimacy by destroying the trust between his regime and politically significant segments of society, efforts to plug in the liberal formula of reformism are exercises either in irrelevance or destabilization. This is what most members of the Carter administration (and I include myself) failed to recognize in both Iran and Nicaragua. The time to insist that the shah open up Iranian political institutions to match the economic and social reforms of his White Revolution was in the 1960s and early 1970s. By the late 1970s, when his regime was in crisis, urging human rights reforms may have been the right thing to do in terms of human suffering, but it was too late to make much difference politically. President Carter's call for reform simply encouraged the shah's opponents.

Similarly, the president's letter to Somoza in June 1978 was misguided in its presumption that sweet talk about his limited reforms could move the Nicaraguan dictator to more significant action. As the widespread rebellions of September 1978 were to show, the time was past when human rights reforms would do anything more than hasten Somoza's departure. The *fuerzas vivas* — the "live forces" — in Nicaraguan politics were nearly united against him. To the Nicaraguans, the issue was not Somoza's reform but his removal.

The time when American policy might most effectively have helped head off later revolution in Nicaragua was many years earlier: in the 1930s, when FDR allowed Somoza García to proclaim himself and his family as America's special friends; in the late 1940s, when the Truman administration backed away from its efforts to divorce American policy from the Somozas; in the subsequent decades of American support for the dynasty; and especially after the earthquake in 1972, when the United States encouraged Anastasio Somoza Debayle to reassume the presidency and allowed him to plunder a suffering nation.

Washington had made the gratuitous mistake it has made so often in the Third World. When the American government decides that its national security interests require support for a friendly but nondemocratic government, there is no reason why we must also embrace its *ruler* — no reason to call Ngo Dinh Diem the Winston Churchill of Asia, to praise the Marcoses and shahs of the world, to allow American ambassadors like Turner Shelton to play the sycophant to a Somoza. Such personalizing of our support for a government only reduces our leverage with its leaders while they hold power and makes it harder to distance ourselves from them when they begin to lose it. Even if the Nixon administration had wanted to push Somoza into reforms, it is doubtful that he would have taken seriously any threat to withdraw American support. Hadn't the administration and its ambassador already told him how important he was to American interests?

For the Carter administration, 1978 was the last time the final crisis might have been averted. Pete Vaky made mistakes during this period, in relying on general rather than specific arguments about how to gain Somoza's resignation and in missing what may have been a signal when Somoza asked about his status in the United States if he decided to leave Nicaragua. But on the central point, Vaky was right: if the United States did not act to gain Somoza's resignation in 1978, it would pay a price later for its caution. The harder question, however, was this: to the degree senior policy makers accepted the truth of Vaky's proposition, could they act on it without incurring costs abroad and at home that they considered unacceptable?

Forcing Somoza's resignation would not have been an easy matter, but as late as 1978 it might still have been possible to find a moderate alternative: the dictator's middle-of-the-road opponents had not yet swung to the Sandinistas, and the Sandinistas themselves were still divided and weak militarily. During the course of 1978, as its Nicaraguan policy evolved, the Carter administration did call, through the mediation effort, for Somoza's resignation. In Vaky's view, however, Washington was not prepared to exercise the influence necessary to achieve this goal. Why was this so?

One of the limitations on the willingness of the Carter administration to act with greater vigor was its belief in principle. President Carter, Secretary Vance, and others deeply believed in the principle of nonintervention in the internal affairs of other nations and in multilateralism as the most effective form of diplomacy. These beliefs were based on more than abstract idealism and respect for international law. Decades of American unilateralism and interventionism had brought real penalties: in the hostility of our southern neighbors when the United States intervened, in the sticky dependency of the rulers we elevated to and kept in power, and in the domestic American political consequences when failure came, at the Bay of Pigs or in Nicaragua in the 1920s. Nor has wielding influence in Central America ever been as easy as some American policy makers have wished. Consider the difficulties the Reagan administration encountered in its efforts in 1988 to oust General Manuel Antonio Noriega from Panama.

In addition, there was a general policy question: if the United States were to decide to remove Somoza through unilateral, nondemocratic means, how many other leaders around the world should also have been ousted? If Somoza, why not Marcos, or Mobutu, or the many other Third World leaders whose rule might breed a revolutionary response? What would be the shape of an American foreign policy that sought the removal of all such leaders?

These concerns led the administration to pursue Vaky's goal

only tentatively. In essence, by emphasizing multilateral diplomacy, it sought to exercise influence while avoiding the American interventionism so resented by Latin Americans. Before each important step, there was careful consultation with other OAS members on strategy and then an effort at cooperative action. The problem was that while sentiment among most Latin American governments was strongly anti-Somoza, it was also strongly against anything that smacked of American military intervention, even if wrapped in a multilateral mantle. Hence the failure of the OAS peace-keeping idea.

In effect, Washington's multilateral approach gave our friends in the hemisphere something close to a veto over American policy. Washington was thus caught by a profound, contradictory Latin American ambivalence: our friends wanted to see us succeed in removing Somoza, but they were also uneasy about the United States' again acting as the arbiter of others' internal politics. They wanted Washington to make things right in Central America, but not through an interventionist exercise of American power, even under cover of the OAS. Thus the importance of efforts by Latin Americans to take the lead in joint diplomatic efforts. When men such as Costa Rican President Oscar Arias take the initiative in international efforts to resolve their region's difficulties, the United States can be seen as adding its weight rather than throwing it around.

Three other factors played an important role in limiting the Carter administration's response during 1978. First, within any bureaucracy there is a natural tendency toward compromise. It is not merely that many bureaucrats seek the safety of "middle options." Compromise flows also from the way of thinking that predominates in many foreign policy discussions. Confronted by a battle between two bureaus, a senior foreign policy maker will naturally look for a synthesis of their views, an Aristotelian mean arrived at by a process of logical deduction. The middle option can produce something close to bureaucratic harmony, and it's tempting to believe that it might convey at least some of the benefits of more radical options while avoiding their pitfalls. Perhaps, with a little luck, Somoza would leave without our forcing the issue.

Second, the tendency toward compromise within the executive branch was reinforced by domestic political pressures. Although there is little evidence of explicitly political concerns surfacing at the White House meetings on Nicaragua (the country did not emerge as an important issue in American public opinion or politics during this period), foreign policy does not need to be driven by politics to be influenced by it. Policy decisions can also be constrained by the anticipated domestic political reaction.

The constraints are contradictory. Since World War II, opinion polls have shown that the American public will hold accountable any president who presides over the fall of foreign territory to communism. However, the public has also penalized any president who violated the popular desire for peace and the promotion of human rights. And since Vietnam, anything more than the briefest American intervention abroad has been unpopular.

So whatever their rhetoric, presidents tend to seek compromises that uphold the American belief in human rights and demonstrate American opposition to the spread of communism while costing as little as possible in American lives and taxes. (Hence one of the dangerous attractions of covert actions abroad: they appear to offer a means of containing communism without evident costs. Moreover, the public is also spared the knowledge that such actions may involve the United States in violations of human rights.)

Few members of Congress became involved on the Nicaraguan issue in 1978. Those who did, however, pushed the Carter administration deeper into the safety of compromise. If the administration had moved actively for the overthrow of an anti-Communist leader such as Somoza, its critics on the right could have had a field day claiming that it had not merely lost Nicaragua, but had voluntarily given it away. On the other hand, if it had done nothing to oppose Somoza, it would have alienated its supporters on the left who had rallied to Carter's human rights banner. Thus, while politics played little explicit role, it provided a context that limited the administration's options.

It is no bad thing that most governments pursue compromise courses most of the time. If they did not, the world would be even more dangerous than it is. Realism requires compromises.

As Adlai Stevenson once put it, "Absolutes are few and black and white rare colors in international politics." Yet the test of a compromise policy is not its intellectual and bureaucratic elegance or its domestic political realism, but its practical consequences. And the harsh fact remains that the policies of the Carter administration toward Nicaragua failed to achieve their purpose.

This raises the third factor in the failure of the administration to act more forcefully in 1978: the estimates of the future provided to policy makers by State Department and intelligence analysts. Policy makers knew that there would be immediate costs in Latin America and at home if they pursued more aggressive policies toward Nicaragua. They did not realize, however, that their compromises would fail, nor did they understand how serious and how soon would be the day of reckoning. With the intelligence community predicting that there would be no crisis in Nicaragua for a few years if Somoza remained in power, why risk an immediate crisis by pushing hard to remove him against his will?

Thus Pete Vaky had an almost impossible task in trying to convince his superiors that they had to act at once. It was a time of intense activity on many fronts: not only in Iran, but also in negotiations on the Middle East, in establishing relations with China, and in talks on arms control with the Soviet Union. In arguing for firm action to remove Somoza, Vaky was in effect telling harassed senior policy makers that they should add another crisis of their own making to the agenda, a crisis that — according to the intelligence community — would not otherwise occur. It was not an attractive proposition.

The reasons for the failure of the intelligence community have already been noted. An important part of responsibility for such failures lies with the policy makers and senior officials at the CIA who failed to allocate the agency's resources effectively or who did not want to hear bad news that might contradict their policy inclinations. It is essential that the director of Central Intelligence be an official who is prepared to present a president with unpleasant information. When the director is a loyalist more than an analyst, an enforcer of the president's ideology rather than a skeptical and independent figure, the result can be disastrous, as was the case with William Casey and the Reagan administration's policies in Central America.

But the intelligence failure goes beyond the CIA. It is instructive to recall just how poorly prepared the State Department was for dealing with the Nicaraguan affair. Recall that in 1977 and 1978 State's office dealing with Central America had no one who could be considered an expert on Nicaraguan politics, that the embassy in Managua was weak in its leadership and thin in its expertise, and that when the crisis erupted in 1979, Washington was forced to send a new ambassador who although highly competent was hardly an expert on the details of the situation on the ground.

STRENGTHENING THE EXPERTS

Here is perhaps the most important lesson of the affair. Sooner or later, presidents and the nation they serve pay a serious price when the voices of the government's middle-level experts are either unclear or ignored. This is obviously true on such grand issues as dealing effectively with the Soviet Union, when knowledge of a foreign leader and his or her society is essential to the design of sensible national security and negotiating strategies. But it is no less true with regard to America's relations with smaller nations such as Nicaragua.

No president or secretary of state has the time or knowledge to do more than set the general direction of policy toward more than 150 foreign nations and dozens of functional problems. They must rely on the middle levels of the bureaucracy in Washington and on American officials working in the far corners of Africa, Asia, Latin America, and the Middle East. When these people fail, it is the president who will be held accountable. When crisis does erupt, a president and other senior officials become all the more dependent on the good advice of their experts. The more the president allows himself to be impelled or constrained by the domestic political pressures that accompany any foreign crisis, the more likely it is that he will pay too little attention to the realities of foreign events and the more likely that he will fail.

This is not to argue that American foreign policy should be left to career officers. In a democracy, public opinion must be the ultimate arbiter of all our policies. But there must be a balance in our foreign policy councils between the experts who bring with them an understanding of foreign realities and the political appointees who promote the president's priorities. Without the former, policies are most likely to fail. Yet it is the political appointees who speak most directly for the people within the councils of government and who are most likely to be personally accountable for any failure.

Successful American foreign policy flows from the same two wells as does our domestic progress: a belief in clear, principled goals and a sense of pragmatism in their pursuit. Either alone must fail. Pragmatism without principle is meaningless, and principle without pragmatism produces mere posturing — or dangerously quixotic policy.

In the past decades, the balance has shifted strongly and dangerously toward the political appointees and their more ideological perspectives. This is true in the White House, where the NSC staff, originally conceived as a group of professional civil servants offering presidents expertise and continuity with previous administrations, has become a place for the most ideologically committed of the president's followers, whether political appointees or career officers. The extraordinary actions of Colonel Oliver North in the Iran-contra affair, held secret as much from the bureaucracy as from the public, were only the culmination of a trend at least two decades old.

This shift in the balance against pragmatic career officials is also marked at the State Department, where the trend over the past six administrations has been to place more political appointees in jobs at the middle and upper levels. Moreover, by 1986 some sixty percent of our chiefs of mission abroad were political appointees, the highest percentage in forty years. (In 1966 fully seventy-two percent were Foreign Service officers.)

Worse still, a purge of Foreign Service officers associated with the policies of the Carter administration was conducted at the beginning of the Reagan administration. The housecleaning even blighted or ended the careers of some officials who had argued against Carter's priorities while loyally serving him. Anticipating that no serious new assignment would be available, William Bowdler retired from the Foreign Service before the inauguration. The relatively conservative views of John Bushnell, the senior deputy assistant secretary in the Latin American bureau and a strong internal critic of Carter's Central American policies, did him no good with the new administration. He was sent abroad but was denied an ambassadorial post, despite his experience and competence.[9]

It would be wrong to suggest that career officials like Bowdler and Bushnell have a monopoly on expertise. Political appointees like Robert Pastor may have a firm knowledge of a region and of American foreign policy (although others do not). The issue is one of perspective. Especially in the early years of an administration, political appointees are much more likely than career officers to assert the importance of one American interest at the expense of others when policy is being designed. In the first year of the Carter administration, policy toward Nicaragua was made almost completely in the context of an overarching concern for human rights. In the Reagan administration, it was made with an eye only on our interest in containing communism.

As Barbara Tuchman once argued, "Any government that does not want to walk . . . into a quagmire, leading its country with it, would presumably [examine] its choices. . . . That, after all, is what we employ Foreign Service Officers *for:* to advise policy-makers of actual conditions on which to base a realistic program. . . . Political passion is a good thing but even better if it is an *informed* passion."[10]

Part of the solution is obvious: to increase the number and influence of career experts in important positions at the State Department and White House — and on the staffs of congressional committees. In addition, it is in the interest of a president to choose his subordinates, whether career officers or political appointees, on the basis of knowledge and pragmatism rather than ideological purity. Unalloyed belief blinds an official to the nature of true loyalty, which involves a willingness to argue as well as to execute a president's policy decisions.

Any president who understands his stake in correcting the current imbalance between career experts and political appointees can easily shape the pattern of his appointments accordingly. One particularly valuable reform would be a partial return to the pattern of the 1950s, when most NSC staff members were career officials chosen primarily for their expertise. An NSC staff that reflected a balance between nonideological career officials and capable political appointees could provide a needed continuity and institutional memory from administration to administration as well as the loyalists a president needs. There should be no doubt that career officers can loyally serve presidents of different parties. When Dean Rusk once remarked to the head of the British Civil Service that he admired the way it remained apart from British politics, the reply was both cynical and encouraging: "Oh no," the Englishman said, "you have it wrong. The British Civil Service supports one political party at a time."[11]

The harder part of the solution concerns the career experts themselves. There is a need to strengthen the ability of the Foreign Service to provide expert opinion — and to present it in a forceful, effective way. The Foreign Service is in trouble. There is no scientific way to measure morale, but despite the large numbers of applicants, there seems little doubt that by the mid-1980s there was a growing sense of malaise and even anger among the State Department's career officials. Perhaps, as someone once said of *Punch* magazine, our Foreign Service "isn't what it used to be — but then, it never was." But the malaise and the problems seem all too real, as reflected in numerous articles about the State Department appearing in *The Washington Post, The New York Times,* and other newspapers.[12]

The life of a Foreign Service officer abroad is more difficult than ever before. As the threat of terrorism and the decline of the dollar have made service abroad less comfortable, the attraction of alternative employment in international affairs has grown. (The international affairs divisions of American banks employ more professionals than does the Foreign Service.) To attract and keep people who will serve in the backwaters of the world, the Foreign Service must in any case offer more than comforts. It must offer a career that can fulfill a sense of commitment to service as well as a thirst for adventure.

Older officers such as Pete Vaky and Bill Bowdler decry the loss of a sense of professionalism that led young Foreign Service officers to work abroad out of dedication more than personal ambition. Both joined the Foreign Service because they were excited about the work. "Now no one even tries to pretend that the Foreign Service is a *profession* and not simply a job," Vaky says. Both he and Bowdler noticed a shift in the 1970s, when young officers became far more anxious about personal advancement than their predecessors had been, and much less willing to serve wherever the Service asked.

Vaky puts some blame on changes in our society and the development of the "me generation," and this is undoubtedly part of the explanation. But it is also true that if young officers are more career-conscious than ever, they have more to worry about than ever before, as political appointees take over an increasing number of the State Department's plum jobs. As Ronald Spiers, under secretary of state for management, put it in a speech in 1986, "[The Foreign Service has] had a net loss of 25 [senior] positions at home and abroad since January of 1981. This may seem an inconsiderable number, but the Service is a relatively small one and shifts of this magnitude can have a large impact on the career outlook for our personnel at all levels. Each time a career position at this level is lost, seven promotion opportunities below it are also lost. The actual impact of a shift of 25 positions is thus 175 promotions and hirings."[13]

The problem of low morale and a loss of professionalism is exacerbated by the acceleration of a trend that began in the mid-1960s: an emphasis within the department on training and promoting generalists and managers at the expense of area experts. As the United States vainly tried to win a political war in Vietnam through efficient military and economic programs, a bureaucratic restructuring in Washington attempted to help the State Department manage interagency decisions on "resource flows" both to Vietnam and around the world. American ambassadors abroad were put in charge of interagency "country teams," again in the name of efficiency. Capturing the spirit of the time, a group of reformist young Foreign Service officers who called themselves the Young Turks urged more managerial training. In a letter to the director general of the Foreign Service in late 1966, they argued that "the habits of diplomacy, characterized by individual brilliance, organizational caution and a continuing effort to widen areas of agreement, are not the habits of the good executive manager."[14]

The new emphasis on management techniques in the late 1960s reflected a widespread view in Washington that was already dated, however. In Vietnam as in the Great Society, a belief in the efficacy of programs tended to divert attention from the realities of international and domestic limits. American competence could not force a transformation of foreign societies any more than Lyndon Johnson's spending programs could put an end to poverty in our own, however useful those programs proved to be. In a new international era, the real challenge to Washington was to compensate for a diminution of our economic and military power by strengthening the effectiveness of our diplomacy. Yet the trend in the State Department was to promote the managers at the expense of the diplomats.

The bureaucratic restructuring of the mid-1960s failed. State Department officials in Washington and American ambassadors abroad were unable (or sometimes unwilling) to assert effective control over the activities and budgets of other agencies. Yet to this day, the training and promotion of Foreign Service officers emphasizes breadth rather than depth in foreign experience. As budget cuts terminated the careers of many Foreign Service officers between 1985 and 1988, the ax seemed to be falling most heavily on those who had specialized on one area of the world, who could speak in the accents of a foreign people rather than the language of the professional manager. To recover some of the lost skills, State reportedly hired some area specialists back as consultants, at a higher cost. As one Foreign Service officer told a reporter from *The Washington Post,* "The question now facing those of us who now are a rung below senior rank is whether you want to really know an area . . . or whether you want an a la carte career where you dabble in many different areas on the theory that you're learning to be a manager. Now to concentrate on a specific area is a recipe for not getting promoted."[15]

All this simply makes no sense. What the nation needs from our representatives abroad, if it is to avoid new Vietnams, Irans, and Nicaraguas, is not managers but men and women who understand foreign societies, who can relate foreign realities to the kinds of policy dilemmas with which Washington wrestles. We need diplomats with the individual brilliance at which the State Department's Young Turks once sneered. Certainly, the Foreign Service needs career generalists who have the breadth of experience to serve in senior positions in Washington. But the primary need is for policy generalists, not managers. And with the training and promotion of such generalists must come greater rewards for those who wish to specialize in one region of the world or on one area of economics or technology. If this is not done, how often will the shortage of expertise that Washington suffered on Nicaragua in the 1977–1979 crises be repeated in the future?

William Bacchus, a respected expert on the State Department, makes an interesting suggestion for building up the number of regional experts in the Foreign Service. Why not, he says, reserve a few hundred positions for men and women who would be recruited specifically to spend their whole careers in certain areas, competing among themselves for positions as ambassadors or for senior positions in the relevant bureaus? Occasional tours outside their areas of expertise and in Washington would combat the dangers of clientitis, of losing their objectivity about the areas in which they serve. There should be no difficulty in recruiting such people: a fascination with Central America or China leads many into a lifetime of specialized study in the academic world. The Foreign Service should be just as attractive to such potential experts.

Another means of bringing more experts into the State Department would be to regularly employ ten or twenty academic specialists for a few years' service in the Bureau of Intelligence and Research, and to create a serious exchange program between the bureau and various academic institutions. (Security clearances would not present a major obstacle.) The department would benefit from the knowledge and fresh perspectives of the academics, and the latter could write about how governments act with some firsthand knowledge of the subject.

Greater expertise alone, however, is not enough. Foreign Service officers also need the competence and confidence to inject another perspective into Washington's policy debates — a perspective worthy of respect, if not ultimate authority. The decision makers who most directly face the judgments of the public deserve the clear counsel of experts with experience in the problem at hand. Thus armed, they can assume the greater responsibility that is theirs.

After the collapse of the mediation effort in January 1979, Pete Vaky was frustrated by the decisions of his superiors. He also questioned himself. Had he failed to make his case for stronger pressures to gain Somoza's departure? Should he have been more aggressive somehow? It would have come as a surprise to his colleagues in the department that Vaky felt such anguish and self-doubt, for he had argued his case clearly and persistently. But he had not conveyed to most of his associates the passion with which he held his views or the depth of his frustration. Few had any idea that more than once, he had been unable to get back to sleep when awakened in the early hours of the morning by his concern about Nicaragua. In all the meetings and arguments, he had maintained his professional calm (except for an occasional outburst on the telephone with Robert Pastor at the NSC). He knew that if he were to explode at a meeting with Deputy Secretary Christopher or Secretary Vance, his views might be discounted as emotional rather than rational. And in any case, Vaky was a professional. In the culture of the Foreign Service, professionalism means calm, understatement, and a degree of detachment.

As Vaky later put it, "The talents that make you a good field officer are not the same as those that make you effective in Washington. In the field, a diplomat's job involves analysis, understanding, and conflict resolution, so the Foreign Service rewards tact and discretion in its promotion system. But in Washington, you need to be able to push harder."

The difference between being a good bureaucrat and being a good diplomat can be seen in the behavior of Foreign Service officers at interagency meetings. A few years ago, a young officer who had not yet been assimilated into the diplomatic culture was encountered just after a meeting at the Pentagon. He was furious. His boss, a senior Foreign Service officer, had been berated by a senior military man who seemed to be treating the department's views the way he would have treated a fumbling young private with an improperly cleaned rifle. Instead of responding in language that might have been understood, the senior Foreign Service officer had expressed his outrage simply by standing up and walking out of the room. In diplomacy, this would have signaled that missiles might soon fill the air; to the Pentagon officials, it probably meant that State's representative was retreating under fire or perhaps simply answering a call of nature. The junior officer had been left alone and outgunned at the meeting.

The distinction between diplomatic effectiveness and bureaucratic effectiveness can also be seen in the written language of the Foreign Service. By the standards of contemporary America, the writing is clear and highly intelligent, but it reflects the function of the diplomat, which is to understand and report complexities, to resolve conflicts. State Department work is complicated and demanding, and uses the elasticity of words to resolve conflicts — if possible on favorable terms. State's subtleties and caution are praiseworthy, since they reflect the complexities and dangers of our world, but to a White House official burrowing through a daily blizzard of memoranda from the agencies, they can also seem like irritating pettifoggery.

Thus it is that the Foreign Service is often misunderstood by presidents and political appointees. Almost every president leaves office believing that the Foreign Service is filled with men and women who are opposed to him politically and ideologically. (Why else would they have been so resistant to his bold initiatives?) Many of the political appointees who work with Foreign Service officers know better, for they encounter in the Service the same proportions of Republicans and Democrats found in the population at large. So for many political appointees, the problem is explained by the adage "There are old diplomats, and there are bold diplomats, but there are no old, bold diplomats."

This is partially true: the recommendations for promotion by the State Department selection boards use criteria that relate more to the skills needed for service abroad than to those most useful in Washington. But there are outstanding exceptions to the adage. Some of the most successful of our recent career officers — men such as Phillip Habib and Lawrence Eagleburger — have been noted for their clout on the Washington scene. And didn't Vaky and Bowdler press for the strongest policy positions in the 1978 debates on Nicaragua?

The problem is more cultural than political or substantive. To political appointees imbued with a passionate commitment to the goals of their president and schooled in the conflict of public debate, the diplomatic style of the Foreign Service officer is often misunderstood as a gray sort of caution. Our dilemma is that we need a Foreign Service that reflects the culture of international diplomacy. We must have representatives abroad who are skilled at understanding others and thus can stand up for the United States in ways that are meaningful to a foreign culture. These must be men and women of sensitivity, of patience and persistence, of a very quiet kind of courage. But we also need a career bureaucracy in the State Department that can forcefully present to our political leaders the opportunities and limiting realities of the world.

The answer to this dilemma lies, in part, in a further shift in the personnel patterns of the Foreign Service — a shift toward informally encouraging certain officers to spend most of their careers as diplomats abroad and allowing those more suited to the jungles of Washington to devote most of their time to service there. Promotion panels should use advancement criteria that are flexible enough to emphasize the risk-taking skills demanded in Washington as well as the diplomatic skills needed for work in the embassies. It is also important that political appointees understand the ways of the Foreign Service, for when they dismiss pragmatism and understatement as obstructionism, they lose the benefit of experience that leavens ideological impulse with a sense of realism.

Beyond restoration of the balance between career officials and noncareer appointees lies a tremendously important challenge for them all: to help promote realistic assessments in the White House, in Congress, and in the public forum. Henry Adams once said that "the Secretary of State exists only to recognize the existence of a world that Congress would rather ignore." Congress is far more involved today than in Adams's time, and many of its members are expert in various facets of American national security. Yet Congress and the public still deserve a realistic picture of the world from the experts at State. For example, there is no reason why a secretary of state could not occasionally participate in the noon briefings in the State Department press room in a way that would educate as well as persuade the nation of the wisdom of the president's policies.

Most senior State Department officials understand the importance of working with key members of Congress. Secretary of State Vance and his deputy, Warren Christopher, certainly did so. But the same attitude does not permeate the rest of the department. To many Foreign Service officers, the Congress means simply a flood of mail to be answered by an overworked desk officer, a congressional delegation to be pampered by embassy staff, or another attack by a congressman on the competence or even loyalty of American diplomats. The Bureau for Congressional Relations seems sometimes to exist only to recognize the existence of a Congress that the Foreign Service would rather ignore.

This view among our professional diplomats is short-sighted as well as elitist. It is admittedly time-consuming and difficult to deal with Congress, especially since the reforms of the 1970s, which diffused power on the Hill and increased the number of congressmen with an interest in foreign policy. But as Brian Atwood, assistant secretary of state for congressional relations in 1979–1980, properly argues, "The time that is wasted in reacting to an uninformed Congress is much greater than the time expended in including the Congress in the first place."

Even if it is no longer possible simply to consult with a few powerful committee chairmen, every assistant secretary of state can identify those five or ten senators and representatives with a particular interest in his area and can arrange to work with them while policy is being shaped and later explained on the Hill. Such discussions are highly beneficial. The executive branch has no monopoly on knowledge — or, certainly, on wisdom — and policy is improved through an exchange of ideas. Indeed, some members of Congress have much greater substantive experience than the assistant secretaries of state with whom they are dealing. In addition, it is better to consult with Congress before a decision than to try to explain it afterwards. Consultation can prevent a nasty political surprise when a congressman who was assumed to be an ally turns on the administration out of irritation at having been bypassed. Moreover, as Atwood observes, "such consultations also force the representatives of the administration to learn to explain their policies in politically relevant terms. This will help it then to explain its policies effectively to the public."

In 1835 Alexis de Tocqueville wrote, "I have never been more struck by the good sense and the practical judgment of the Americans than in the manner in which they elude the numerous difficulties resulting from their Federal Constitution."[16] Our government retains its vitality precisely because the Constitution on which it rests did not establish clear lines of authority among its institutions. In the making of foreign policy, its invitation to struggle between the Congress and the executive branch ensures that policy will flow from the clash of ideas and from political competition, as it should in a democracy.

But the struggle between presidents and lawmakers must be waged on even ground and conducted with "the good sense and the practical judgment" upon which Tocqueville remarked, or it becomes destructive ideological warfare. Similarly, within the executive branch, without a balance between the limiting caution of career officials and the policy priorities of political appointees, we are deprived of the full benefits of a system that encourages constructive debate.

These essential balances are being lost. They should be restored.

Notes

Index

Notes

2 / Washington and the Somozas

1. Bernard Diederich, *Somoza and the Legacy of U.S. Involvement in Central America* (New York: E. P. Dutton, 1981), p. 24.
2. Ibid., pp. 153–54.
3. From a March 10, 1978, press conference. Cited by the PBS *Frontline* television program "Crisis in Central America: Revolution in Nicaragua," transcript, p. 8.
4. Richard Millet, *Guardians of the Dynasty* (Maryknoll, N.Y.: Orbis, 1977), pp. 148–61.
5. Lester D. Langley, *The Banana Wars: An Inner History of American Empire, 1900–1934* (Lexington: University Press of Kentucky, 1983), p. 218.
6. Millet, *Guardians,* p. 197.
7. Diederich, *Somoza,* p. 50.
8. Millet, *Guardians,* p. 197.
9. Department of State, *Foreign Relations of the United States, 1945,* vol. 9 (Washington, D.C.: U.S. Government Printing Office, 1969), p. 1230.
10. Department of State, *Foreign Relations of the United States, 1946,* vol. 11 (Washington, D.C.: U.S. Government Printing Office, 1969), p. 1076.
11. Cited by James Chace, *Endless War: How We Got Involved in Central America — And What Can Be Done* (New York: Vintage Books, 1984), p. 54.
12. Department of State, *Foreign Relations of the United States, 1952,* vol. 4 (Washington, D.C.: U.S. Government Printing Office, 1983), p. 1372.
13. Ibid.

14. Ibid., p. 1375.
15. Millet, *Guardians*, p. 255.
16. Shirley Christian, *Nicaragua: Revolution in the Family* (New York: Random House, 1985), p. 36.

3 / In Christopher's Back Office

1. Robert A. Pastor, *Condemned to Repetition: The United States and Nicaragua* (Princeton: Princeton University Press, 1987), p. 60.
2. Ibid., p. 62.
3. Ibid., p. 63.
4. Ibid., pp. 64–65.
5. James A. Thomson, "How Could Vietnam Happen? An Autopsy," in *Readings in American Foreign Policy: A Bureaucratic Perspective*, ed. Morton H. Halperin and Arnold Kanter (Boston: Little, Brown, 1973), p. 102.

4 / Questions from the 1920s

1. William Kamman, *A Search for Stability: United States Diplomacy toward Nicaragua 1925–1933* (Notre Dame: University of Notre Dame Press, 1968), p. 10.
2. James Chace, *Endless War: How We Got Involved in Central America — And What Can Be Done* (New York: Vintage Books, 1984), pp. 28–29.
3. Richard Millet, *Guardians of the Dynasty* (Maryknoll, N.Y.: Orbis, 1977), p. 23.
4. Lester D. Langley, *The Banana Wars: An Inner History of American Empire, 1900–1934* (Lexington: University Press of Kentucky, 1983), p. 169.
5. *Arbiter* is Robert A. Pastor's term. See his *Condemned to Repetition: The United States and Nicaragua* (Princeton: Princeton University Press, 1987), p. 22.
6. Langley, *Banana Wars*, p. 217.
7. Dana G. Munro, *The Five Republics of Central America: Their Political and Economic Development and Their Relations with the United States* (New York: Oxford University Press, 1918), p. 251.
8. Chace, *Endless War*, pp. 40–41.
9. Kamman, *Search for Stability*, p. 83. Kamman's history of this period in American policies toward Nicaragua is probably the best full account available.
10. Ibid., p. 123. Kamman cites Sandino's brother.
11. Gregorio Selser, *Sandino* (New York: Monthly Review Press, 1981), pp. 117–19.
12. Ibid., p. 97.
13. Ibid.

14. Kamman, *Search for Stability*, p. 123.
15. Ibid., p. 126.
16. Ibid., p. 169.
17. See, for example, the 1928 Democratic party platform.
18. Kamman, *Search for Stability*, pp. 223–24. Kamman's analysis of the period offers a compelling argument about the declining importance of economic factors in explaining American intervention in Nicaragua.
19. Ibid., p. 227.
20. Memorandum of January 2, 1927, cited by Millet, *Guardians*, p. 52.
21. Kamman, *Search for Stability*, pp. 76–79.
22. Millet, *Guardians*, p. 63.
23. Department of State, *Foreign Relations of the United States*, 1927, vol. 3 (Washington, D.C.: U.S. Government Printing Office, 1942), p. 329.
24. Department of State, *Foreign Relations of the United States*, 1925, vol. 2 (Washington, D.C.: U.S. Government Printing Office, 1940), pp. 627–28.
25. Millet, *Guardians*, p. 118.
26. Langley, *Banana Wars*, p. 197.
27. Millet, *Guardians*, pp. 118–19.
28. His *Guardians of the Dynasty* is probably the best history of American policy toward Nicaragua up to 1977.

5 / State: The Bureaus

1. Raymond Bonner, *Waltzing with a Dictator: The Marcoses and the Making of American Policy* (New York: Times Books, 1987), p. 181.
2. In a conversation in November 1978 with William Jorden, as secretly recorded by Somoza and published in the memoir Somoza wrote with Jack Cox, *Nicaragua Betrayed* (Boston: Western Islands, 1980), p. 313.
3. Wade Matthews, "Human Rights and the National Interest: Our Policy in Central America and the Philippines," Department of State Executive Seminar in National and International Affairs, 1979–1980, p. 6.
4. Ibid., p. 9.
5. James Fallows was a White House speechwriter.
6. PD/NSC-30, February 17, 1978.
7. See Pastor's *Condemned to Repetition: The United States and Nicaragua* (Princeton: Princeton University Press, 1987), pp. 66–68, for his account of this affair.
8. James A. Thomson, "How Could Vietnam Happen? An Autopsy," in *Readings in American Foreign Policy: A Bureaucratic Perspective*, ed. Morton H. Halperin and Arnold Kanter (Boston: Little, Brown, 1973).
9. Somoza, *Nicaragua Betrayed*, pp. 137–38.

6 / State: The Embassy

1. Letter from Dana Munro, August 29, 1928, as cited by William Kamman, *A Search for Stability: United States Diplomacy Toward Nicaragua 1925–1933* (Notre Dame: University of Notre Dame Press, 1968), p. 223.
2. This function was transferred from State to the Commerce Department in 1980.
3. Bernard Diederich, *Somoza and the Legacy of U.S. Involvement in Central America* (New York: E.P. Dutton, 1981), pp. 23–24.
4. See Shirley Christian, *Nicaragua: Revolution in the Family* (New York: Random House, 1985), p. 44.
5. Martin Mayer, *The Diplomats* (Garden City, N.Y.: Doubleday, 1983), p. 136.
6. Gerald Jordan in *The Philadelphia Inquirer*, March 27, 1987, p. 9-A.
7. See Robert A. Pastor, *Condemned to Repetition: The United States and Nicaragua* (Princeton: Princeton University Press, 1987), p. 72.
8. The best accounts of this incident, as of events in Nicaragua throughout 1978–1979, are to be found in John A. Booth, *The End and the Beginning: The Nicaraguan Revolution* (Boulder: Westview Press, 1982), and in Christian, *Revolution*.
9. Mayer, *Diplomats*, p. 75. His statistics covered 1977; since then, the cable traffic has continued to increase.

7 / The Sixth Floor and the EOB

1. For an account of this development see chapter 4, "Courtiers and Barons: The 'Inside' Politics of Foreign Policy," in I. M. Destler, Leslie H. Gelb, and Anthony Lake, *Our Own Worst Enemy: The Unmaking of American Foreign Policy* (New York: Simon and Schuster, 1984).
2. Harry S. Truman, *Memoirs*, vol. 2, *Years of Trial and Hope* (Garden City, N.Y.: Doubleday, 1956), p. 60.
3. Martin Mayer, *The Diplomats* (Garden City, N.Y.: Doubleday, 1983), p. 73.
4. *The WPA Guide to Washington* (New York: Hastings House, 1942), pp. 247–48.
5. The descriptions of this and subsequent interagency meetings rely primarily on Pastor's *Condemned to Repetition: The United States and Nicaragua* (Princeton: Princeton University Press, 1987), augmented by other sources and interviews. Pastor's account of most meetings is more detailed than mine.
6. See Pastor, *Condemned*, pp. 87–91, for a complete account of this extraordinary affair.
7. Ibid., p. 91.

8 / Mediation in Managua

1. *Report of the International Commission of Friendly Cooperation and Conciliation for Achieving a Peaceful Solution to the Grave Crisis of the Republic of Nicaragua,* March 1979, p. 3. The description of the course of the negotiations contained in the remainder of this chapter is drawn from this report; from Robert A. Pastor's *Condemned to Repetition: The United States and Nicaragua* (Princeton: Princeton University Press, 1987), chapters 5 and 6; from John A. Booth's *The End and the Beginning: The Nicaraguan Revolution* (Boulder: Westview Press, 1982), pp. 165–68; from Shirley Christian's *Nicaragua: Revolution in the Family* (New York: Random House, 1985), chapter 5; from newspaper accounts; and from interviews with participants in the events described.

2. See Pastor, *Condemned,* pp. 105–6, for his recollections of the meeting.

3. Ibid., p. 106.

4. Remarks at a breakfast with members of the White House Correspondents Association, December 7, 1978, and at a breakfast with the National Finance Council of the Democratic National Council, December 9.

5. Cited by Pastor, *Condemned,* p. 109.

6. Cited by Booth, *End and Beginning,* p. 166.

7. Pastor, *Condemned,* p. 111.

8. This is according to Luis Pallais, in an interview with Pastor. See *Condemned,* p. 111.

9. *United States Policy Toward Nicaragua,* Hearings before the Subcommittee on Inter-American Affairs, House Committee on Foreign Affairs, June 26, 1979, p. 44.

10. As cited by Bernard Diederich, *Somoza and the Legacy of U.S. Involvement in Central America* (New York: E.P. Dutton, 1981), p. 236.

11. See Pastor, *Condemned,* pp. 118–19, for an account of this rare failure of President Carter to track the course of an issue he was following.

9 / State: The Press Briefing Room

1. Quoted by Eleanor Randolph in "Hearing Between the Lines in the Briefing Room," *The Washington Post,* page A23, July 9, 1986.

2. Haluk Sahin, Dennis K. Davis, and John P. Robinson, "Television as a Source of International News: What Gets Across and What Doesn't," in *Television Coverage of International Affairs,* ed. William C. Adams (Norwood, N.J.: Ablex, 1982), pp. 233–40.

3. Robert A. Pastor, *Condemned to Repetition: The United States and Nicaragua* (Princeton: Princeton University Press, 1987), p. 123.

10 / On Capitol Hill

1. *Congressional Record: Proceedings and Debates of the United States Congress* (Washington, D.C.: U.S. Government Printing Office, February 21, 1979), p. 2965.
2. See Lars Schoultz, *Human Rights and United States Policy toward Latin America* (Princeton: Princeton University Press, 1981), pp. 58–64, for a description of these groups and their activities. This summary draws primarily on that account, together with interviews and the annual reports to Congress by the U.S. attorney general conveying statements by those groups as required by the Foreign Agent Registration Act.
3. Ibid., pp. 59–60.
4. *Congressional Record*, September 21, 1978, pp. 30750–51.
5. See Robert A. Pastor, *Condemned to Repetition: The United States and Nicaragua* (Princeton: Princeton University Press, 1987), pp. 114–15.
6. See Cindy Arnson, "Congress and Central America: The Search for Consensus" (Ph.D. diss., Johns Hopkins School of Advanced International Studies, 1988), chapter 2, for a description of this incident.
7. As quoted by *The Washington Post*, December 7, 1978, p. 26.
8. Pastor, *Condemned*, p. 115.

11 / Slow Intelligence

1. Robert A. Pastor, *Condemned to Repetition: The United States and Nicaragua* (Princeton: Princeton University Press, 1987), p. 130.
2. John Ranelagh, *The Agency: The Rise and Decline of the CIA* (New York: Simon and Schuster, 1986), p. 24.
3. Pastor, *Condemned*, p. 140.
4. See Pastor, *Condemned*, chapters 8 and 9, for an excellent, more complete description of this as well as other interagency meetings on Nicaragua during June and July of 1979.
5. Martin Mayer, *The Diplomats* (Garden City, N.Y.: Doubleday, 1983), p. 141.
6. Harry S. Truman, *Memoirs*, vol. 2, *Years of Trial and Hope* (Garden City, N.Y.: Doubleday, 1956), p. 105.
7. Drafts of this speech may be found at the Carter Presidential Library in Atlanta, Georgia.
8. See Pastor, *Condemned*, pp. 147–48, for an account of these events, based in part on Brzezinski's diary.
9. Tommie Sue Montgomery, "Making the Same Old Political Mistakes," *The Atlanta Journal/The Atlanta Constitution*, November 22, 1987, p. 10-J. Also, telephone interview with Wipfler.
10. Pastor, *Condemned*, p. 168.

12 / End Game in Managua

1. Somoza was secretly taping his conversations with American diplomats, and later published some of the transcripts in his attack on the Carter administration, *Nicaragua Betrayed*, written with Jack Cox (Boston: Western Islands, 1980). The transcript of this meeting with Pezzullo is on pp. 333–49. My account draws also on Pezzullo's cable to Washington (since declassified) reporting the conversation, and his memories of the meeting. Since Somoza knew the tape recorder was running, he was speaking for posterity as well as to Pezzullo. Thus, by his own standards, this was Somoza at his best.

2. Robert A. Pastor, *Condemned to Repetition: The United States and Nicaragua* (Princeton: Princeton University Press, 1987), p. 154.

3. See Pastor, *Condemned*, pp. 159–66, for a fascinating account of these events — including the tale of Torrijos's inebriated flight to Florida on his way to Washington.

4. Bernard Diederich, *Somoza and the Legacy of U.S. Involvement in Central America* (New York: E.P. Dutton, 1981), p. 297.

5. Karen De Young, "Somoza Agrees to Quit, Leaves Timing to U.S.," *The Washington Post*, July 7, 1979.

6. Pastor, *Condemned*, p. 178.

7. The following account of events from July 17 to July 19 is based on interviews with participants and on the descriptions by Pastor in *Condemned* and by Shirley Christian in *Nicaragua: Revolution in the Family* (New York: Random House, 1985).

8. Diederich, *Somoza*, p. 320.

9. Ibid., p. 326.

13 / Afterthoughts

1. See John A. Booth, *The End and the Beginning: The Nicaraguan Revolution* (Boulder: Westview Press, 1982), p. 105. Most of the data here about the Nicaraguan revolution are drawn from his excellent study.

2. Omar Cabezas, *Fire from the Mountain: The Making of a Sandinista* (New York: Crown, 1985), pp. 5–11.

3. Ibid., p. 209.

4. Bernard Diederich, *Somoza and the Legacy of U.S. Involvement in Central America* (New York: E.P. Dutton, 1981), p. 207.

5. Hannah Arendt, *On Revolution* (New York: Viking Press, 1963), p. 112.

6. Booth, *End and Beginning*, p. 219.

7. Pastor, *Condemned*, p. 76.

8. Jeane Kirkpatrick, "Dictatorships and Double Standards," *Commentary*, September 1979.

9. For a full account of the purge, see the four-part series in *The Washington Post* on "America's Fading Foreign Service," beginning with "Clout and Morale Decline: Reaganites' Raid on the Latin Bureau," by John M. Goshko, April 26, 1987, p. 1. See also George Gedda, "A Dangerous Region: Association with Carter's Central American Policies Proved Hazardous to the Careers of Several FSOs," *The Foreign Service Journal*, February 1983, p. 18.

10. Barbara Tuchman, address before the Foreign Service Association, January 1973.

11. Cited by Nathaniel Davis in "Diplomacy Is a Game for Professionals," in *Conflict in American Foreign Policy*, ed. Don L. Mansfield and Gary J. Buckley (Englewood Cliffs, N.J.: Prentice-Hall, 1985), p. 191.

12. For example, see "America's Fading Foreign Service" in *The Washington Post*, cited in note 9 above, and Elaine Sciolino, "Austerity at State Department and Fear for Diplomacy" in *The New York Times*, November 15, 1987, p. 1. In 1986, of 226 Foreign Service officers who responded to a questionnaire in *The Foreign Service Journal*, only 14 percent said they would encourage new American diplomats to consider the Service as a lifetime career. The survey was reported in *The New York Times*, September 25, 1986, p. B10.

13. Ronald I. Spiers, "The Management Challenge at the Department of State," in the Department of State *Newsletter*, June 1986, p. 5.

14. *The Foreign Service Journal*, November 1966, p. 26.

15. John M. Goshko, "Tradition Bows to the Demand for Management Skills," *The Washington Post*, April 27, 1987, p. 1.

16. Alexis de Tocqueville, *Democracy in America* (New York: Vintage Books, 1945), vol. 1, p. 173.

Index

and press corps, 181
Vaky on Nicaragua policy of, 116
and Wilson, 204
and women in foreign service, 98
Casey, William, 215, 279
Castro, Fidel, 159, 227. *See also* Cuba
Catholic Church, and FSLN appeal, 268
Central American initiative, 135–36, 137–38
Central Intelligence Agency (CIA), 213–16, 278–79
  in Arbenz overthrow, 17, 234
  National Guard commander candidates found by, 252
  in Nicaragua embassy, 95
  Somoza estimates by, 212–13, 216–18, 219
  see also Intelligence
Chace, James, 48, 53
Chamorro, Emiliano, 16
Chamorro, Pedro Joaquín
  assassination of, xiii–xiv, 3, 6, 7, 9–10, 23–24, 25, 82, 98, 99–100
  vs. Somoza family, 9, 50
Chamorro, Violeta de, 219–20, 228
Cheek, James, 19, 142, 161
Chiang Kai-shek, 65, 271
Chile, overthrow of Allende government in, 115–16
Chinese revolution, 268, 269
Christopher, Warren, 5, 36–37
  and Brzezinski, 32
  and Carter letter to Somoza, 85
  and Central American initiative, 135
  and Congress, 289
  and foreign aid loans, 82–83, 208
  and House hearing, 200
  and Inter-Agency Group on Human Rights, 82
  McDonald's aggravating of, 198
  and mediation effort, 138, 142, 144, 148
  and Nicaraguan dilemma, 46–47
  and OAS resolution, 225
  and Pérez reply, 26, 34, 35, 39–42
  policy problems as concern of, 81
  and PRC meeting, 153–54

and press relations, 175–76, 182
and reconciliation proposals, 226, 242
and sanctions, 149
and Somoza appeal to Carter, 250
and Somoza-Pezzullo meeting, 240
Somoza pressured by, 256–57
on Somoza's ouster, 117
staff of, 38, 39
and swivels war, 71–72
and Vaky, 123
and Vance, 39–40
Wilson's attacks on, 206, 207
CIA. *See* Central Intelligence Agency
Classified documents, 106–8, 185
"Clientitis," 27, 29, 108–9, 285
Cold War, and U.S. attitude to Nicaragua, 16. *See also* Anticommunism; Communism
Colombia, 139, 140, 244
Communism
  need to prevent fall to, 277
  and Somoza-Pezzullo meeting, 233, 234
  Somoza as cause of, 139
  and Somoza on U.S., 137
  and Urcuyo on junta, 254
  see also Anticommunism; Radicalism
Congress, U.S.
  and compromise solutions, 277
  and foreign assistance, 22, 82–83, 204–6, 207, 208
  influence of, 198, 209–10
  Somoza allies and enemies in, 193–94, 198–99, 220–21
  Somoza lobbyists with, 196–97
  State Department relations with, 197–98, 289–90
  see also Politics, domestic
Contras, and Bay of Pigs, 261
Coolidge administration, 54, 55, 59
Corinto, 62–63, 94
COSEP, 248
Costa Rica
  and Sandinistas, 138, 211, 213, 220, 240, 270
  see also Carazo, Rodrigo
Cramer, William, 196–97
Cranston, Alan, 193, 209

Somoza falling :

E 183.8 .N5 L35 1990   258360

Lake, Anthony   Von Canor

Southern Virginia University

DATE DUE

GAYLORD   #3522PI   Printed in USA